THE ARCHAEOLOGY OF
NORTHEAST CHINA

THE ARCHAEOLOGY OF NORTHEAST CHINA

Beyond the Great Wall

Edited by Sarah Milledge Nelson

London and New York

First published 1995
by Routledge
11 New Fetter Lane, London EC4P 4EE

Simultaneously published in the USA and Canada
by Routledge
29 West 35th Street, New York, NY 10001

Typeset in Garamond by
J&L Composition Ltd, Filey, North Yorkshire
Printed and bound in Great Britain by
Biddles Ltd, Guildford and King's Lynn

British Library Cataloguing in Publication Data
A catalogue record for this book is available from the British Library

Library of Congress Cataloging in Publication Data
The Archaeology of Northeast China: Beyond the Great Wall
edited by Sarah Milledge Nelson
    p.   cm.
Includes bibliographical references and index.
1. Manchuria (China)—Antiquities.   I. Nelson, Sarah M.
DS782.5.B49 1995
931–dc20   94–9966

ISBN 0–415–11755–0

CONTENTS

CONTENTS

FIGURES

TABLES

CONTRIBUTORS

Guo Da-shun is Director of the Liaoning Province Archaeology and Cultural Relics Institute, Shenyang, China.

Xu Yu-lin is Researcher, Liaoning Province Archaeology and Cultural Relics Institute, Shenyang, China.

Liu Zhen-hua is Researcher, Jilin Province Archaeology and Cultural Relics Institute, Changchun, China.

Liu Jing-wen is Researcher, Jilin Province Archaeology and Cultural Relics Institute, Changchun, China.

Tan Ying-jie is Director of the Research Office, Heilongjiang Province Archaeological Institute, Harbin, China.

Sun Xiu-ren is Researcher, Heilongjiang Province Archaeological Institute, Harbin, China.

Zhao Hong-guang is Assistant Researcher, Heilongjiang Province Archaeological Institute, Harbin, China.

Gan Zhi-geng is Researcher and Deputy Director of the Heilongjiang Province Cultural Relics Management Committee, Harbin, China.

ACKNOWLEDGEMENTS

The idea for this book germinated in the summer of 1987, when I went to the Dongbei for the first time with Ardith Hunter. We visited sites and museums in Liaoning, Jilin, and Heilongjiang provinces. The amount of new and interesting material was astonishing, and I realized it should be written up for a western readership. I mentioned the possibility of a book with chapters written by local archaeologists to my hosts in the three provinces, Guo Da-shun in Liaoning, Jiang Peng in Jilin, and Gan Zhi-geng in Heilongjiang, and the idea was well received.

The following year I received a Visiting Scholar grant from the Committee on Scholarly Communication with the People's Republic of China, for research in Jilin and Liaoning. During that time I was able to discuss the book further with my hosts, and specific chapters and their contents were decided upon. Some of these changed for various reasons, but the basic concept of the presentation of Dongbei archaeology to the west by Dongbei archaeologists was adhered to.

As the articles arrived over the next two years, it became apparent that a book spanning Paleolithic to Iron Age would be far too long. I therefore chose the middle sections, as those most applicable to my work and perhaps with the most audience appeal in the west, and returned the other chapters that had arrived. In the summer of 1989, Mingming Shan, who had been my interpreter in the Dongbei the previous two summers and therefore was involved in the book discussions, came to pursue graduate studies at the University of Denver. She began the translations in 1990, as soon as manuscripts began to arrive. In 1991 she was joined by another graduate student, Peng Ke, who with his wife Du Jie translated further chapters. By the summer of 1992, all the translations were completed and edited, and returned to their authors for corrections. As these returned, I did another round of editing. The semi-final copy was sent to Katheryn Linduff and Lothar von Falkenhausen for their extremely helpful comments and suggestions. They are of course not responsible for any remaining errors, but I am very grateful to them for those they brought to my attention.

ACKNOWLEDGEMENTS

Many other people had a hand in the book in various ways. Thanks are due to Carol Taylor of the University of Denver Faculty Computer Lab, who made the maps, and to Cris Wolf for redrawing some of the figures which did not arrive in usable shape. Megan Bryant typed endless revisions into the computer, with help from Natasha Psenicka and Suzanne Currie. Kathy Williams was also very helpful. My gratitude is extended to all who worked on the book.

S.M.N.

INTRODUCTION

Sarah M. Nelson

Although the Great Wall of China was not erected until well after the time period with which this book is concerned, it makes a convenient geographical demarcation familiar to most readers. The region with which this book is concerned is known in China as Dongbei – the northeast. Now entirely within the People's Republic of China, the Dongbei is nearly identical to the territory which historically has been known as Manchuria. The Dongbei consists of three provinces: Liaoning, Jilin, and Heilongjiang, to list them from south to north. This region is of interest for its contributions to the formation of China south of the Great Wall as well as its non-Chinese inhabitants, and its connections in the distant past with Siberia, Mongolia, and beyond.

Archaeologists from the Dongbei, whose papers are the heart of this book, believe that connections between Dongbei and central China are important to emphasize, hence they often focus on common themes, similar art motifs, and ceremonial commonalities between the two sides of the Great Wall. Time periods in the "historical" era (that is, beginning with the Shang dynasty) are given with reference to the central Chinese dynasties (e.g. Shang, Warring States) reinforcing the trend toward interpreting the northeastern area in terms of the present center. On the other hand, the contrasts between archaeological sites north and south of the Great Wall are another important theme – the archaeology of ethnic groups, or "nationalities" in Chinese parlance, beyond the Chinese frontier. In as much as the Dongbei was at times partly or completely outside the sphere of China proper (the *Tianxia*, or all under heaven) for much of the period covered by this book, as well as in recent historic periods, the region needs to be viewed from two perspectives – that of central China, and that of the "barbarians," non-Chinese people with external ethnic affiliations. Peoples in the Korean peninsula and Japanese islands also have had connections to the Dongbei at various times. Thus both Chinese antecedents and non-Chinese groups are represented in Dongbei archaeology.

In recent centuries, the vast territory of the Dongbei has been known as

1

Manchuria, the homeland of the Manchus, who spoke a Tungusic language unrelated to Chinese. Before the rise of the Manchus this region was largely occupied by other Tungusic speakers, wholly or in part Manchu ancestors (Lattimore 1932, Spence 1990). The Manchus conquered the Ming dynasty in 1644, forming the non-Chinese dynasty known as Qing, and joining their home territories to China. When the central authority in China weakened toward the end of this period, and ultimately failed in 1911, various warlords seized power in the northeast. Both Russia and Japan entered Manchuria to take advantage of the situation with the result that some of the early archaeology in this region was done by Japanese and Russian researchers, as well as by Chinese archaeologists.

The three provinces of the northeast are largely inhabited by Han Chinese at present. However, significant minorities of Koreans, especially in the Yanbian Autonomous Region, and of Mongols in villages near Mongolia, are present in the Dongbei. A few Manchu pockets survive, and even an occasional Manchu-speaking village, but the Manchu population has largely been assimilated into the Han Chinese majority, and Manchus are not easily distinguished from Chinese.

Much that has been written about this region at any period, whether by westerners or Chinese, is seen from the perspective of China. As a result, we in the west are accustomed to thinking of Mongolia and Manchuria as comparable lands of non-Chinese nomads beyond the Great Wall, and to lumping all non-Chinese cultures together. For example, Owen Lattimore's *Inner Asian Frontiers of China* (1932) and William Watson's *Cultural Frontiers in Ancient East Asia* (1971) each discuss the cultures on China's periphery separately, but nevertheless leave the impression that there are characteristics which tie these frontiers together, especially a client relationship to China alternating with border raiding. Often this is made into an opposition of nomads versus farmers – a perspective which, as we shall see, is erroneous with regard to Manchuria in the Neolithic and Bronze Age. More recently Thomas Barfield's *The Perilous Frontier* (1991) has the advantage of making a distinction between the grasslands of Mongolia and the Manchurian forests.

For the purposes of this book, therefore, a Sinocentric approach is not altogether appropriate, nor is it the one taken by the Chinese archaeologists who have written the substantive chapters. Since the focus is on Manchuria, which is strikingly different from Mongolia, not only in the ethnic affiliations of the past and present inhabitants, but also in environment, it is important to highlight those differences. It is time to unpack the nomads-on-the-frontier notion. Archaeology has important data for this project.

The vast grasslands of Mongolia, so appropriate for herds of horses, cattle, and sheep, do not extend into the Dongbei, except on its western fringes. Even in early Neolithic times, few of the archaeological sites indicate that the occupants of Manchuria were nomadic. Liaoning and Jilin provinces border Inner Mongolia in the west, and Heilongjiang abuts Outer Mongolia, but mountain ranges have kept the grasslands pastoralists for the most part on the western side of the border. In contrast, the forested mountains and hills of Manchuria slope down to the Manchurian plain, which even today is one of China's major agricultural regions (Whitaker and Shinn 1972).

The Dongbei, while having fringes which ecologically belong to other regions, is basically a coherent whole. The three northeastern provinces each center on the vast Manchurian plain with mountains on the east and west. In Liaoning province, the hilly Liaodong peninsula is an extension of the Changbai mountain range which borders North Korea to the east. On the west side is the southern end of the Greater Xingan range, and the Yanshan, or Yan mountains. The Great Wall of China is south of Liaoning, in Hebei, but it touches Liaoning as it arrives at Bohai Bay. The rivers of Liaoning drain into the Manchurian plain. Beyond the mountain ranges on the west lies Inner Mongolia. The major cities of Liaoning – Shenyang, Fushun, and Anshan – all lie in the plain. Dalian is on the tip of the Liaodong peninsula, while Yingkou and Dandong flank its west and east edges, where the peninsula joins the continent.

The major cities of Jilin province, Changchun and Jilin city, are also at its center in the plain. The province becomes sandy and marshy in the west. It is mountainous in the southeast where it touches North Korea, and likewise extends into the Xingan range in the west. The plain is wider in Jilin than in Liaoning province.

The province of Heilongjiang has an even broader plain, in which the reported Neolithic and Bronze Age sites are located. Harbin and Qiqihaer are its two largest cities. In the western edge of the Manchurian plain, the land is marshy and filled with sand dunes, similar to western Jilin province. The plain is closed off by the Lesser Xingan mountains which run northwest to southeast. Thus, the archaeological sites of the Neolithic and Bronze Age are found either in the arable Manchurian plain or in the mountains that border either side.

The agricultural nature of Manchuria is worth emphasizing. Rice is now grown in the river basins, and maize, soybeans, and sorghum on the hill slopes. As noted above, Manchuria and Mongolia are too often conflated in prehistory as well as history. Because northern invaders from beyond the Great Wall created dynasties within China on several occasions, these are often lumped together and presented as nomadic depredations upon the settled Chinese farmers. One still hears and reads that the Great Wall was constructed to keep the nomads out, but the archaeology of this area demonstrates that this is by no means an accurate account in the Dongbei. Northeast of Beijing lived farmers, not nomads, well back into prehistory. Settled agricultural villages in Liaoning province have radiocarbon dates in the same time range as the millet-growing villages of the Zhongyuan, and probably also grew varieties of millet. The cultures beyond the Great Wall in the northeast were different from those of the Ordos region as well as the Mongolian grasslands.

CHINESE AND WESTERN APPROACHES TO ARCHAEOLOGY

Because this book has been written, edited, and assembled for readers in the English-speaking world, it will be useful to examine both theoretical and methodological differences between Chinese archaeology and that of the west. It should be borne in mind that Chinese archaeology is just beginning to consider theory as a topic for discussion, and that the lengthy debates on method and theory which have occurred in the west have touched Chinese archaeology little.

For example, although the Marxist paradigm used in China bears super-ficial resemblance to the evolutionary paradigm which has been dominant in western archaeology for several decades, there are important differences, and these differences have implications for the methodology of site excavations, artifact analysis, and interpretations. The Chinese Marxist perspective on the prehistoric past is that cultures unfolded in predictable ways – matriarchal tribes inevitably turning into patriarchal clans, ancient slave states followed by feudal society. The particulars may be demon-strated archaeologically, but according to Chinese lights it is not *necessary* to do so. The pattern itself requires no explanation, although any deviation from the pattern needs to be explained. This paradigm is similar to the western model of the succession of bands, tribes, chiefdoms, and states (Fried 1967, Service 1975) (although different in detail), in that the levels themselves are often treated as if they were inevitable, and are not seen as requiring any explanation. However, the Chinese Marxist paradigm is unlike the evolutionary paradigm in leaving the differences between these stages or levels, and the processes of change, undeveloped theoretically. While western archaeologists have concerned themselves with the transitions between stages, and the causes for movement from one stage to the next, as well as discussing both the necessary and incidental characteristics of each level, Chinese archaeologists generally have not engaged in debate or refinement of this nature.

The lack of evolutionary or developmental theory in Chinese archaeology is related to the fact that Chinese archaeology has social and culture history as its stated goals. For the same reason, there has been little concern for the role of the environment in the formation of sites or selection of site locations, or for ecological or environmental explanations of archaeological cultures. It should also be noted that China was cut off from the west for an entire generation, with a deliberate policy of developing on its own.

Although this policy was mainly applicable to other fields, it affected Chinese archaeology as well. Falkenhausen (n.d.) reminds us that archaeology in China as elsewhere responds to its current social and political environment, and that constraints on the ways archaeology is pursued are both obvious and subtle.

The very notion of what makes a "culture" in Chinese archaeology is not well described. It is possible to glean from the Chinese literature the notion that cultures are larger than sites, that they exist over time and in space, and that they are the minimal unit of interaction among groups of sites. In general, the cultures are not seen as requiring explanation, for delineating the complex web of cultures in time and space is sufficient.

Western notions of what qualifies as "historic archaeology" are different from those in China. The length of time in China that is treated as historic is much longer. Although the Paleolithic is a separate area of study, joined to paleontology, the discipline of archaeology from the Neolithic onward is frequently placed in departments of history. The weight of roughly three thousand years of written history in China is responsible for the fact that a great deal more attention is paid to documents than we in the west are accustomed to, except in classical archaeology and the most recent European protohistory.

In the west, with an emphasis on ecological and evolutionary paradigms, "culture history" became a pejorative expression in the 1960s. Archaeologists were enjoined to go beyond the mere connecting of pottery types in time and space, and consider the *anthropoloy* of the past. Indeed in some places (e.g. the American Southwest), with the time/space systematics thoroughly sorted out by means of highly developed and precise techniques such as tree-ring dating, it has become possible to accomplish sophisticated analyses of relationships between sites and within sites. From this perspective, Chinese archaeology may be viewed as unsophisticated, but by this criterion so is archaeology in most of the rest of the world, where chronologies and site relationships are also still under development.

As noted above, the interaction between border regions and the Yellow River sites in both archaeology and history is particularly emphasized in Chinese interpretations. Named groups of "barbarians" appear in Chinese ancient histories, and the assignment of sites to specific ethnic groups or "nationalities" is an important question in China. Reference to ancient texts is common in archaeological site reports in China (e.g. Chapter 8). These references include texts obscure to many western scholars, for there are more documents than those that have been translated into English (see Wu 1982 for a compilation of these sources).

The sheer volume of archaeological sites in China is staggering. The effort of making a coherent and logical "story" from the diverse and fragmentary but numerically large prehistoric sites is in itself a major contribution to world prehistory. However, as in all regions with an emergent rather than an established archaeological data base, the urgent matter is the tedious and time-consuming work of discovering sites, excavating them carefully, and piecing together the framework of the past. Without this framework, this three-dimensional trellis of knowledge relating sites to each other, all sophisticated studies aspiring to transcend a single site must be suspect. However, because the goals of Chinese archaeology, as noted above, are more historical than anthropological, the framework is not merely a necessary first step, but within China it may be an end in itself.

Further goals in addition to space-time systematics are those of the identification of ethnic groups and the movements of peoples – other topics which were declared uninteresting by processual archaeology, but which are now being revived in some western archaeological circles. More recent archaeological approaches including post-processual and Marxist standpoints will find grist for their mills in the data presented here, although ready-made explanations are not forthcoming. Chinese archaeologists are interested in ideology, especially as it may reflect ethnicity, but do not extend this to discussions of human agency, nor do they consider the interplay of domination and resistance.

Although the Chinese authors in this book use terms translated as "Neolithic" and "Bronze Age," it is necessary to underline the fact that these terms become problematical when applied to the Dongbei. In China, as elsewhere in Asia, "Neolithic" simply indicates the presence of pottery. Even ground stone tools, the original defining characteristic of the Neolithic, are not necessarily found in these sites – in fact, microliths and larger chipped stone tools continue into the Bronze Age, alongside ground stone. It is not known whether all sites with pottery in Manchuria also contain cultivated plants, since evidence is not consistently collected, but no *assumption* of such a connection is implied by calling the sites Neolithic.

The designation "Bronze Age" is a historical marker, although the approximate time of origin of a Bronze Age varies by author as well as by region. The term, as used in the chapters of this book, implies that bronze is present within China at the same time in similar sites, not necessarily on the site being described. Because bronze appears to have been locally produced from its earliest appearance in the Dongbei, yet bronze-casting was an industry making only small tools, weapons, and ornaments, the addition of bronze does not seem to have changed the economy in these northern regions in any definitive way, at least in the beginning. With historical connections more important than technological stages, "Bronze Age" can be taken to mean any site that is contemporaneous with Xia, Shang, or Zhou. (The authors in this book assume that the historicity of the Xia dynasty has been demonstrated by excavations in the

Zhongyuan, especially Erlitou. By using the term Xia here and in the succeeding translated chapters, I am simply reflecting that usage.) The amount of actual bronze use or bronze-casting at any site under discussion is irrelevant to its designation as Bronze Age. However, bronze is not late in the Dongbei, in fact it is present in some sites in the Dongbei as early as elsewhere in China.

METHODOLOGY

Excavation techniques, as reported in these chapters and by my own observation at sites I have visited, are similar to those used in the west. On Neolithic and Bronze Age sites, 5 m squares with 1 m baulks between them tend to be used. Artifacts are left in the ground until a floor is established, which is then drawn and photographed. A house and its contents are recorded as a unit, as is a grave. Plans and profiles are drawn for each unit.

Stratigraphy is established by means of house floors or changes in the soil matrix. These archaeological levels are then analyzed according to their artifactual content, and the site is divided into two or three (or rarely more) cultural levels. While these might be referred to as phases, we have retained the more literal translation. However, individual artifacts may be assigned to a cultural level by perceived style, rather than by stratigraphic location. This procedure is justified by the fact that the major purpose of excavation is to place the site in time, and to relate it culturally to other nearby sites. Underlying assumptions about changes from simple to complex, and crude to refined, may take precedence over the actual locations in the ground. In this case we use the term "phase."

Precise quantification of data is not a standard inclusion in site reports. The relative amount of different types of pottery, stone, or bone tools is frequently indicated, along with the range of sizes, but counts or percentages are not usually included. Detailed descriptions of each class of artifacts are reported, rather than named types. The Chinese format is related to the lack of development of a typological concept for pottery which could apply across sites. The use of types is likely to be missed by western archaeologists, even though types have been considered merely a sort of convenience to by-pass repetitive descriptions. Although some comparisons are made with reference to specific characteristics (usually pottery, stone, and other tools), features such as dwelling floors and burials are divided into groups which apply to a specific site only. Thus, comparisons across sites require careful reading.

The reader is cautioned that all Chinese dates are based on a half-life of 5570. Table 1 and Table 2 include all the radiocarbon dates mentioned in the book, assembled for the convenience of reference, although they will also be found at the appropriate places in the text.

Table 1 Neolithic dates in the Dongbei

Site	Lab. No.	C_{14} date 5730 Half Life	Calibrated	Source	Reference
Niuheliang	ZK-1352	4975±85 BP	3771–3519 BCE	charcoal	Kaogu 1984(4):94
Dongshanzui	BK-82079	489±70 BP	3640–3382 BCE	charcoal	Kaogu 1986(7):657
Chahai	ZK-2138	6925±95 BP	5712–5530 BCE	charcoal	Liaohai Wenwu Xuegan 88.1
Xinglongwa	ZK-1392	7240±95 BP	6032–5760 BCE	charcoal from dwelling floor	Kaogu 85.10
Fuhegoumen	ZK-0188	4735±110 BP	3510–3107 BCE		Kaogu 64.1
Xiaoshan	ZK-2061	6150±85 BP	4996–4784 BCE	F2 carbonized sample	Kaogu 87.6
Lower Houwa	BK-84002	5600±110 BP	4370–4159 BCE	charcoal	Wenwu 89.12
Daliudaogou	ZK-0282	2220±75 BP		charcoal	Kaogu 1978(4):284–285
Jingu	ZK-0785	4465±100 BP	3094–2890 BCE	charcoal	Dongbei Kaogu Yu Lishi 82.1
Zuojiashan	BK-85061	6100±80 BP	4936–4773 BCE	first phase	Kaogu Xuebao 1989(2):209
Zuojiashan	BK-85060	4375±80 BP	2921–2703 BCE	third phase	Kaogu Xuebao 1989(2):209
Dongshanzui	BK-82079	4895±70 BP	3640–3382 BCE		Kaogu Xuebao 1989(2):209
Zuojiashan	BK-85061	6100±80 BP	4936–4773 BCE	Period I	Kaogu Xuebao 1989.2
Wujiacun	BK-78064	4830±100 BP	3627–3350 BCE	G1F1	Kaogu Xuebao 1981.1
Lower Guojiacun	ZK-0414	5015±100 BP	3780–3530 BCE		Kaogu 1979(1):89
Yaojingzi		4726±79 BP		ox bone from AT2	Bowugwan Yanjusuo 1990(3):58
Bashan	ZK-1375	4870±80 BP	3634–3374 BCE	human bones from M1	Kaogu 1988(12):1084
Yinggeling	ZK-0089	3025±90 BP	1310–1008 BCE	charcoal from F1	Kaogu 60.4, 81.6
Yinggeling	ZK-0088	2985±120 BP	1300–920 BCE	birch bark from F1	Kaogu 60.4, 81.6
Xinkailiu	ZK-0424	5430±90 BP	4239–3995 BCE	M5 human bone	Kaogu Xuebao 79.4

Table 2 Bronze Age dates in the Dongbei

Site	Lab. No.	C₁₄ date 5730 Half Life	Calibrated	Source	Reference
Zhizhushan	ZK-0176	3965 ± 90 BP	2466–2147 BCE	charcoal	Kaogu 1974(5):336
Fengxia	ZK-0153	3550 ± 80 BP	1886–1681 BCE	middle layer	Kaogu 1977(4):2000
Dadianzi	ZK-0402	3390 ± 90 BP	1685–1463 BCE	grave No. 454	Kaogu 1978(4):285
Dadianzi	ZK-0480	3420 ± 85 BP	1735–1517 BCE	grave No. 759	Kaogu 1979(1):89
Gaotaishan	BK-77018	3370 ± 90 BP	1678–1444 BCE	T1H1 charcoal	
Wanliu	ZK-2268	3085 ± 75 BP	1392–1127 BCE	charcoal	Kaogu 89.12
Baijinbao	ZK-0324	2790 ± 65 BP	918–810 BCE	charcoal	Zhongguo Kaogu-xue Nienji 87
Hanshu II	BK-78001	2380 ± 100 BP	481–213 BCE	charcoal	Dongbei Kaogu Yu Lishi 82.1
Beishan	WB-87-18	2165 ± 75 BP		burials	
Xingxingshao	ZK-0679	3055 ± 100 BP	1389–1030 BCE	human bone	
Yangtun	WB-81-08	2590 ± 70 BP	796–446 BCE	middle phase	Wenwu 73.8
Yangtun	ZK-0093	2165 ± 75 BP	347–3 BCE	later period	Dongbei Kaogu Yu Lishi 82.1
Jingu	ZK-0675	3270 ± 155 BP	1630–1300 BCE		Zhongguo Kaogu-xue Nienji 87
Xingcheng	ZK-2252	3585 ± 115 BP	1932–1687 BCE	charcoal, lower F3	Zhongguo Kaogu-xue Nienji 87
Baijinbao	ZK-0324	2790 ± 65 BP	918–810 BCE	ash-pit No.1	Zhongguo Kaogu-xue Nienji 87
Baijinbao	ZK-2156	3110 ± 115	1420–1100 BCE	charcoal	Kaogu 89.12
Pingyang	ZK-1349	2385 ± 70 BP	410–364 BCE	M40 and M41	

The presentation of data in the chapters of this book as well as in Chinese journals follows a set form, as the reader will perceive. This format enables detailed comparisons of sites, levels, and assemblages. However, because verbal descriptions can be misleading no matter how carefully constructed, and because reading these descriptions can be tedious, some written details have been omitted from the chapters as they were submitted, and illustrations provided instead.

DONGBEI ARCHAEOLOGY

This volume includes only Neolithic and Bronze Age sites, although the original intent was to include Paleolithic and Iron Age as well. Early on it was evident that such a book would be far too long. Paleolithic sites were omitted because they were recently treated in another book (Wu and Olsen 1985), and Iron Age was considered largely historic, leading into discussions of Dongbei politics which touch delicate sensitivities. These sites deserve a book of their own, or several books.

Neolithic

In general the nature of Dongbei Neolithic sites is different from those along the Yellow river, but similar to the earliest pottery-bearing sites in Hebei province, especially those of the Cishan and Peiligang cultures. The similarities include incised and impressed brownish pottery, semi-subterranean houses, and the addition of ground stone tools to small and large chipped stone implements.

The earliest known Dongbei Neolithic sites are located in the Liaodong peninsula and the Manchurian plain, dated about the same time as Peiligang (Yang 1988). These sites all appear to partake in an early pottery horizon which occurred throughout the northern Pacific shores, from Kyushu, the southernmost island of Japan, to coastal China. The most common shape of pottery in the early Dongbei sites is simple – a tall, flat-bottomed, straight-sided pot with a direct rim, which was produced in various sizes. This pottery is decorated over all or most of the exterior surface with incised or impressed geometric designs. Closely related pottery is found throughout northeastern Asia, including coastal Siberia, Korea, and Japan. It differs in construction and decorative techniques from pottery further south in China which may be equally early.

Although few of the earliest sites in northern China have direct and unequivocal evidence of domesticated plants or animals, they contain indirect evidence which is consistent with plant cultivation, along with clear evidence of permanent villages. Even the site with the earliest date for the Dongbei – Chahai – is a village site with houses constructed in rows, as if the entire population had settled the site at once. While domesticated pigs are found in the Peiligang culture, their presence is not attested in the earliest Dongbei sites. However, pig bones are found in the Dongbei by the following stage.

An interesting characteristic of Dongbei Neolithic sites is that "jade"-working is present at the earliest sites. The term jade, as used in China, does not refer to specific raw material such as nephrite and jadeite; any colored stone which can be carved and polished may be considered jade. At Chahai, for example, white stone earrings were simple in design, with a slit through an annular shape in which to insert the ear lobe. These ornaments have a pleasing appearance and are polished to a high sheen. Later, jade artifacts and ornaments became increasingly more complex in shape and more sophisticated in the surface treatment, and the raw material selected was more varied in color, but they are nevertheless stylistically related to the Chahai jades. Quarry sites for most of the Dongbei jades are not known, but it is surmised that the raw material was obtained from increasingly far afield, to account for the increasing variations in color and improvement in the quality of the jade used.

The Chinese chapters translated here use two different words for a method of stone-processing which westerners might call chipping or flaking. One of the terms applies to the processing of microliths and retouching of projectile points; this word has been translated as "flaking." The other refers to larger pieces reduced from a core; we have translated this as "chipping." Further distinctions are made between the first processing of ground stone and the final grinding. We have translated the first as "pecking," since this term is more commonly used in English, but the literal meaning in Chinese is "carving," the same word applied to jade-processing. The second step we call "grinding." Since in English we tend to think of carving as more applicable to wood and other softer materials, the term has not been used for hard stone, but has been retained for jade, since this is a customary usage.

Stone tool assemblages are frequently a mixture of microliths, flaked stone, and ground stone in the same level of the same site. This occurs in so many sites that it cannot be attributed to accidental mixing of levels. In any case, a progression from microliths to chipped stone to ground stone is not present in Neolithic sites, rather, these techniques are all present at once, although the relative amounts may change. The various reduction techniques were applied to different types of stone, and the raw material seems to have been selected specifically for a given end product. For example, cryptocrystalline stone was selected for flaked microliths which were used as insets in bone handles, or as projectile points, silt stone was used for chipping larger tools such as hoes and plows, sandstone was selected for grinding stones, and dense, heavy stone was made into ground stone objects such as axes, adzes, and chisels.

Bone tools were mostly produced by techniques of grinding and polishing. They include forms such as needles, awls, knives, and spatulas. Some shell is also found, fashioned into bracelets and knives, probably reduced in the same manner as bone.

Various house forms are found, but the semi-subterranean house is by far the most common. These dwellings are relatively small, nuclear-family sized, and grouped into villages. The houses often include square hearths, a feature which is also found in Korea and coastal Siberia.

Regional differences can be specified, although usually no sharp boundaries can be drawn. Three important Neolithic regions are characterized as Liaodong (eastern Liaoning, including the Liaodong peninsula), Liaoxi (western Liaoning sites), and the Xinle culture, which includes the region around Shenyang and sites to the north. These regions are not equally discussed in the following chapters. Except for the Houwa site where the Liaodong sites are referred to, the Liaodong peninsula sites are not described in detail.

The peninsular sites have been divided into levels where appropriate, usually two or three to a site. With the help of C14 dates they have been ordered by time and as cultures. The lowest levels feature brownish pottery with incised and impressed designs, often in the shape of tall, flat-bottomed, wide-mouthed pots. Sites in the Liaodong peninsula thus partake of the general characteristics of the Dongbei Neolithic in the earlier levels, but their upper levels have many similarities with the Longshan culture as it appears in Shandong, especially in terms of pottery shapes and surface designs. For example, tripods and pedestal vessels appear, along with limited painted vessels and black polished ware.

Lower Xinle and other sites to the north are discussed as "Pre-Hongshan" sites. Jade carving is noticeable in many sites, as it is also in Liaoxi. Sites of this sort are found as far north as Jilin province. Some evidence of cultural complexity is already apparent, in differential house sizes and distribution of artifacts.

The earliest Neolithic sites in the Dongbei are probably not derived from China south of the Great Wall. The C14 dates are similar in age, giving no clear precedence to one region or the other. In both regions it is likely that native grains such as millets, buckwheat, and/or echinocloa were cultivated. Thus, either or both could be centers of incipient agriculture. However, the generic similarity of the pottery over this whole area suggests widespread interaction of peoples. The distribution of sites implies that ideas were diffused and populations moved along the coasts and rivers, in boats.

Another kind of typological problem is noted in the Bronze Age chapters from both Jilin and Heilongjiang – the difficulty of distinguishing purely Neolithic sites from later ones that have no obvious bronze. The careful attention to the pottery from these sites has allowed archaeologists to make this distinction whether or not bronze is present at a specific site. This is a milestone in understanding the cultural chronology of these regions.

The Neolithic sites mentioned so far are simple villages, with no visible hierarchy of sites, no development of complexity, and little that could be interpreted as craft specialization. While the lower component at the Xinle site has two different-sized houses, few other indications of complexity are present. All this changes with the Hongshan culture, within the large area that it covers. While still lacking metals (although one mold has been found recently [see Chapter 1] and an earring partly made of copper wire has been excavated from a Hongshan tomb [Han 1993]), the Hongshan culture has a great many features of complex society. Most obvious are its highly worked jades, its elaborate burials, and its complex ceremonial precincts, but Guo Da-shun argues further for craft specialization in painted pottery, jade, and bronze.

Two particularly notable ceremonial precincts have been described. The first, known as the Goddess Temple, had fragments of statues of sitting female figures of various sizes, as well as indications of pig and bird statues. These were made from unbaked clay, and were preserved only by the application of fine clay on the surface, topped by a layer of paint. The building itself was constructed in an asymmetrical lobed shape. Footings show elaborate geometric designs made with clay in high relief on the inside, and painted yellow, red, and white. Another ritual area has both round and square earth and stone platforms reasonably designated as altars, a human skeleton interpreted as a human sacrifice, and a number of smaller figurines, broken but clearly representing nude females. These are of great importance in interpreting Dongbei prehistory.

Because of the time frame, and the perceived need to associate sites with Chinese history, the Hongshan culture is related to the legendary Yellow Emperor, one of the sage kings in predynastic history/legend. This is a topic of more interest within China than outside, but it is worthy of note that Chinese legendary history includes a suggestion of inequality at this time period. However, the legends are almost entirely silent on the question of goddesses (Nelson 1993).

The formation of the Hongshan culture on an ecotone, between the Mongolian grasslands and the Manchurian plain, is probably significant for the development of cultural complexity there. The ceremonial sites and elaborate burials are in the hilly land, while villages are found along the rivers, with evidence of both plow agriculture and cattle, as well as sheep and pigs. Furthermore, exotic items suggest long-distance trade. The presence of jade, turquoise, and other non-local materials locally worked into unique expressions of the culture shows that contact with distant regions occurred, although it may have been sporadic and ephemeral. The existence of painted pottery, the first to appear beyond the Great Wall, has been interpreted as relating to contact with the Yangshao sites of the Zhongyuan.

The complexity of Hongshan cannot be derived from Yangshao,

13

however. Hongshan is complex in ways that differ from Yangshao or any of its known variants. So far there is nothing comparable to the Hongshan ceremonial centers in Yangshao sites, and no female figurines occur. Human depictions in other Chinese Neolithic sites are generally only heads, whereas Hongshan sculptures include the entire body. Sculptures elsewhere are often stylized, while the Hongshan sculptures are realistic (Yang 1988). The exact nature of the complexity of Hongshan is not completely understood, yet it appears to be quite other, unique and *sui generis* in the region.

It is also interesting to note that the population base for Hongshan ceremonialism is neither in cities nor in clusters of villages, but in farming villages strung out along rivers which so far show few traces of the traits of the ceremonial centers, other than red painted pottery and occasional jades. Guo (Chapter 1) argues that Hongshan is a civilization, but even if that is accepted the appearance of Hongshan remains unexplained.

The Hongshan culture is an anomaly in several ways − it was not clearly refered to in Chinese legendary history, it does not fit the Marxist paradigm, and it fails to conform to western ideas of chiefdoms or incipient states. The female figurines suggest to the Chinese a matriarchal society, but complex society ought to be patriarchal according to received tradition. This problem is raised by Guo (Chapter 1), but is not discussed at length. Perhaps not surprisingly, it is also difficult to squeeze Hongshan into western notions of a chiefdom (Nelson 1993), although characteristics of complex society are definitely present. The Hongshan culture may ultimately be useful in widening our understanding of the paths to complex society.

Furthermore, there are important gender questions which have not yet been posed (but for a tentative beginning, see Nelson 1991). What is the meaning (or multiple meanings) of the female figurines? Did women have power and/or rank? Were women the mediators with the spirit world? Did the figurines reflect a previous era of gender equality, now attenuated or vanished? Sexing of the burials at Niuheliang is imperative to begin answering these questions.

The Bronze Age

The Bronze Age has its own set of problems. To consider just when a Bronze Age began north of the Great Wall is only one of the problems, and arguably the least critical. China seems to have drifted into a Bronze Age slowly and uncertainly, with more than a millennium passing between the earliest appearance of bronze, cast on the spot it would seem, and the intensive use of bronze. In fact, the Chinese Bronze Age is often described in terms of the ceremonial use of bronze, rather than reflecting efficient technological improvements brought by bronze tools, or more effective warfare produced by bronze weapons. The bronze vessels which were dedicated to the mortuary complexes of the royal ancestors in the Shang dynasty and perhaps earlier are a frequent focus of study. A large part of the production of bronze was diverted to conspicuous consumption, or to ceremonial needs, rather than used for the production of implements or even weapons. There is little evidence that farmers profited from better tools, for example, although as I have argued elsewhere (Nelson 1992), bronze is fully recyclable, and its absence in archaeological household contexts may not mean that it was not present. Bronze weapons definitely were much used by the Late Shang period – battle-axes, knives, and halberds are among the early components of warfare, and of course the Shang war chariot depended to some extent on bronze fittings. While the potential of bronze for changing the face of warfare was not ignored, it developed only slowly.

North of the Great Wall, there is the merest hint of bronze in the Hongshan culture, which remains to be corroborated by further finds. However, the Lower Xiajiadian culture, contemporaneous with the Erlitou site of the Xia culture (as demonstrated by both C14 dates and cross-dating of artifacts – see Chapter 5) was a bronze-using culture. The concept of "Northern Bronzes" was created to discuss the bronzes found in Inner Mongolia, especially the Ordos region, but it is here applied to Liaoning province. Few of the discoveries have any site context (see Chapter 6), but they are known to be at least contemporaneous with the Erligang phase, and some may be earlier. The finds of bronze in the Dongbei are not dissimilar to those found in Inner Mongolia and south of the Great Wall, so that bronze-working itself appears to tie these sites loosely together, as jade-working continued to do.

An interesting factor among sites in Liaoxi is the rhythm of the rise and fall of cultures. Rather than a steady progression from simple to complex, the sites suggest that complexity was achieved in fits and starts. The Hongshan culture is the first flowering in the region, but it is followed by a decline, a period with fewer sites, lacking both ceremonial centers and elaborately worked jade. The next highly developed culture – the Lower Xiajiadian – has some characteristics that suggest antecedents in the Hongshan, some continuity with the local past, but also new exotic features which appear to arrive fully developed. The walled sites suggest either an intrusive population with reason to fear local enemies, or a local population with raiding neighbors. The elaborate burials are quite different in detail from those that preceded them, suggesting the former interpretation. The ceremonial pottery of Lower Xiajiadian is one of its most striking features, with elaborate shapes painted with pastel pinks and yellows in ornate curvilinear designs. It has no obvious antecedents.

Another hiatus follows Lower Xiajiadian, filled only with ordinary-looking sites, unless the Northern Bronzes are the only discovered remains of continuing complexity. The context of the Northern Bronzes is largely unknown (see Chapter 6). By the time of the Late Shang dynasty, the Upper Xiajiadian culture flourished north and south of the Yanshan, across which later was built the Great Wall.

Various ethnic groups inhabited the region north of the *Tianxia*. Chinese histories give names to these groups at various times, and to some extent describe them, but the northern peoples have no written histories of their own. Identifying specific sites with the customs of particular barbarians produces some heated debates in Chinese archaeological journals, and some of these various opinions are considered in the Bronze Age chapters. It is particularly interesting to note that the custom of covering the face of the deceased, either with a cloth decorated with bronze bosses or with jade covering the eyes and mouth, known to have been practiced by Tungusic groups, is present at various sites in the Bronze Age of the Dongbei (Lin 1985 and Chapter 8).

One archaeological manifestation of the Dongbei which is treated lightly in these chapters is that of dolmens. The Chinese term is *shipeng*, stone huts, which indicates both their size and their construction with four upright stone slabs topped by a much larger capstone. Dolmens are most numerous in the Liaodong peninsula, where they tend to be large and well made, with polished stones rather than the raw slabs that characterize Korean dolmens. One dolmen near Yingkou, for example, was large enough to have been reused as a building. The interior is 2.8 by 2.6 m while the cover slab is 8.6 by 5.7 m. Dolmens are known as far north as Jilin province (Chapter 7). Although most likely used for burials, they are too obvious in the landscape and too accessible to tomb robbers for burials in them to have remained intact for modern archaeologists to find and excavate. Scatters of red polished potsherds have been found in an excavation outside one dolmen, suggesting close connections with the Korean dolmens in contents as well as construction.

Similarities between the Liaodong peninsula and the Korean peninsula in the Neolithic are noted in Chapter 2, and this relationship continues through the Bronze Age. The dolmens, thought to be Bronze Age structures in the widest sense, are one such manifestation, for dolmens are considerably denser in Korea than in Dongbei. Other similarities in pottery can also be found throughout the Bronze Age, helping to date Korean sites, which have few independent dates, especially those in North Korea.

Bronze Age sites on the Song-Nen plain in Jilin province have just begun to be differentiated from those of the Neolithic (Chapter 7). The most important group of sites is known as the Xituanshan culture, featuring many slab-lined-grave cemeteries, with offerings of pig heads which seem to link them loosely with sites from Upper Xiajiadian to the Liulihe site in Beijing. Although bronze is scarce, it is present often enough to identify these sites as part of the world that knew and used bronze.

Heilongjiang province in the Bronze Age had an even more tenuous grip on actual bronze, but there are a number of interesting sites which show that even at this distance from the *Tianxia* complex society was to be found. The sites are dated with reference to the Central Plain, not to Upper Xiajiadian in its more immediate neighborhood, reflecting the customary usage in Chinese archaeology.

In general, as bronze appeared in the Dongbei, it is represented by small objects, and, as can be seen by the presence of sandstone molds and slag, locally produced. Did itinerant smiths ply their trade in the Dongbei? Did the knowledge of bronze-working instead spread among these various groups, with local individuals becoming bronze workers? Where were the sources of copper and tin, and perhaps zinc, and how were the metals distributed to the casting sites? These are important questions surrounding the Dongbei Bronze Age which remain to be answered.

It is fair to say that Dongbei archaeology is at the necessary and important stage of creating the temporal framework on which to hang additional studies in the future. These chapters are thus offered as a wealth of detailed information on Dongbei archaeology, with a spatio-temporal scheme on which further studies can be based.

REFERENCES

Barfield, Thomas J. (1989) *The Perilous Frontier, Nomadic Empires and China.* Oxford: Basil Blackwell.

Chang, K. C. (1986) *The Archaeology of Ancient China*, 4th ed. New Haven, CT: Yale University Press.

Falkenhausen, Lothar von (n.d.) The Regionalist Paradigm in Chinese Archaeology, in *Nationalism and the Practice of Archaeology*, ed. P. Kohl and C. Fawcett. Cambridge: Cambridge University Press. Forthcoming.

Fried, Morton (1967) *The Evolution of Political Society.* New York: Random House.

Guo Dashun and Ma Sha (1985) Neolithic Cultures in the Liaohe Valley and Its Vicinity. *Kaogu Xuebao* 1985(4): 417–444 (in Chinese).

Han Rubin (1993) Recent Metallurgical Achievements at the University of Science and Technology, Beijing. Paper presented at the International Conference on Chinese Archaeology Enters the 21st Century, Sackler Museum, Beijing, May 29, 1993.

Lattimore, Owen (1932) *Manchuria, Cradle of Conflict.* New York: Macmillan.

Lin Yun (1985) The Tuanjie Culture. *Beifang Wenwu* 1985(1): 8–22 (in Chinese).

Lin Yun (1986) A Re-examination of the Relationship between Bronzes of the Shang Culture and of the Northern Zone, in *Studies of Shang Archaeology*, ed. K. C. Chang, pp. 237–273. New Haven, CT: Yale University Press.

Nelson, Sarah M. (1991) The Goddess Temple and the Status of Women at Niuheliang, China, in *The Archaeology of Gender*, ed. D. Walde and N. Willows, pp. 302–308. Proceedings of the 22nd Annual Chacmool Conference, Calgary, Alberta, Canada.

Nelson, Sarah M. (1992) A New Understanding of Korean Bronzes in the Light of Northern Chinese Bronzes, in conference papers, Vol. III, unpaginated.

International Academic Conference on Archaeological Cultures of the Northern Chinese Ancient Nations, Hohhot, Inner Mongolia, August, 1992.

Nelson, Sarah M. (1993) Ideology and the Formation of the Early State in China, symposium on Ideology and the Emergence of the Early State, at the International Congress on Anthropological and Ethnographic Sciences, Mexico City, August, 1993.

Service, Elman R. (1975) *Origins of the State and Civilization.* New York: W. W. Norton.

Spence, Jonathan (1990) *The Search for Modern China.* New York: W. W. Norton.

Wagner, Maike (1992) Impromptu talk with slides at the International Academic Conference on Archaeological Cultures of the Northern Chinese Ancient Nations, Hohhot, Inner Mongolia, August, 1992.

Watson, William (1971) *Cultural Frontiers in Ancient East Asia.* Edinburgh: Edinburgh University Press.

Whitaker, Donald P. and Rinn-Sup Shinn (1972) *Area Handbook for the People's Republic of China.* Washington, DC: US Government Publication DA Pam 550–60.

Wu, K. C. (1982) *The Chinese Heritage.* New York: Crown Publishers.

Wu Rukang and John W. Olsen (1985) *Paleoanthropology and Palaeolithic Archaeology in the People's Republic of China.* Orlando, Fla: Academic Press.

Yang Xiaoneng (1988) *Sculpture of Prehistoric China.* Hong Kong: Tai Dao Publishing.

Part I

NEOLITHIC

1

HONGSHAN AND RELATED CULTURES

by Guo Da-shun

EDITOR'S INTRODUCTION

Guo Da-shun's chapter is ambitious in scope and coverage. It is given the lead-off position in the section on the Neolithic because, although it focuses on Hongshan at the end of the Neolithic, the chapter covers a long temporal span and most of Liaoning province. It is thus a somewhat unusual but effective introduction to Dongbei Neolithic.

Guo argues for the centrality of the Hongshan culture for understanding the Neolithic and Bronze Age in the Dongbei, and sees Hongshan as a turning point in Chinese culture, suggesting that the Hongshan should be considered "the dawn of Chinese civilization." While Hongshan may not be earlier than other emergent polities in China, it is important to call attention to the unusual features of Hongshan. Guo also argues for local continuities, perceiving Lower Xinle and earlier Neolithic cultures as the antecedents of Hongshan. He also sees Lower and Upper Xiajiadian, and even possibly the Shang dynasty, as the successors of Hongshan. He proposes these connections not merely as a temporal sequence but as a continuity of culture, of changing but linked traditions.

This chapter includes a wealth of detail about Hongshan sites and other archaeological sites in Liaoning. The so-called Goddess Temple is a major unexpected discovery, with its odd shape and painted walls. The statuary, too, is surprising, especially the female face with blue-green jade eyes, as well as the enormous size of some statues hinted at by the ear that is three times life-size, and the presence of statues of both pigs and birds. The elite tombs also have unusual and interesting features, with their subsidiary burials, their rows of bottomless pots, and their emblematic jades. The jades have become world-famous for the fineness of their execution, but more ordinary sites have their importance as well; for example, the stone plows that indicate the intensification of agriculture in the Hongshan period. Another feature of interest is the black-on-red painted pottery, which is seen as a link between Hongshan and the Yangshao Neolithic of the Zhongyuan. The odd fact of the grave pottery being bottomless is not addressed in the chapter, but one of my students suggested the pots might have held candles or flares, like luminarias, surrounding the grave with light in its final ceremony. It seems as good an explanation as any, and could be tested.

Guo argues for the continuity of the altar, temple, and cairn, begun at Niuheliang, through Chinese history right up to the Qing dynasty. The reader is invited to judge the arguments on their merits. The most compelling of these for me is the continuity of the outdoor altar, which is not only characteristically Chinese, but is different from ceremonial sites elsewhere in the world.

Pre-Hongshan sites specifically mentioned are Chahai east of Hongshan near Fuxin, the oldest Neolithic site discovered so far in the Dongbei, and the Xinglongwa culture which overlaps Liaoning province and Inner Mongolia and is closer to Hongshan geographically. Both are dated in the sixth millennium BCE, equivalent in age to the earliest Neolithic sites in the Zhongyuan.

Nearby cultures contemporaneous with Hongshan, Fuhe and Zhaobaogou, are also discussed for their similarities to and differences from Hongshan.

Post-Hongshan sites in western Liaoning no longer have ceremonial centers and large square cairn burials. The pottery is different, including the appearance of the thunder pattern and pedestal vessels. Echoes of Longshan are notable. Although these sites reflect a less intensive cultural development, they are seen as a link between Hongshan and Lower Xiajiadian.

Finally, Guo notes the contact between Hongshan and Yangshao in the region of the present Great Wall. He concludes by invoking some documents of legend and history which include the far north as part of the imperial realm.

S.M.N.

This chapter focuses on the Hongshan culture, although it touches on several other cultures as well: "Pre-Hongshan" culture and "Post-Hongshan" culture, Neolithic cultures located in the same region, and other cultures contemporary with Hongshan. The main distribution of the Hongshan culture is in western Liaoning between 4000 and 3000 BC.

HISTORY OF DISCOVERY AND RESEARCH

The term Hongshan culture is derived from the site called Hongshanhou in the suburbs of Chifeng, Inner Mongolian Autonomous Region. This site was first excavated by Hamada Kosaku and Mizuno Seiichi in 1935, and published as *Chifeng Hongshanhou* in 1938.[1] Earlier, in 1908, Torii Ryuzo made a related survey along the bank of the Yingjin river in Chifeng,[2] and in 1923, the Swedish geologist J. G. Andersson discovered similar remains at the site of Shaguotun Cave in Jingxi county, Liaoning province.[3] In 1930, Liang investigated a similar site in Linxi county in the eastern region of Inner Mongolia and along the valley of the Yingjin river.[4] Liang Si-yong, along with two other Chinese archaeologists, Yin Da and Pei Wen-zhong, studied this culture carefully. Painted pottery and pottery with Z-shaped comb-patterns coexisted, as well as ground stone and microlithic tools, indicating the existence of dual cultural factors from the north and from the central plains of China.

In the 1930s, although archaeological data were insufficient, Liang was already predicting that the difference between the areas south and north of the West Liao river should be dealt with as an important topic. He also realized the importance of the fact that the Great Wall zone is where the southern and northern cultures meet.[5] In the 1940s, Pei proposed that the integration of the painted pottery culture of central China with the microlithic culture of northern China created a mixed culture.[6] In the early 1950s, Yin made an analysis of Hongshan culture, based upon Liang's proposal. He further suggested that this was a new type of archaeological culture resulting from contact between the Neolithic cultures of the south and the north. He then named it Hongshan culture and hypothesized that this new culture would be of great significance for studying the relationship between the areas south and north of the Great Wall in the Neolithic.[7]

Very little research was done on Hongshan and related cultures in the 1950s and 1960s, compared with the large-scale work in central China. The related sites were mainly discovered by Beijing University students who did their practical training at the Hongshan site.[8] The archaeological team of the Inner Mongolia Autonomous Region surveyed along the valleys of the Sharamurun and Laoha rivers. The excavation of the Fuhegoumen site by the Inner Mongolia Team of the Archaeological Institute of the Chinese Academy of Social Sciences was both large-scale and complete, providing a great deal of data on this dwelling site of the microlithic cultural system.[9] The research design focused on differentiating various types of microlithic cultures, and Hongshan culture was formally separated from Fuhe culture.[10] Until that time, the common understanding regarding Hongshan culture was that it was a Late Neolithic culture in North China, greatly influenced by the Yangshao culture in central China, with a date roughly corresponding to Late Yangshao.

In the 1970s, discovery and research entered a new stage, not at first deriving from the discovery of new archaeological sites, but rather from the recognition and reappraisal of a group of jade objects which had been scattered all over the world and neglected. These jade objects were already recorded in publications of the Qing dynasty.[11] There were also examples in the collection of the Fogg Museum [since moved to the Sackler Museum] at

Harvard University, and museums in San Francisco, Paris, Australia, Tokyo University and elsewhere.[12] Some of these jade objects were also found in China, in such places as the Tianjin Municipal Art Museum, Chifeng Municipal Museum in Inner Mongolia, and Liaoning Provincial Museum, as well as located in antique shops.

In 1975, at Hutougou village in Huashige township, Fuxin county, Liaoning province, one source of such jade objects was discovered.[13] Several jade ornaments in the shapes of tortoises, birds, and fish were unearthed from a stone grave under the edge of the east bank of the Mangniu river. A burial of the Spring and Autumn period (800–400 BCE) was superimposed upon this grave. The coffin in which the jade was found was surrounded by stone slabs, around which was standing a row of eleven painted cylindrical vessels without bottoms. This stone grave was very unusual in terms of its structure. It was quite different from most earth-pit burials, because the entrance to the grave was unclear. In addition, this group of jade objects had special shapes as well as advanced techniques. No one had ever thought of dating the jades by the painted pots from the cemetery. The first archaeologist to make this connection was Sun Shou-dao, who treated the stone wall, the painted cylindrical pots under the wall, and the grave with the jade objects as a complete unit.[14]

In 1979, a stone cist grave with similar jade objects was discovered at Sanguandianzi[15] in Lingyuan county. Many painted potsherds were scattered over the grave. Contrasting the jade dragon excavated from nearby Hongshan sites at Sanxingtala, Wengniute Banner, Inner Mongolia,[16] and considering the numerous jade pendants excavated from Hongshan culture sites at Nasitai, Balinyouqi[17] and others, Sun Shou-dao and Guo Da-shun submitted a paper in 1981 (published in *Wenwu* three years later[18]) arguing that this group of jade objects belonged to the Hongshan culture. In 1979–1981, after the sacrificial site and the pottery human figures of Hongshan culture were discovered at the Dongshanzui site, in the Mongolian Autonomous county of Kelaqinzuoyi (hereafter called Kezuo county), we realized that Hongshan culture was more complex than previously thought, and should be re-evaluated.[19] The discovery of the Goddess Temple and the clusters of stone tombs at Niuheliang led to the hypothesis that the dawn of Chinese civilization was five thousand years ago.[20]

At about the same time, the three excavations at Xinglongwa Aohan Banner, Inner Mongolia,[21] at Zhaobaogou,[22] and at Xiaoshan,[23] artifacts were found which were earlier than the Hongshan culture. Therefore the category of Pre-Hongshan culture was proposed. The discovery of Nantaidi site at Baisilongyingzi, Xiaoheyan township, Aohan Banner, and that of Danangou cemetery in Wengniute Banner led to the proposition of Post-Hongshan culture.[24]

The understanding and knowledge of Hongshan culture have deepened to a great extent over the last ten years. In the following, I will deal with Hongshan culture, Pre-Hongshan culture, Post-Hongshan culture and related cultures in that order.

HONGSHAN CULTURE

Distribution and types of site

The boundaries of the distribution of Hongshan culture are not yet completely clear, but the northern boundary seems to be beyond the Sharamurun river. At such places as Nasitai at Balinyouqi, Haijinshan and other sites on the north bank of the river, typical Hongshan sites were found; further north along the valley of Wuerjimulun river the red pottery and painted potsherds characteristic of the Hongshan culture have also been collected. At the Yangjiayingzi site, and Lindong in the valley of the same river, layers of the Hongshan culture have been excavated as well.[25] Thus it can be seen that the Hongshan culture extended into the Mongolian plateau. The eastern boundary is located beyond Yiwulu mountain. Although there are fewer sites of the Hongshan culture there, yet farther beyond Kangping county in northern Liaoning, close to the lower reaches of the Liao river, Hongshan painted pottery can still be seen. The southern boundary is divided into two sections, the east and the west. The eastern section extends to the coast of Bohai Bay, but there are many fewer red vessels and no painted pottery, and there are differences in the shape as well. The western section goes beyond the Yan mountains [Yanshan] to the northern China plain, abutting the distribution area of the Yangshao culture and forming an area of contact between Yangshao and Hongshan. A similar situation occurs at the upper reaches of the Sanggan river in Wei county, where the remains of the Miaodigou type of Yangshao culture are dominant, although the painted pottery of Hongshan culture also occurs. This region can be regarded as the western boundary.[26]

In terms of density, typical sites of the Hongshan culture are found most often along the middle and upper reaches of the Laoha river, including Hongshanhou, Zhizhushan[27] and Xishuiquan[28] and Shandaowan, Aohan Banner[29], along the valley of the Yingjin river in a suburb of Chifeng city and Nasitai at Balinyou Banner along the valley of Sharamurun river. They are all located on heights, mostly on hills approximately 10–40 m above the river level (Figure 1.1).

After the discovery of the Goddess Temple and the cairn burials at Niuheliang, we further investigated the locations and distribution of Hongshan culture. We have found that to the north of Niuheliang the culture goes as far as Chifeng via the Laoha river, to the east to Chaoyang and Fuxin via the Daling river, to the northeast to the Aolai River valley via

25

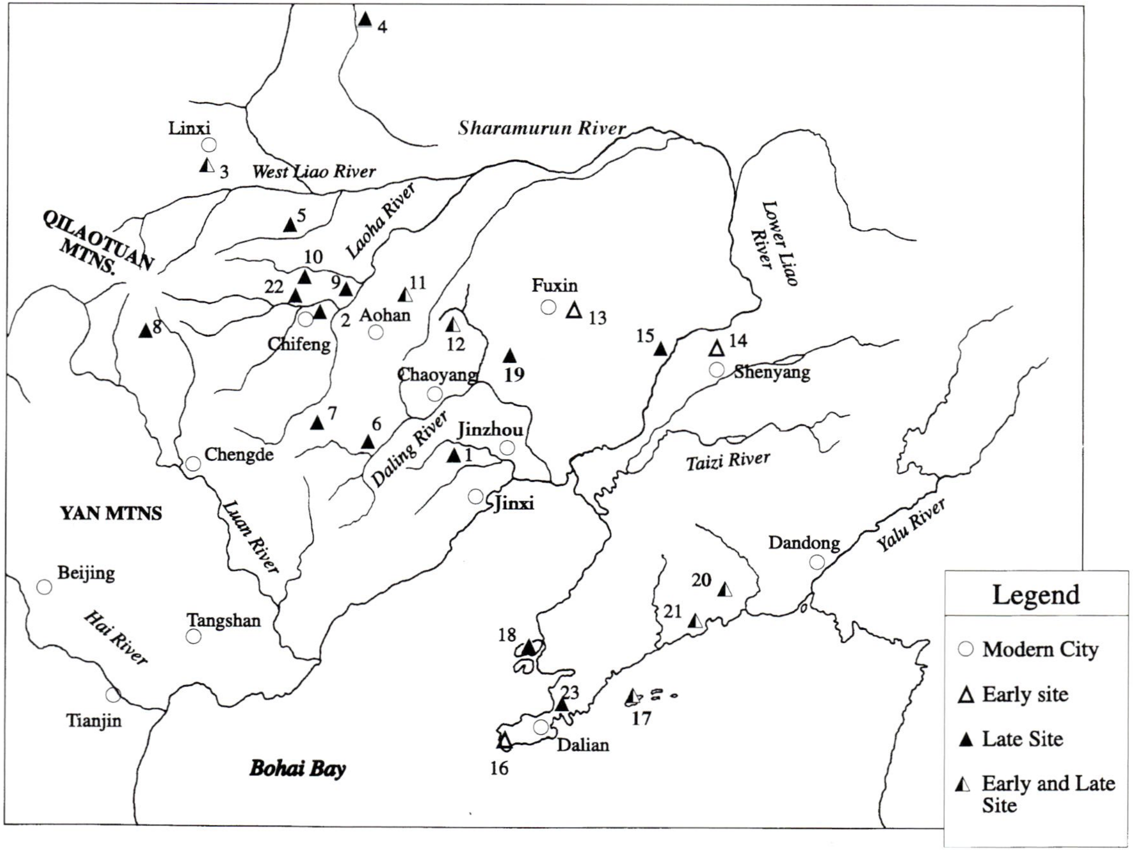

Figure 1.1
Distribution of the
Hongshan culture
and other Neolithic
cultures in Liaoning.
Key
1) Shaguotun
2) Hongshanhou
3) Shawozi
4) Fuhegoumen
5) Sanxingtala
6) Dongshanzui
7) Niuheliang
8) Weichang
9) Xiaoheyan
10) Danangou
11) Zhaobaogou
12) Xinglongwa
13) Chahai
14) Xinle
15) Pianbao
16) Guojiacun
17) Xiaozhushan
18) Santang
19) Hutougou
20) Houwa
21) Beiwutun
22) Xishuiquan
23) Dajuzi

Nuluerhe valley, to the southwest to Chengde and south of the Yanshan, and to the Bohai Sea via the west and south branches of the Daling river. Niuheliang is located in the center of a network leading to all the regions of the Hongshan culture. Thus it is demonstrated that Niuheliang is one of the centers of Hongshan culture.

As to the outlying Hongshan culture, its features vary. This is quite obvious mainly along the basins of the Daling and Xiaoling rivers and along the basin of the Laoha river as well as in the zone to the north. For instance, cairns are found only along the basins of the Daling and Xiaoling rivers where they are quite densely located, while along the Laoha river and to the north there are none. However, many densely distributed dwelling sites are seen in the Laoha River basin, whereas there are fewer along the valley of the Daling and Xiaoling rivers. These are just some of the differences in the sites between these two adjacent regions. For example, stone plows [si] are more often seen in the Hongshan sites along the basin of the Laoha river, whereas along the Xiaoling river there are very few. Fish-scale patterns painted on pottery are mainly found along the Liaoha river and the painted pottery with a motif of plant-like designs is quite common along the valley of the Daling and Xiaoling rivers. These differences have great significance for the chronology. Based upon the current knowledge of the dates of Hongshan culture, the Laoha River basin includes remains of the Hongshan culture from the early period to the late period, while the clusters of cairns along the basins of the Daling and Xiaoling rivers arose in the late period. However, regional differences cannot be excluded, so that archaeological sites of the Hongshan culture in these two regions must be dealt with separately. The Hongshan culture along the Laoha river is therefore named the West Hongshan culture, while that along the Daling and Xiaoling rivers is the East Hongshan culture.

Dates and chronology

The chronology has been difficult to determine, since most of the known Hongshan culture deposits are very thin. In addition, full-scale exposure of sites is uncommon, nor are intact vessels available in large groups. According to Zhang Xing-de, the Hongshan culture can be divided into three phases. The first phase is represented by Zhizhushan site and Xishuiquan (Tomb F17) in Chifeng, with numerous fine-clay red vessels and red-rimmed bowls. The cylindrical pots are mostly thick-lipped, and the black-and-red painted pottery has a motif of scale designs. More chipped than polished stone tools are found. The second phase is represented by Shandaowan (H1) in Aohan Banner as well as the second level of Chengzishan in Lingyuan county, with characteristics including ring-footed bowls, plain bowls, basins, thinner-lipped cylindrical pots, black painted pottery and cylindrical pots with patterns of connected hooks, and an increase in polished stone tools. The third phase is typified by Dongshanzui and Niuheliang, with black pottery, waisted stone hoes, and painted pottery with connected hook and plant designs. During this phase, cairns and jade animal figurines began to appear in great numbers, along with tripods and ring-footed vessels. Stone-constructed buildings and clay deity figures emerged, as well.

In terms of the chronology of the Hongshan culture, compared with the Yangshao culture in the Zhongyuan, the early period is close to the Hougang type, that is, the same time as the Early Yangshao culture; the late period is synchronous with the Miaodigou type, corresponding to the Late Yangshao culture. Four Late Hongshan C14 dates show that the Goddess Temple at Niuheliang (T113) is 4975 ± 85 BP, calibrated at 3740~3520 BCE, and Dongshanzui is 4895 ± 70 BP (3650~3420 BCE).[30] It is therefore inferred that the time period for Hongshan culture is between 4000 and 3000 BC.

Contents

In addition to stone tools, pottery, house floors, and burials, which are commonly encountered in the Neolithic, Hongshan also has jadeware, clay human figures, and other features. Therefore the contents to be described here are richer and more varied than the Neolithic usually contains.

Stone tools

In Hongshan sites, stone tools have several notable features (Figure 1.2). 1) Many kinds of stone tools are found in these sites, and there are more stone objects than in earlier Neolithic sites. Some sites have more stone objects than pottery. 2) Polished stone tools, chipped stone tools, and microliths coexist. Polished stone tools are the most common, chipped tools are second, and microliths are rarest. 3) Very large stone tools occur. The main types include rectangular grinding slabs, grinding stones with a D-shaped cross-section, narrow-bladed stone axes with an oval cross-section, chipped shouldered stone hoes, and stone adzes chipped into a long rectangular shape. Polished stone plowshares [*si*] are common Hongshan stone tools. They can be classified into two types: Type I, which has a long willow-leaf shape, 30–35 cm long, is usually made of granite; and Type II, which is wide and short, is usually made of limestone. 4) The techniques of both grinding and polishing are developed. Of the polished stone tools, some of the materials are carefully selected, with some almost jade-like.

The technique of manufacture is very fine. For example, the perforated stone knife in the shape of a bay leaf has a thin body, smooth surface, and regular shape. The small jade adze is finely polished, and the four edges and

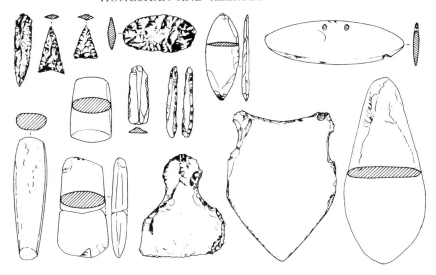

Figure 1.2 Stone tools from the Hongshan culture

the blade are sharp, although the selected material is extremely hard. These examples indicate that although in the Hongshan culture people had a good command of stone-polishing technology, and a wide range of polished stone tools was used, the technique for chipping stones did not deteriorate. On the contrary, flaking was also widely used to create tools and the technical level of production is evident in the careful selection of material such as slate, most of which is very hard, but good for flaking. The tools are symmetrical with bifacial flake removal. Tool shapes are standardized; for example, long-square adzes and shouldered hoes are flaked into the same shapes as the polished stone tools, but with sharper blades than the polished examples. These were made by first polishing and then chipping the blade, in order to achieve the twin results of standardization and sharpness. 5) Microliths are made of materials such as flint, jade, agate, crystal, and other similar hard stones. One typical shape is a triangular arrowhead with an indented base. Microliths, long and narrow blades about 3–4 cm by 0.5–1.0 cm, are mostly used as inlaid stones for composite tools. Conical cores are the main type of core from which they are detached.

In the Hongshan culture, very large stone tools are mostly related to agricultural production. Tools for plowing the earth and cutting implements are common, whereas there are relatively few hoes for tilling. This may indicate that cultivation is both intensive and extensive. Some of the thin sharp-bladed chipped tools and some microlithic blades probably were used for cutting skin and meat, suggesting that animal husbandry played an important role. The frequent appearance of stone arrowheads also bespeaks the existence of hunting. Bones of cattle, sheep, pig, and other domesticated animals as well as wild deer and other animals are found, reflecting a mixed economy.

Hongshan sites are distributed on the edge of the transitional belt where the grassland extends to the forest. The sites are located at higher elevations, and the cultural deposits are very thin. These conditions indicate that Hongshan had a mixed economy of farming and animal husbandry.

Pottery

Pottery is mainly red or grey with sand temper. Most of the grey pottery was fired at a high temperature, while red clay vessels tend to be made of coarse, thick paste. However, a very few are made of fine paste and painted red. By late Hongshan, some clay vessels have pure grey paste and some have black paste. The dark grey vessels are hand-made. Although the paste is soft, the inner and outer surfaces are polished, with regular shapes. The walls are thin, demonstrating that pottery technology was advancing toward a new stage. Most of the sandy grey-brown tall cylindrical pots are decorated with impressed Z patterns (rocker-stamping), comb-dot Z patterns, and incised designs. In addition a vessel is found with a mouth which slants down on one side, making a kind of scoop. Its purpose is not clear yet. There are some other more complex vessels made from this coarse paste, such as vessel lids resembling an upside-down basin. Although the lids are large, they are well manufactured, with Z patterns not only on the lid surface but also on the wide band. Loop handles were attached where the surface is decorated with hook-shaped patterns. The decorative patterns on this type of pottery vary, with some having impressed Z designs whose vertical lines overlap the horizontal lines, and others with horizontal lines on top of the vertical lines. In terms of the Z patterns, there are arc-shaped, vertical, and wavy lines as well as dotted lines (comb pattern). This kind of impressed Z pattern is found not only on the sandy grey pottery, but also on the bodies of red narrow-necked jars. In the late period this design is mostly restricted to black pottery, when the decorations became even more delicate (Figure 1.3).

Red clay pottery and sandy grey pottery are found in approximately equal amounts, although some sites have more red pottery than grey pottery. Common shapes of pottery include bowls and jars with two handles and straight collars. The bowls include narrow-mouthed with short walls and bent shoulders, and straight-mouthed, and others. Red-rimmed bowls were reddened on the rim when the pottery was stacked for firing while the rest of the body remained grey. They are found in most sites, and are characteristic of the Hongshan. Among the basins, there are bent-shouldered vessels with short and pointed rims, and globular vessels with short and pointed rims, straight-collared vessels with thick round rims, as well as narrow-mouthed vessels with folded rims.

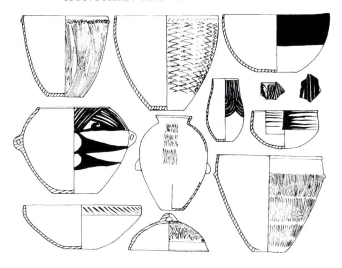

Figure 1.3 Typical pottery from the Hongshan culture

Outstanding painted pottery is found in Hongshan. The paint is mostly black, but red and purple also occur. The most characteristic patterns include fish-scales and connected floral hooks (Figure 1.4). The former is mainly found along the valley of the Laoha river, the latter along the Daling and Xiaoling rivers. The fish-scale patterns are painted on the walls of small-mouthed jars. They consist of concentric bands filled with scale patterns. This method is very similar to that used to decorate the dragons on some bronze vessels in the Shang dynasty, therefore it has attracted particular attention. Other painted pottery commonly has a design of parallel horizontal bands, either single or multiple. The motifs include matchstick-like lines, parallel slanting lines, connected triangular hooks with swirls, elongated triangles and diamonds, and others. Generally speaking the patterns are well organized, and the designs are regular. In Late Hongshan, the inside of a lid-shaped basin was painted with more than twenty concentric circles, all executed skillfully. The wall thickness of the painted pottery cylinders found at the Goddess Temple in Niuheliang is 2–2.5 cm, the diameter is over 1 m, and the geometric patterns are very regular.

Polished black pottery is mainly found at sites of the Late Hongshan culture along the Daling and Xiaoling rivers, including small tripod cups and large vessels with ring-feet.

At the Silengshan site in Aohan Banner, six kilns have been discovered where sandy clay pottery was found.[31] Each kiln consisted of three sections: pottery chamber, fire channel, and fire pit. Two kinds of kiln were found: single-chamber kilns and connected-chamber kilns. The single

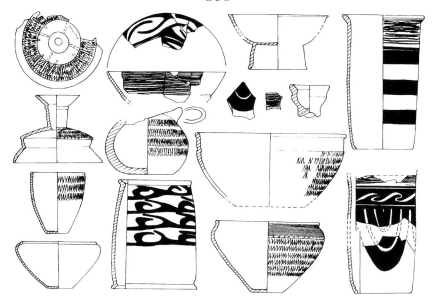

Figure 1.4 Pottery from the Late Hongshan culture

type has two or four pillars inside. For example, Y1 is a U-shaped single-room kiln, 1.4 × 1.38 m. The kiln chamber and the pillars are made of rocks, the surface of which is smoothed with clay paste mixed with straw. The pottery chamber is 1.2 m long and 0.6–0.8 m wide, slightly slanting.

An example of a connected-chamber kiln is Y6, which has double pottery chambers, with a rectangular plan. It is 1.0 × 2.7 m, with eight pillars. The kiln chambers as well as the pillars were made of earth and stone, with the surface smeared with clay paste mixed with straw. Two pottery chambers were located at each side, 1.8 m long, 0.8–0.95 wide, and 0.6–0.9 m high. These kilns are more advanced than the single-room kilns discovered in the Yangshao culture.

Dwellings

Hongshan sites discovered along the Yingjing River valley are often located on high terraces on southern or eastern slopes, generally about 10–40 m above the river level. The cultural accumulations are comparatively thin, varying from 0.5 to 2.0 m or so. Relative to the Lower Xiajiadian culture in the same region, the artifact scatter of each site is smaller and the sites are farther apart. Within a range of 180 km along both sides of the Yingjin river, only eighteen Hongshan sites have been discovered. The Xishuiquan site in Chifeng, for instance, is located 9 km north of Chifeng, on a hill between the Yingjin and Zhaosu rivers. The hill is 3 km long and the site is on the east slope of the hill. The site is 15–30 m above the modern river level, with a cultural deposit less than 1 m thick.

Dwelling sites of the Hongshan culture are found at the Xishuiquan and Yangjiayingzi sites in Balin Left Banner. Another was discovered at Dongshanzui in Kezuo. These dwelling floors are all square and subterranean. The house at Xishuiquan was built into the hill slope, with each side about 4 m long. The dwelling floor seemed to have been stamped, with a gourd-shaped hearth at the center. The hearth has a sloping fire tunnel, whose wall was plastered with mud mixed with straw. On the west side of the fireplace, rectangular river rocks were placed, which look like stone-bricks, either chopped or cut out of rocks. No post holes were found. A larger house floor is 9 × 11.7 m, with the long axis north-south. Slightly south of center a large gourd-shaped hearth with plastered walls is 0.9 m deep. The slightly sloping house entrance faces south. Within these dwellings there are often several complete sets of agricultural implements such as stone hoes, knives, arrowheads, axes, adzes, grinding stones, and grinding slabs. Whole sets of living utensils, such as cooking pots, containers, and storage containers, were also found. This suggests that these large dwellings might include several households.

Graves and accompanying jade artifacts

So far, Hongshan graves have only been found along the valleys of the Daling and Xiaoling rivers in the southern section of the Hongshan region. The grave structure is mainly of the cairn type. This type of cairn is often situated on a high hill. Generally one or two cairns were erected on one hill, but occasionally the number exceeds five. A large grave is usually found at the center of the cairn, whose construction begins below ground. A stone cist was built inside an earth-pit with a single body buried extended and supine, head toward the east. Several smaller ones were ranged around the central grave, mostly placed on the ground surface. The large tomb has very clear boundaries, which are marked neatly with stones in either square or circular shape. Both inside and outside the boundaries stand rows of cylindrical painted objects, like pots without bottoms. Stones and earth were piled on top of the grave to seal it. White limestone was often used for this purpose.

Some examples are Chengzishan at Sanguandianzi in Lingyuan, and Locality 2 at Niuheliang[32] (Figure 1.5). The cairn has not been completely exposed at Chengzishan. One large grave at the center has a burial chamber made of stone slabs. The chamber is 2.54 m long, 1.5 m wide, and 1.2 m deep with the head end wide and the foot end narrower, and the bottom larger than the opening. The opening is 2 m long, 0.45 m wide, and 1.6 m high. The bottom is 2.1 m from the ground surface. Slabs cover the bottom and top of the grave chamber. The human bones had decayed. Nine pieces of jade were recovered: one jade pendant in the shape of a hooked cloud at the chest, above it a jade hoop in the shape of a horse hoof, and two large jade *bi*, and below it three jade rings, one jade bead, and a bird-shaped jade.

Locality 2 at Niuheliang includes five stone tombs on a hill, numbered from west to east. No. 1 has a rectangular stone boundary wall. Although the central part was destroyed by an irrigation ditch, the north section of the wall is well preserved. One section of it is 35 m long, with cylindrical pots placed in a row inside. If each pot had a diameter of 30 cm, this line of pots would number over 100. Surrounding the central grave and touching each other, 16 small stone cist burial pits were excavated (Figure 1.6). In some burials there are from one to five jade objects. Grave 4, for example, has an opening 1.98 × 0.4–0.55 m, with a height of 0.5 m. Three jade objects were found, including a hoof-shaped jade hoop under the head and a pig-dragon-shaped jade decoration on the chest. The body seems to be a male. The large central burial in this cairn has not been found. Cairn 2 has a

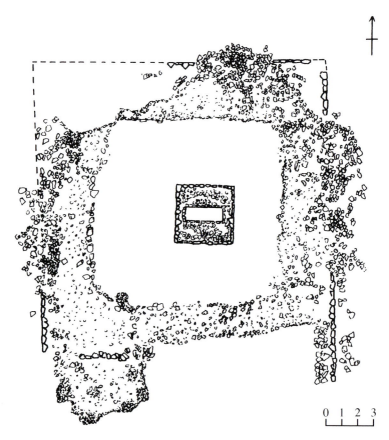

Figure 1.5 Plan of cairn with stone tomb at Niuheliang, Hongshan culture

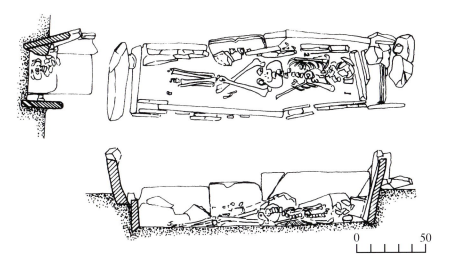

0   50

Figure 1.6 Plan view and cross-section of stone slab grave at the center of cairn at
Niuheliang

square boundary wall, the side facing south is 16.4 m long. This cairn does
not have attached small burials. The central grave is a square platform, with
a stone slab coffin. Each side is 3.6 m long, and the inner coffin is 2 m
deep. No human bones or burial objects were found. Most of the earth and
stones covering the top had already been removed; probably at an earlier
time the burial was robbed or moved to another place. Cairn 3 is like a
round earth altar with red granite stones used for the boundary walls,
forming three concentric circles, each higher as they go inward. The
diameter of the exterior circle is 19.2 m. No trace of either graves or
burials has been discovered at the center. This cairn has a different
structure from the others. It is more like an altar than a burial. Cairn 4 is
a double cairn with two linked together. The ground plan of the cairn at the
west is square at the bottom and round at the top, whereas the one at the
east is square at the south and round at the north. The whole cairn, 30 ×
30 m, is the largest of all. Cairn 5, whose surface was exposed, has a
rectangular boundary wall. The five cairns discussed above are all quite well
made and the structures on the ground are also well designed with many
features, suggesting that this place might have been used to hold sacrificial
ceremonies at the graves.

So far all the jade objects belonging to the Hongshan culture which
have clear excavational context have been found in cairns at Niuheliang,
Sanguandianzi, and Dongshanzui in Kezuo. Along the Laoha River valley,
jade objects are frequently discovered also, but although contexts are often
given, the connections are not clear. As no official report on cairn discovery

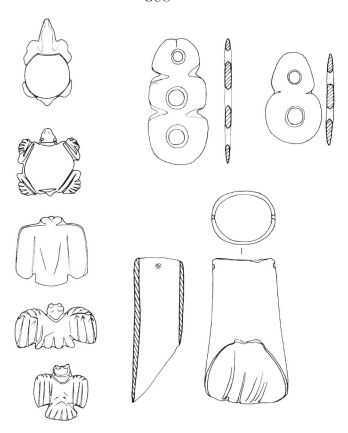

Figure 1.7 Hongshan culture jade turtles (upper left), jade birds (lower left), jade *bi* (upper right), and jade hairband (lower right)

along the Laoha River valley is available, these excavated jade objects need to be studied further. Summing up all the information and the material that we have available on Hongshan jade objects, the following features are salient.

1) Shapes: In addition to the common shapes of the Neolithic, such as beads, rings, semi-annular jade pendants [*huang*], and *bi*, animal shapes are found, such as dragons, tigers, pigs, tortoises, birds, and cicadas (Figure 1.7, left). In terms of the jade *bi*, which is usually round, there are also double-ring *bi* and three-ring *bi*, hook-cloud jade pendants and hoof-shaped jade hoops. Most of these jade objects are clothing ornaments, although the jade hoop might be for binding hair together. Some of the jade objects are very large. The largest is a jade dragon unearthed from Sanxingtala, Wengniute Banner, Inner Mongolia (Figure 1.8, right). This jade dragon is 26 cm long.

36

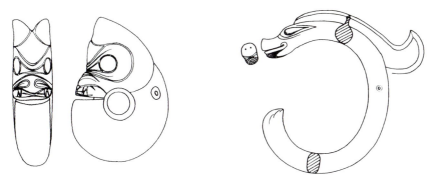

Figure 1.8 Hongshan culture jade pig-dragon (left) and jade dragon (right)

Jade pendants are usually about 10 cm in diameter; and jade hoops are 15 cm long with a diameter of 8 cm or so.

2) The jade source is not yet clear. It is often said that the material is serpentine from Xiuyan county in the east Liaoning mountainous regions, because that source of very pale green "jade" is quite well known. However, the material selected for Hongshan jade artifacts is soft jade, whose colors are light green, milk white, and dark green, therefore the source for this jade material remains to be discovered. Ornaments made of a turquoise-colored material were also found; for example, a fish and a bird. These are the two earliest animal objects made of turquoise known so far in China. Although these turquoise objects are few compared with jade artifacts, they serve well for ornament or decoration, so that they should be considered as valuable artistic objects.

3) The manufacturing technique is unique. Usually jade objects are plain, without surface designs. For thin jade objects like the hook-cloud jade pendant, the edge is polished into blade shape from both facets, and on the body, shallow hook lines are engraved parallel to the shape of the object. These hook lines, reflected from different angles, produce a decorative beauty, flickering under the light, preventing a flat appearance. In terms of carved animals and birds, the elaborate carving is not obvious at first glance, but if carefully observed, the feet, wings and head are very well made, indicating a high artistic technique. Furthermore, the mysterious effect of this group of jades is enhanced.

Sacrificial sites and statues

At Niuheliang, located at the border between Lingyuan and Jianping counties, and Dongshanzui, Kezuo county, sacrificial sites of the Hongshan culture have been found. There is a distance of 50 km between these two sites. Niuheliang is much the larger, but the two might be considered roughly as a single unit.

Dongshanzui is located on the west bank of the Daling river, 4 km southeast of Kezuo county. The site is at the exact center of a terrace on a hill ridge north of the village, with dimensions of 60 m long and 40 m wide. It is 50 m or so above the river-bed. The main part of the site consists of a round, altar-like structure in the south and a square structure in the north. The round building is 2.5 m in diameter, paved neatly with stone slabs on the four sides, and the altar floor is paved with pebbles. Nearby, painted pottery lids, small dark tripods, and pottery statues in small and medium sizes were excavated. Northeast of the round altar a complete human skeleton was found, supine with the head pointing east. The midsection was covered with huge potsherds. It is speculated that this might be a human sacrifice.[33]

The square structure is 11.8 m long from east to west, and 9.5 m wide. The four remaining sides are paved with from two to four layers of stones. The exterior is smooth, and the technique of paving is similar to that of the stone boundary walls of cairns. In the middle of the southern part of the square structure there is a round pile of stones, which consists of erect tall stones. The square structure, along with its inner circular stone pile, stands on the same axis from south to north as the round structure in the south, just 15 m distant. Judging from the location, the geographic features of the whole site, the structures, and the patterns as well as the artifacts of non-daily life, this site is different from usual living sites, and should be regarded as a ritual site.

The large site of Niuheliang is located on the border between Jianping and Lingyuan counties. It is on a loess ridge extending from east to west for over 5 km. It was named for the nearby Mangniu river, a tributary of the Daling river. In this region there is much loess. Within a range of 50 km^2, over ten sites of various kinds have been discovered. The Goddess Temple and the huge platform at the top of the major mountain ridge constitute the center of the whole cluster of sites. In the surrounding hills, clusters of cairns are distributed, among which the one just to the south of the temple (Locality 2 mentioned previously) is the largest. Looking far to the south, Mulan mountain, whose main peak resembles a pig's head, may be a related site, also.

So far only the surface layer of the Goddess Temple has been uncovered. It is 25 m long from south to north, and 2 to 9 m wide. It is subterranean, with multiple chambers: a main chamber, a north chamber, right and left side-chambers, a south triple chamber and a south single chamber, making altogether eight units. Six to seven individual pieces of human clay statues have been excavated from the temple, including one head, ears, noses, hands, breasts, upper arms, legs, etc. Parts of clay animal figures, such as pig-dragon feet and bird claws, were excavated, as well as large painted pottery vessels with openwork, and the lid of an incense burner with comb patterns. The human clay figures excavated from both Dongshanzui and Niuheliang can be divided into three scales: large, medium, and small. The largest ones are mostly found in the Goddess Temple at Niuheliang. Although complete statues have not been restored yet, judging from the remaining fragments they were sitting cross-legged, nude, with the back of the body attached to the wall. The human clay figures are life-sized, and some of the broken ears are twice as large as life-size. At the center of the main chamber, some excavated broken pieces of noses and ears are surprisingly three times as large as life-size. The most precious object unearthed was a likeness of a complete human head, excavated from the west side of the main chamber. The surviving length of the head is 23 cm. The eyes are slanting and filled with blue-green jade pieces for irises, making them very lifelike. The corner of the mouth turns outwards, with a smiling expression as if wishing to speak. The cheekbones are raised and wide, the ears are small and thin, the face surface is smooth. This face seems to have many female features. In addition, the square face, the slanting eyes, the low and short nose-bridge and the round nose-tip are all characteristics of Mongoloids.

A medium-sized clay statue was found at Dongshanzui, including a torso and a lower body belonging to the same individual. The upper fragment is 18 cm high, 22 cm wide, and 0.9 cm thick. It is a torso from the chest to the abdomen with the left arm missing but the right arm present, the two arms placed across the abdomen. The left hand is in a fist, the right hand holding the wrist of the left hand. The fingernails of the right hand are long. The lower piece is 12.5 cm tall, 22 cm wide. It is hollow, with a 3–4 cm thick wall. It is sitting with legs crossed, right leg on top of the left. The right foot is missing. The left foot and toes are bare, but the surface of the sole is decorated with mat patterns.

Figurines were found at Dongshanzui, Niuheliang, and Xishuiquan (Figure 1.9). All the heads are missing. Two pieces were found at Dongshanzui, one 5 cm tall, the other 5.8 cm tall. Both are nude standing figures, with large abdomen and hips and a clear indication of the vulva. The left arm is bent, with the left hand on the abdomen. These features suggest pregnant women. The figurine at Xishuiquan has particularly large breasts.

Clusters of deity statues are a hallmark of Hongshan culture. Such statues are not found in other Neolithic cultures of China, but they have much in common with human statues found in other parts of the world in the Neolithic. Considering the discovery of the clay statue clusters as a benchmark, we are beginning to take a completely new look at the position of Hongshan culture in China, in northeast Asia and in a wider range.

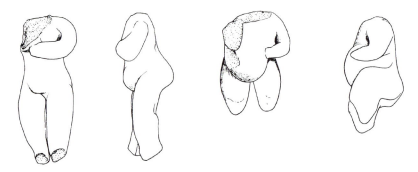

Figure 1.9 Clay female figurines from Dongshanzui, Kezuo

Preliminary analysis of social formation

It has been commonly considered that the period of Hongshan culture (around 3500 BC) belongs to a primitive society, like that along the Yellow River valley. In other words, it is the transitional period of primitive clan communities in which matriarchal clans were declining in prosperity. Furthermore, it was thought that in the surrounding regions, societies developed later than in the Zhongyuan. Hongshan culture has long been considered to be a mere branch culture in a remote region, so that it was impossible to consider that it might surpass the developmental stage of the nuclear region. However, in the light of the contents of Hongshan culture, it seems necessary to re-evaluate the social relationships of the Hongshan culture.

Production tools and subsistence

Stone tools were the main production tools of primitive agriculture. They are quite similar to those of the Neolithic cultures in the Zhongyuan, but there are some unique features, and furthermore Hongshan shows a degree of additional advancement.

The techniques of skillful polishing and chipping are combined. This shows that the technology met the demands of agricultural development for more efficient production tools. Correspondingly, the materials used for stone tools were chosen according to different qualities of hardness and texture. The masterful skill, plus careful selection of the materials, have helped the production of stone tools become patterned and specialized. The stone tool inventory of the Hongshan culture can be divided into axes, knives, plowshares, adzes, chisels, hoes, choppers, pickaxes, grinding stones and slabs, etc. Within each category they can further be divided into several types, demonstrating a comparatively formal division of agricultural tasks, such as preparing the soil, plowing, tilling, and harvesting. There are more stone tools in Hongshan dwellings than in all the sites in the Zhongyuan at the same time, especially large stone tools and choppers. This suggests that there was increasing demand for expanding cultivated land. Therefore the amount of stone implements is a very important phenomenon. Another outstanding feature is the extensive utilization of the stone plow. Although large stone plows for tilling the soil are seen occasionally in the Zhongyuan, they do not play a very important role. In Hongshan culture they appear in great numbers. There have been disagreements as to whether these objects did function as plows; however, they have sharp tips for plowing points, and arc-shaped side wings, and they are long (usually over 30 cm); the other dimensions and weight demonstrate that the object could not have been attached to a short handle, and in addition the narrow and long back and waisted sides were made to attach it to a large fixed wooden tool. Most of the plow blades bear use marks, and they must have been the main plowing tools of this culture. Also the use-wear groove in the sharp point is long, gradually increased with constant use of the long side. These facts suggest that they were used as plowing tips, instead of for other purposes. This is consonant with the growing demand for plowing in response to rapid expansion of cultivation. Thus it should be considered that as a consequence of extensively using this kind of plow, Hongshan had already taken a significant step into plow agriculture.

Another difference between Hongshan stone tools and those in the Zhongyuan lies in the fact that there are a great many cutting tools, in addition to microlithic blades for composite inlaid blades and as scrapers; some of them are made of very hard material. The choppers with sharp blades, as well as the stone axes, are also related to cutting and scraping of hides. In Hongshan sites, many pig and sheep bones were excavated, showing that animal husbandry played an important role. The combination of plowing and stock-raising is characteristic of the Hongshan economy. It was also an advantage to the Hongshan culture, because the culture is distributed in a transitional region between the Mongolian grassland, which is a pure herding land, and the Yellow River valley where agriculture is practiced on a large scale.

Three handicraft industries and social division

Bronze

The most important handicraft industry in Hongshan culture is bronze metallurgy. Whether or not Hongshan people practiced casting and using metals still remains a question. On January 10, 1988, *People's Daily* carried a report on the discovery of a bronze-casting mold at the Xitai site in Xishuiquan, Aohan Banner, Inner Mongolia. The mold consists of two joinable pieces. It is made of dark pottery with red slip, the exterior outline is squarish, and at one side there is a runner and an exhaust hole. It might have been used to make bronze items such as simple bird-shaped bronze buttons. A Japanese edition of *People's China* also disclosed the news of a bronze-casting site at Niuheliang.[34] So far, the most important discoveries of large-scale bronze-casting have been found in the Erlitou and Erligang cultures, in the Zhongyuan. Several bronze artifacts were also unearthed from pre-Shang sites, most of which are copper, but bronze also is found. For instance, in the Qijia culture in the northwest region, which is contemporaneous with the Longshan culture, and at Lower Xiajiadian culture in the northern regions, there are also metal artifacts, most of which are true bronze. Bronze artifacts were found much earlier beyond the Zhongyuan, such as the bronze knife discovered at Majiayao in Donglin town, Gansu province,[35] with a date of about 3000 BC. The discovery of related bronze-casting in the Hongshan culture is therefore one of the earliest, and in addition, the two-piece mold was already in use. Thus bronze casting already existed around 3500 BC or so, and bronze-casting technology in this place was already quite impressive.

Pottery

The largest output of a handicraft industry now preserved in the Hongshan culture is pottery production. After the common pottery vessels for daily life, the largest amount of pottery comes from cairns. Painted cylindrical pots stood in rows surrounding the interior walls in the cairns at Niuheliang. Some cairns had more than one line of vessels. If the average mouth diameter of each pot is estimated as 30 cm and each side of the dividing line as 30 m, there would be 100 pots on each side, and each cairn would exceed 300–400 pots. Around 30 cairns have been located at Niuheliang, for which over ten thousand pots would have been used. Furthermore, this type of pot is very large, and painted, so that it can be inferred that there must have been a large, specialized workshop, which is yet to be found.

The pottery kiln found at Xiaoheyan in Aohan Banner, Inner Mongolia is more complicated in structure than the one from the Yangshao culture in the Zhongyuan which consisted of a single chamber and a horizontal pit. The Hongshan kilns are more systematic, and have a clearer division of labor, indicating a relatively advanced level. Besides, in the ritual sites at Dongshanzui and Niuheliang, a group of very delicately made pottery objects was unearthed; for example, a small polished bowl made of dark pottery decorated with neat comb-dot Z patterns. The largest tubular vessels have a diameter of 1 m across, while the wall is only 2 cm thick, and the paste has a very hard and dense quality. The exterior suface is painted bright red, and the inner paste also has a bright and pure color. To achieve this result requires great skill. This type of pot with such an excellent technique demonstrates that the pottery-making technique of Hongshan had entered an advanced stage.

Jade

The jade object production in Hongshan culture reflects the highest level of skill. Analyzing the type, the shape, the material, and the technology of several hundred jade objects leads to several conclusions. Since there was a great demand for the raw materials, and definitive working procedures included selecting the material, designing, carving, engraving, and polishing, the production required strict and specialized division of labor and a variety of specialized tools. In addition to tools for cutting, boring, etc., a primitive emery wheel and a simple machine with axle and transmission gearing may have been used. At Niuheliang the jade material which was used for carving and the raw material left after the object was carved off were both found, implying a workshop nearby. Several jade implements unearthed from the graves at Chengzishan in Sanguandianzi were made of chunks of jade material, but some of them are not of good quality. This might suggest that the making and using of jade implements had become in some degree commercialized.

The bronze-casting, pottery-making, and jade-carving mentioned above are the three major industrial accomplishments of the Hongshan culture. Large-scale production and specialized division of labor suggest that in addition to farming and animal husbandry, a large group of people was already engaged independently in handicraft industries. As this group of people understood the technology and organized and managed it, they became a special class which arose from primitive agriculture. Since these three industries all made products which were closely related to rituals, it is possible that those who organized, understood, and managed the key technologies became the elite in the society.

As the social division of labor develops into specialties, exchange must accordingly occur. Exchange in the Hongshan culture had developed into a new stage, the major landmark of which is the appearance of a medium of exchange – shell-like jade money. Shell was the earliest currency used in China, and the jade shell currency discovered at Niuheliang is the earliest so far found there. In the Shang dynasty, on oracle bones, the written character for wealth and money includes a shell. However, the currency shells which are found in the early periods by archaeologists are difficult to distinguish from shells used for decorative purposes. Shells definitely identifiable as currency are imitation shells. Previously imitation shells made of bronze were discovered at Anyang in the late Shang dynasty. The delicate jade imitation shells found at Niuheliang show that before bronze imitation shells were used as money, there was a period when jade shells had that function. This relates to the development of the exchange economy of the Hongshan culture. Farming and animal husbandry were both attractions to the Yellow River valley where only farming was practiced. In addition, the jade implements and the pottery which was used in quantity for rituals in the Hongshan culture also provided a condition for ritual objects to become commercialized.

Altar, temple, and cairn, and the origin of China's civilization

The economic development and the characteristics of Hongshan culture discussed above surpassed greatly the level of primitive clan communes. Moreover, the religious constructions in the combination of altar, temple, and cairn, which appeared on the basis of social production, reflect social stratification which had entered into the civilization stage.

As previously discussed, the exploration of the origins of civilization in the western Liaoning region was pursued in order to identify the jade objects of Hongshan culture, and it was first notable when jades were found in ritual sites at Dongshanzui and Niuheliang. The jade objects which were excavated and identified as Hongshan are obviously superior to those found at other places at the same time, because, first, the faunal images of specific types such as bird and animal became even more spiritual and, second, their production and use were more standardized. Although they were all unearthed from graves, they were no longer merely decorative but suggest symbols of class and status. A few of the objects might be symbols of power and authority. This suggests the division into classes among group members, and it is also the basis for raising the possibility of "primitive civilization." In addition, the ritual site built with stones at Dongshanzui had a pattern with a north-south axis, round in the front and square in the rear with two wings, of which one is more important than the other. This is very different from common dwelling sites in the Neolithic. Thus, although among the human figures unearthed from Dongshanzui the female figurines were objects symbolic of matriarchal clan society, we have noted signs of incipient civilization. Following the discovery of the Goddess Temple and the cairns at Niuheliang, the Hongshan culture is understood as representing a new stage, and in many aspects the discoveries reflect the origins of civilization.

Furthermore, we observe that, although the Niuheliang region has an area of nearly 50 km^2 located in a hilly region and varied in geographic features, all the sites are designed according to a definite pattern. The Goddess Temple with multiple chambers located at the center of the site is close in the north to a large stone platform. The platform and the temple are oriented in the same direction, and the central axis from the south to the north along the temple platform extends farther to the south, overlooking Zhushan, "Pig Mountain." Three big cairns and ritual altars are

located between them. This forms a primary pattern of the temple platform, stone altar and "Pig Mountain," in a line from south to north. Even
though there is a 20 degree difference due to the geographic location of the
mountain, the plan for their design from south to north is quite clear. The
rest of the site is built around this main axis, making this construction huge
in scale, including the altar, temple, and other locations where rituals were
to be conducted.

In addition, Niuheliang, with temple in the center and the combination
of the temple, cairn, and altar, suggests a complete unit for a ritual such as
worshipping ancestors. Locality 2 of Niuheliang, for example, has five big
cairns, lined up east to west. The round altar-like construction between the
East Cairn II and the West Cairn II, the three circles built with stone walls
which from exterior to interior increased in height, are considered to be a
ritual construction. In addition, a burned floor is found on the south side of
each cairn and a paved stone floor on the north side. All these are
important indications of ritual activities held at the graves. The ritual
activity held at the cairn locations was probably for sacrifice to deceased
ancestors, but the Goddess Temple at the center of the cairn clusters must
have been a ritual location of a higher level. The Goddess Temple was
made to a pattern which became traditional, with multiple differentiated
chambers, indicating that the ideology of worshipping ancestors within a
temple was already established. The several statues of various sizes also
show differentiation into primary and secondary within the statue complex.
The largest ones would be two to three times life-size, thus indicating
that they are the most important statues. Smaller statues imply lesser gods.
They also suggest the worship of multiple gods with a main one at the
center.

Moreover, although Niuheliang is located at the center of the Hongshan
culture, no dwelling sites have been found nearby. This suggests that this
ritual location was chosen to be distant from the dwelling quarters for the
sole purpose of a sacrificial place. Its scale is too large for only one clan or
tribe to own it, therefore it must have at least represented worship of a
common deity by this common culture. It is generally believed that the
worship of ancestors originated from the period of patriarchal family clan
communities, and when it entered the civilization stage, the family temple
became the symbol of power and authority. Throughout the history of all
dynasties in China, worship of ancestors has been very important, although
there has been little evidence of ancestral temples from prehistory to
history. The discovery of the Hongshan culture has shown that the worship of ancestors in the form of tombs and temples as an ideological system
may have been already very mature as early as five thousand years ago.

Third, the evidence indicates that the Hongshan culture entered the level
of civilization and established a social relationship with one individual at the
center. The pattern of a temple at the center with a complex of main deities

reflects this social relationship, and it is reflected even more obviously in the Hongshan tombs. One of the most salient features of the cairns is the central tomb. This tomb is huge in scale, and required a great deal of labor and expense. It contains superior-quality jade objects, and is surrounded by small graves with clear differentiation of the primary and the secondary. The covering earth, stones, and dividing stones as well as the cylindrical pots are designed specifically to make the large grave more outstanding, thus forming a "mountainous tomb," and fully indicating the authority and power of one individual who was superior over all others. The cairns have superceded the previous order of a common public graveyard under the clan system, and based on the prevalence of this system among Hongshan cairns, the system of opposing social relationship had been firmly established.

The indicators of the beginning of a civilization include: the formation of cities, the invention of a written language, and bronze metallurgy. However, these criteria are derived from the beginning of Western civilizations. China, as a center of Eastern civilization, embodies several features which are quite different from Western civilizations, so that the hallmarks for the beginning of Chinese civilization should not be limited by these three criteria. In connection with the Hongshan culture, it is the combination of the altar, the temple, and the cairns which shows the dawn of civilization, because the pattern is identical to that of the Ming Heavenly Altar, Temple, and Ming Shishan tomb several thousand years later. This is not simply coincidental, but suggests that the origin and development of Chinese civilization had their own tradition and features, and furthermore, that this tradition was repeated from generation to generation. In the meantime, the origin of a civilization as a great leap for human societal development should be seen to be a process whose beginning is traced back to the beginning of the clan system, from prosperity to disintegration, so that the earliest beginning of a civilization should be sought in this process. Thus the appearance of the altar, the temple, and the cairns in the Hongshan culture is a milestone in this process.

PRE-HONGSHAN, CONTEMPORANEOUS AND POST-HONGSHAN CULTURES

It is obviously critical to know how and why the Hongshan culture developed and what direction it took, since it is an archaeological culture with very rich content which played an important role in the origin of China's civilization and history. In recent years, within the area of Hongshan culture, including its central region, some new cultures related to Hongshan have been discovered, raising the possibility of studying the subject systematically. Some of the related cultures are earlier than Hongshan, therefore providing data to study its origin; these are called "Pre-Hongshan culture."

Others are later than Hongshan culture, and thus are helpful in assessing its continuing development; these are called "Post-Hongshan culture." In addition, some cultures within the same range and period as Hongshan culture have influenced and affected each other's development in the same process. These cultures will be covered in the following sections. Pre-Hongshan culture sites include Chahai and Xinglongwa.

Pre-Hongshan culture sites

Chahai [36]

The Chahai site is located at the eastern edge of the western Liaoning mountainous region. It is connected to the Song-Liao Plain in the east, under the jurisdiction of Sala township, Fuxin county, 5 km from Chahai village to the west. The site is in an open and gently sloping field. In the south runs a seasonal stream called Quanshuigou, and 5 km to the northeast stands the highest mountain of the region called Chahai mountain, 200 m or so above sea level. The site extends 200 m from south to north and 150 m from east to west. There is no modern village at the site and very little farmland, so that it remains in a natural state. The western portion of the site has been excavated, in an area of 2000 m^2. The cultural accumulations consist of yellow-brown soil above and grey-brown soil below, 60–70 cm altogether; below this stratum lies bedrock. House floors, pottery, stone tools, and jade implements have been discovered at the site.

Eleven houses have been found, all square with rounded corners. The site is oriented slightly to the west of south, and the houses are densely packed, with only 1 to 2 m between houses. Furthermore there are obvious size differences among the houses, with a large house in the center surrounded by small ones. The central house is 8 m long on each side, with the interior divided into rooms.

A pit and a hearth were found in the middle of each building, as well as a post hole at each of the four corners. Potsherds were scattered all over the dwelling floors. These potsherds are all of sandy clay, baked at low temperature. Neither red clay nor painted pottery sherds were found. The main shape is the cylindrical pot, with some bowls and tall jars, basins, cups, etc. Most of the pottery vessels are decorated, mainly with impressed patterns such as the Z pattern, the net pattern, and parallel slanting lines. The Z pattern is more common than impressed dots. Short impressed parallel lines forming "Z-like patterns" might be related to its beginning.

There are many chipped waisted stone axes, stone hoes, grinding stones and slabs, and also polished stone axes and adzes. Some of the small adzes are very finely polished. In addition, irregularly shaped flaked choppers are found. A group of jade objects was excavated. The shapes mainly suggest earrings, but jade spheres were also found. This group of jade objects is pure white in color, with regular shapes and a single hole bored from both faces, well polished on the whole body. The technique is very well developed. The earliest carbon date for the site is 6925 ± 95 BP [ZK-2138], which calibrates to 5712~5530 BCE, much earlier than the Hongshan culture.

Xinglongwa[37]

The Xinglongwa site is located on a hilly field in the eastern part of West Liaoning Province, in the upper reaches of the Mangniu river, under the jurisdiction of Baoguotou town of Aohan Banner, Chifeng, Inner Mongolia, and adjoins Beipiao county, Liaoning province, in the south. The archaeological site is about 1.3 km from Xinglongwa village in the southeast. It is on a low hill, about 20 m above the valley level, sloping from east to west. A spring flows from the base of the hill in the southwest, and about 1.5 km to the east of the hill a river channel was cut. Dwelling sites belonging to the Hongshan culture are found from the northeastern slope to the western slope, while the remains of the Xinglongwa culture are distributed on the southwestern slope of the hill, which is currently farming land. This is a comparatively intact settlement, with no sign of later disturbance. The "ash-earth circle" of each house, as well as an ash band surrounding the village, were exposed by plowing. The ash band formed an irregular circle, which might be considered the boundary of the village. The village is 183 m

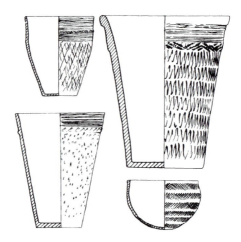

Figure 1.10 Pottery excavated at Xinglongwa

long from northeast to southwest, and 166 m wide. In the upper area a ditch, 1.5–2.0 m wide and 0.55–1.0 m deep, was disturbed by houses of the Hongshan culture. Over a hundred ash circles are lined up roughly from southeast to southwest, about eleven to twelve lines with ten ash circles per line.

The houses are subterranean, square with rounded corners, and the walls and floors of the houses are of native earth. The floor surfaces were rammed with tools, and there is a round hearth at the center of each house, some of them outlined with stones. Some of the houses are large, such as F1 (8.5 m long, 7 m wide); small ones like F2 are 5.1–5.4 m long and 3.5–3.8 m wide. Most of the artifacts, such as pottery, stone tools, and bone objects, were found in the houses.

The clay vessels are sand-tempered and hand-made (Figure 1.10). They are constructed by coiling, and on the outside of the rim extra clay strips were attached. Baked at low temperature, they lack pure colors, being either grey-brown or yellow-brown. The pottery types are like those of the Chahai site, mostly cylindrical jars, with straight rims, straight or slightly everted and thick round lips, straight sides and thick walls. Some of the jars are as tall as 50 cm. There are also pottery bowls. The designs consist of three to five varieties, mainly impressed or raised patterns. The compositions are very regular. They generally include: 1) impressed and raised patterns below the rim, with either impressed cross or net patterns on the body; or 2) impressed Z patterns, more commonly vertically impressed. Horizontal lines are rarely seen. Impressed dotted lines are more common.

In terms of stone tools, the most common are chipped shouldered hoes, whose shapes are somewhat irregular; next are disk-shaped implements and handled axes, as well as grinding stones and slabs. A kind of chopper is made from a stone core with only a few flakes removed. Polished stone tools, such as axes and adzes, are very finely made, with four definite edges. The long flaked blade, 10–18 cm long, 3–4 cm wide, and 1 cm thick, was attached to a bone handle. One kind of bone dart has three slots on one side where a line of microliths was inlaid. There are also bone awls and arrowheads. The arrowhead is long and conical, with a three-edged point (the original report called it an awl) (Figure 1.11).

Also unearthed from the dwellings were bones of animals such as deer, badger, and pig. Chestnuts have been identified among the plant remains. As to the date of the site, because the surrounding ditch was covered by house floors of the Hongshan culture, its date is assumed to be earlier than Hongshan. The C14 date for a sample from the dwelling floor of F119 is 7240 ± 95, the calibrated date is 6032~5760 BCE [ZK-1392].

In terms of the cultural contents, Chahai and Xinglongwa are very similar to each other, as well as nearly contemporaneous. Thus, the discovery of these two sites is of great significance for understanding the early formation of ancient western Liaoning culture, for the following reasons.

1) The subsistence base of these two sites is an integration of primitive agriculture with animal husbandry, fishing and hunting, and a sedentary life-style. These are the most primitive settlements known so far in the Liaoxi region.

2) Both sites are between 5000 and 6000 BCE, which is contemporaneous with the Cishan-Peiligang culture in the Yellow River basin. The dates are also close to those of some early sites in northeast Asia, including the Korean peninsula and the Japanese islands. Since they have much in common in terms of cultural features, it is no wonder that they are of great significance for studying early agriculture and culture and its relations around Bohai Bay.

3) From present knowledge, a related site to the north is the Fushunyong site in Keshiketeng Banner, Inner Mongolia, north of the Kelamulun river; to the east there is the Shengfuquan site in Naiman Banner, Zhelimumung on the left bank of the middle reaches of the Aolai river. A roughly similar overburden lies between them and the Hongshan culture. The cultural contents, with Z pattern as the main decoration of the pottery, link them closely to Hongshan culture, therefore they provide excellent sources for tracing the origin of the Hongshan culture, both the Z-patterned pottery and agriculture in Liaoxi. The Chahai site in particular, where Z patterns are dominant, should be regarded as a precursor of Hongshan culture.

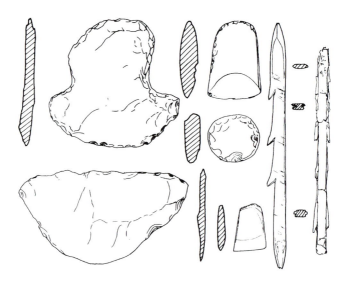

Figure 1.11 Stone and bone tools excavated at Xinglongwa

50

Contemporaneous cultures

Fuhe culture

Typical sites of the Fuhe culture are mostly found north of the Sharamurun river; for example, Jinguishan, Yangjiayingzi, and Fuhegoumen. Fuhegoumen, the type site,[38] is located 150 km north of the Sharamurun river, on the east bank of the Wuerjimulun river and on the southern slope of a hill north of Fuhe village, 25–60 m above the current river. The site covers 200 m from south to north and 300 m from east to west. "Ash circles" were exposed as house floors. There are about 150 houses which all face the sunny side on the south slope. Thirty-seven houses have been excavated, among which four are round, and the rest are square. The dimensions are 4–5 m from east to west and 3–5 m from south to north. They are quite densely distributed, with the distance between houses 2–3 m from east to west and 4–8 m from south to north. The walls on the slope side are higher, and there is a row of post holes. The dwelling floor has been rammed and fired. There is a square hearth in the center, which consists of an earth-pit outlined with stone slabs. Slanting-mouthed pots were placed by the hearth. They might have been for storing kindling. Round pits were found in some houses. Stone tools outnumber bone implements. The stone tools excavated from Fuhegoumen amount to about 2,700 items, which makes them the most common kind of artifact for this culture.

Stone tools

Stone tools can be divided into two categories: very large and microlithic (Fig. 1.12). Most of the very large stone tools are bifacially chipped; some blades were polished afterwards. The edges are quite regular, and the tools are in specific shapes. They include choppers, axes, rectangular adzes, chisel-like tools, shouldered hoes, pointed tools, and scrapers. Most of the tools are made of shale, but grinding slabs and stones are made of volcanic material such as basalt or tuff. The microliths were mainly used as insets in composite tools. The longest blade is 13 cm, reflecting the skillful technology of detachment from stone cores. Secondary processing is by pressure flaking. Other kinds of microlithic tools include arrowheads with either indented or flat bases, and round scrapers. Most of the bone implements are awls, but a few bone knife-handles, needles, harpoons, fish-hooks, and toothed tools for making impressed patterns on pottery were also found.

Pottery

Pottery consists mainly of tall cylindrical vessels of grey-brown sandy clay with impressed Z patterns (Figure 1.12). The pottery walls are thinner and smoother compared with the same kind of vessel from the Xinglongwa culture. The impressed Z patterns are horizontal impressions forming vertical bands. Some comb-dot patterns are also found. A few standard bowls have small ring-feet.

Many kinds of animal bones were excavated from the site. Some were burned and discarded after the meat was consumed, others were broken for the marrow, and still others are the remains of bone tool production. There are bones of wild boar, cervids (including musk and elk), Mongolian gazelle, fox, badger, and some birds. Deer account for 50 percent of the bones, wild boar 17 percent, and badger 9 percent. All the animals are mountain-forest types of the modern northeastern animal regions, with few grassland ungulates, nor are there any large animals. It is difficult to judge whether any animals are domesticated. These data indicate that at this time the area was very different from the modern desert-grassland regions, rather it was forested, and its primitive economic life mainly included farming, hunting, and fishing.

The Fuhe culture is largely scattered north of the Sharamurun river, with very few sites found on the south bank. The Hongshan culture also penetrated this region, indicating that there was an area along the Sharamurun river where these two cultures mingled. At Yangjiayingzi, the superposition of Hongshan culture above Fuhe layers was described. However, considering the commonalities and the differences of these

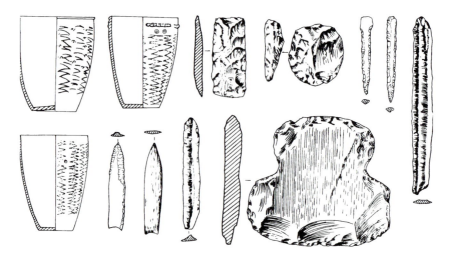

Figure 1.12 Pottery and stone tools excavated at the Fuhegoumen site

two cultures, there is a great likelihood of their coexistence. A C14 date from Fuhegoumen is 4735 ± 110 BP, the calibrated date is 3510~3107 BCE [ZK-0188], which is near the late period of Hongshan culture. However, with regard to the combined dates of several Neolithic sites in Liaoxi and Liaodong, the date for Fuhe culture could be pushed to an earlier point, so that it belongs to the same period as Hongshan culture. Fuhe and Hongshan are two cultures, one in the north and the other in the south, but they influenced and mingled with each other in Liaoxi between 3000 and 4000 BC. The Hongshan culture was influenced by the Fuhe culture from the north during the process of its development.

Zhaobaogou culture

Typical sites include Zhaobaogou, Xiaoshan and Anxingzhuang in Qianan, Hebei.[39]

Xiaoshan is located 1.3 km east of Xinglongwa village, in Baoguotu county at the southeast boundary of Aohan Banner, 140 km east of Chifeng, belonging to the upper reaches of the Mangniu river. The site is 467 m above sea level; to the east and south of the site it is low and hilly, while to the west and north it is low and flat. The site is located on the low southeastern slope of the hill. Some 500 m east to Shilishan where the land is saddle-shaped there are Hongshan sites, and between there is a spring. The Mangniu river is 2 km from Xiaoshan.

Two house floors were excavated. F1 is subterranean, rectangular with round corners. Oriented 20 degrees, it is 6.9 m long from east to west and 4.75 m wide, covering an area of 33 m^2. Burned mud lumps are scattered on the stamped earth floor. A shallow pit, almost round with a diameter of 0.9 and a depth of 0.13 m, was in the center of the house. Within the pit three pots were found. On the dwelling floor, 19 restorable pots were excavated, along with 16 stone tools and 3,058 stone flakes. The implements were concentrated at the center of the dwelling floor, with a grinding slab and stones in the eastern section. A *zun* [see below] and other fine vessels lay in the west side of the house, while rough sandy pottery was in the east. From the west section of the south wall, a fine-polished stone axe was excavated. To the east of the axe there was a stone with 2,183 stone flakes on and around it. This distribution suggests that ordinary activities took place at the edges of the house, whereas production, living, and ceremonies were conducted in the center.

The stone implements include both polished stone tools and microliths. Among the polished tools, the greatest number are axes, but there are also some chisels, and *si* [plow] as well as ring-shaped tools. A finely polished long stone axe, with a single hole and evidence of binding on the handle, was excavated from the south wall of the house. At the top there is a hafting area upon which a human face was carved, and the round blade was made of tuff. It is 18 cm long and 4–5.4 cm wide. The object is well made but the blade is blunt. Another finely polished tool is a chisel with four precise edges and a sharp blade. Among the microliths, most are blades, which generally run about 5 cm long, 1 cm wide, and 0.1 cm thick without retouch. There are also conical cores as well as flat square scrapers. Many grinding slabs and stones were found as sets on the house floors. The grinding slabs are often rectangular and the grinding stones are long and thin.

Pottery vessels are mainly of rough sandy clay or fine clay mixed with sand. There are a few clay bowls and red-rimmed bowls. The rough sandy pottery mainly includes cylindrical pots with Z patterns. They have straight mouths and slightly curved sides, decorated with short and dense Z patterns. The finer vessels are black-grey or yellow-brownish in color. The shapes include wine vessels, basins, bowls, and vessel covers as well as short ring-footed bowls. There are also vessels on oval bases. The impressed spirals are very striking, because they have a style of broad composition which covers the whole vessel, varying with the vessel's curve. The motifs include diamonds, F-shaped, S-shaped, and diamond thunder patterns, with a few examples of connected clouds. *Zun* vessels are the typical containers of this culture. They have three parts: the body is like a bowl, connected above to a straight collar and supported below by a pseudo ring-foot. Thus, this vessel has a very formal look, and in addition has delicate decorative patterns. In particular there is one vessel whose whole body is decorated with designs of the "Four Spirits," including deer, bird and pig; the fourth animal is damaged and unclear. The heads of these animals look very realistic, but the bodies are twisted and altered into strange shapes. The outline of the body is drawn with thin lines, and dense cross-hatching fills the interior. The eyes, the pig tusks, the deer ears, and the deer hooves retain a polished appearance. The pig-headed dragon has slender eyes, long mouth, and uplifted nose with a scaly snake body; the deer head has rhombus eyes, peach-shaped ears and hooves; the bird head has a crest, round eyes, hooked beak and the body prepared for flight; the other animal, although damaged, also looks like some sort of deified spirit. Thus, they are interpreted as the "Four Spirits." The vessel cover is also unusual, with a knob like a ring-foot which could also be used as a container, so that it seems to be paired with the *zun* wine vessels (Figures 1.13 and 1.14).

The Zhaobaogou site is located in eastern Aohan Banner, Chifeng, west of Xinglongwa and Xiaoshan. It is in the foothills 2 km northwest of Zhaobaogou village, surrounded by mountains, covering an area of 90,000 m^2. Seventeen houses have been excavated, in square, rectangular, and trapezoidal shapes. Each generally covers about 20 m^2, but the largest house is 100 m^2. The bigger houses are stepped, with the north section higher than the south. North of the center of the house there is a

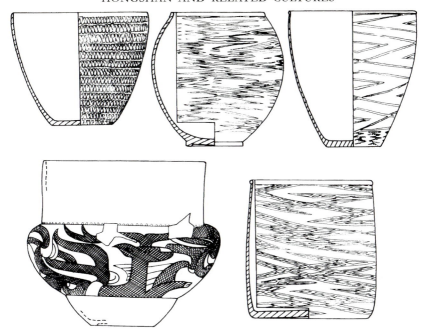

Figure 1.13 Zhaobaogou culture pottery from Xiaoshan site (lower left) and
Zhaobaogou site (lower right and above)

square hearth, with two post holes, one in the south and one in the north.
Some houses have an entrance in the middle of the south wall. The pottery is
like that of Xiaoshan, in that in addition to wine vessels, cylindrical pots, and
bowls, there are also oval straight-sided pots, ring-footed and globular jars,
and tall ring-footed bowls. A new decorative pattern is an impressed dense
design as background upon which geometric thunder designs were made.
The stone implements discovered include a complete stone plow [*si*], 15.4
cm long. An indented notch in the top indicates that this culture hafted
their plows. The rest of the stone tools, including axes, and microlithic
flakes, are similar to those from the Xiaoshan site (Figure 1.14).

The most typical artifact of the Zhaobaogou culture is polished pottery
decorated with geometric thunder designs, which is quite different from the
neighboring culture of Xinglongwa as well as different from the Hongshan
culture. This design ranges north to Daqintala in Naiman Banner,
Zhelimumung, Inner Mongolia, and south to Anxingzhuang in Qianan
county, Hebei province, so that it coincides with part of the Hongshan
culture. With regard to the dates, five C14 dates are available. The carbonized samples from F2 of Xiaoshan are 6150 ± 85, and 5980 ± 85, within
the range of 4996 ~ 4784 BC [ZK-2061], equal to early Hongshan, but later
than Xinglongwa. Therefore, some scholars point out that the typical vessel

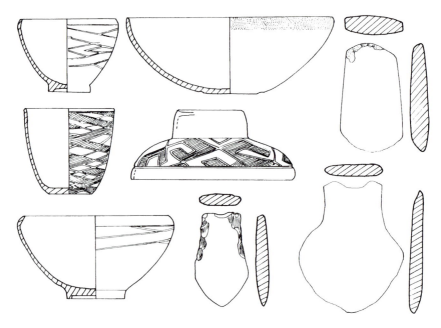

Figure 1.14 Zhaobaogou culture pottery and stone tools from Xiaoshan site (upper and middle center) and Zhaobaogou site (all others)

[*zun*] of Zhaobaogou type is more advanced in terms of the shape, which is close to that of post-Hongshan culture. At present this culture can be considered to have coexisted, mingled with, and influenced Hongshan culture. What is more, due to the advanced polished pottery with geometric thunder patterns and the Four Spirits, it might be inferred that it exerted great influence upon the formation and development of the Hongshan culture.

Post-Hongshan culture

Typical published sites include Shaguotun in Jingxi, Shandaojingzi in Chifeng, Shihushan in Shiyang, Aohan Banner, Baisilongyingzi in Xiaoheyan, Aohan Banner and Danangou in Wengniute Banner.

Shaguotun site in Jingxi was discovered in July 1921 and excavated by Andersson.[40] Two pieces of pottery can be defined as belonging to Post-Hongshan culture according to the published materials: one, the grey, cylindrical, sand-tempered pot, whose body is decorated with cord marks in diamonds and two decorated raised bands below the rim, which are obviously different from the cylindrical pots with Z patterns from Hongshan culture (Fig. 1.15); the other, a bowl of grey sand-tempered pottery, decorated with slanting cord marks.

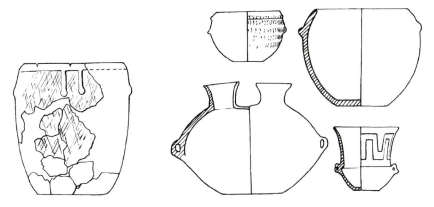

Figure 1.15 Pottery vessel excavated from a cave at Shaguotun, Jingxi
Figure 1.16 Pottery excavated at Shihushan, Shiyang, cemetery

The publication of Shandaojingzi in Chifeng is in *Chifeng Hongshanhou* along with the publication of the Hongshanhou site. Typical pots include cylindrical jars of sandy clay decorated with cord marks, pottery decorated with simple colorful bands, and pottery bowls. Since all these vessels are complete and constitute a set, they might have come from the same burial.

At Shihushan in Aohan, a pottery set in a burial has some dual-handled *zun* painted in red with geometric diamond patterns, two-handled and double-mouthed necked jars of grey sand-tempered pottery decorated with incised herringbones (Figure 1.16), some microlithic arrowheads with indented bases and a few stone rings. Some relevant reports have noted that this group of pottery, in terms of its shape, painted patterns, and designs, is quite different from the Hongshan culture, so that it is hypothesized that the date of this grave is later than Hongshan.[41]

The Nantaidi site in Xiaoheyan, Aohan,[42] is located on the first terrace west of Bailangyingzi village. The terrace is 20–25 m above the Laoha river. The site is 242 m long from east to west, and 85 m wide from south to north. After the formal excavation, four houses were defined as belonging to Post-Hongshan culture. They are either round or oval with a diameter of 3 m or so, subterranean, with a stone-built hearth in the center as well as symmetrical dual post holes. There is one house with a partition which forms two rooms on the east and west. A group of pottery excavated from the site has further suggested on the whole the features of Post-Hongshan culture: cylindrical pots made of sandy pottery decorated on the body with fine cord marks in diamond patterns, frequent two-handled and ring-footed vessels, such as dual-handled small-mouthed jars, dual-handled big-mouthed jars, *zun*-shaped vessels, the painted *dou* [pedestal vessels] with tall stem and shallow plate, and engraved black *dou*. The painted pottery is mainly black, with some red paint, brushed with white slanting lines marking the boundaries, within which it is filled with black, red, and purple, forming diamonds, triangles, octagons, net and other geometric patterns, with some simple inner painting (Figure 1.17). Among the stone implements microliths occur, but polished shovels also appear. Since this group of artifacts from Nantaidi is easy to define, this type of relic has been formally separated from Hongshan culture and called "Xiaoheyan Type" since the discovery of this site, with a view that it is a culture between Hongshan and Lower Xiajiadian cultures.

Danangou cemetery[43] is located in Erdao Zhangfang village in Wengniute Banner, 25 km north of Chifeng. It is hilly land between the northern bank of the Yingjin river in the Laoha river's upper reaches and the Yangchang river. The cemetery is on the southern slope of a hill 800 m or so above sea level, with a loess layer. At the north ridge of the hill there is a seasonal stream. Hongshan sites as well as Lower Xiajiadian culture sites are found nearby. Seventy-seven burials were excavated, divided into three sections. Each section has burials lined up along the terrain, and within each section the front, the middle, and the back portions could be seen, so that it is possible that each grave section was formed contemporaneously. The three sections could have represented three large independent family clans each occupying one of the three public graveyards. The burials are earth-pits, some with an extra pit in the side wall. People were buried lying on their backs with bound limbs. Each grave is about 150 cm long and 70–80 cm wide. Probably it was customary to burn the body before burial, since there are marks of fire on the burial, the fill, and the human bones. The burials are mostly adults, with few child burials. Among the 38 sexed skeletons, there are more males than females. Peculiar burials are quite common, such as headless burials and graves without a skeleton. These burials frequently contain many burial objects, therefore they might represent a special custom rather than a punishment. There are two graves with dual burials. The manner of burial is exceptional. Rather than a side-by-side burial, the two bodies were buried in a line, with the heads in opposite directions and the legs across each other. Many grave goods were found inside. These burials must have been for special members of the clan. One of the graves of this kind contained a man and a woman buried together. The accompanying burial objects include pottery, stone, and bone tools, as well as ornaments. Three pottery basin, jar, and pedestal vessels make a set. The stone and bone implements include battle-axes, axes, adzes, chisels, bone-handled knives, bone chisels, and bone arrowheads. The stone and bone implements mentioned above are only found in the men's graves. In female burials, only pottery vessels and stone spindle whorls were found. Ornaments include stone rings, which the male wore on the neck, while the female wore them on the wrist. There are also shell arm-rings and shell hairbands.

Another cemetery is 2.5 km away. Six burials there all have features of the

Figure 1.17 Pottery excavated at Sidaojingzi, Chifeng and Xiaoheyan, Aohan Banner

late period, supplying the missing part of the pottery for the late period in Danangou.

Summing up all the information belonging to Post-Hongshan culture, including the data from Danangou, the following points can be made with regard to Post-Hongshan culture.

1) The characteristics of continuity and change in artifacts and features are quite obvious. For instance, there are changes in the basin shape, changes in the pottery design from the scale pattern to the spiral pattern, etc.

2) Many new features appeared, such as the replacement of Z patterns on sandy pottery by the spiral design made with cord marks. In the later period, square and basket designs appear. The number of *dou* increases greatly, with an increase also in black pottery and the appearance of vermilion paint and painted pottery.

3) The early period pottery is quite similar to Late Yangshao culture, with painted bowls and *dou*. The late period is related to Early Longshan culture; for example, in the appearance of the banded basin, the basket and the

59

square designs, which suggest that Post-Hongshan culture had developed for several hundred years, to around 2500 BC or so.

4) There is a clear relationship to the Hongshan culture, especially in the early and the middle periods. With the rapid appearance of new cultural factors, sites become more like Lower Xiajiadian culture, representing the transition between Hongshan culture and Lower Xiajiadian culture in Liaoxi.

CULTURAL RELATIONSHIPS

Hongshan and its related cultures cover Pre-Hongshan culture through Post-Hongshan culture, dating from 6000 BC to 2500 BC. To this period, in terms of the transmission of cultural characteristics, belong the origin and development of comb pattern and impressed Z patterns, the rise of agriculture and animal husbandry, the advance of jade-carving, clay sculptural arts, temples and religious ceremonies, and in addition it reflects the disintegration of primitive clan communities, entering the threshold of civilized society. All these important events, relevant to economic, cultural, and social formation, are reflected in this ancient culture; there are several causes of course. The interrelationship between Hongshan and other cultures discussed above promoted the development of Hongshan culture itself on the one hand, and on the other hand the active neighboring cultures also played important roles.

The cultural relationships of Hongshan are a huge subject which need further study, and will only be briefly addressed here. First of all, there is the issue of the relationship with the northern grassland culture. As mentioned previously, the northern boundary of Hongshan impinged upon the northern grassland, and its cultural contents include many features of the northern grassland, such as microliths and a subsistence base including both agriculture and animal husbandry. It is distributed among other cultures, and coexists along with Fuhe culture on both banks of Sharamurun river. Thus, it can be considered that Hongshan, which was in close contact with Fuhe as well as the ancient culture of the northern grassland region, absorbed and retained some of the northern grassland cultural features.

Second, there is the relationship with the Neolithic culture in Liaodong (see Chapter 2). The pots with straight sides and impressed Z patterns were a common feature of the ancient cultures from both Liaoxi and Liaodong. Given the earlier origin of the impressed Z patterns in the Hongshan culture, its continuous development, longer duration, and greater variability, we may say that this culture showed stronger viability. As a result, Hongshan and related cultures in Liaoxi played a more important role than those in Liaodong. Relevant to this issue, Akiyama hypothesized that the pottery sculptures in Hongshan culture are due to contact with western cultures through the broad grassland, and they also influenced the development of the pottery idol sculptures in the late Jomon period in Japan. This view can be regarded as a summary of the cultural relations from the northern grassland to northeastern Asia through Liaoxi and Liaodong.[44]

The relationship with the ancient culture of the Yellow river agriculture regions was also a decisive factor in the development of Hongshan culture, therefore this chapter concludes by briefly addressing this relationship. As previously mentioned, in the primary period of the development of Hongshan culture, scholars have observed contact and mutual influence between cultures south and north of the Great Wall region, but the influence of Yangshao culture upon Hongshan culture has received the most comment. With the progress of research on Hongshan culture itself, attention has been given to its internal development, and it was realized that the relationship with Yangshao is not one-sided, but rather that the two influenced each other. This view was further reinforced when excavating Sanguan in Wei county, Zhangjiakou district, Hebei province. From this site, typical pottery of the Miaodigou type of Yangshao culture was found; for example, the painted basin with flower designs, the small-mouthed, pointed-base jar, and so on. It is the northernmost point of Yangshao distribution, but with the inclusion of pottery with Z patterns and typical painted pottery with scale designs of the Hongshan culture, it is also the southernmost point for the Hongshan culture. This site is therefore the contact region for these two cultures. Judging from the cultural materials from both areas, the time period is Late Hongshan, suggesting that before 3000 BC these two cultures had come into contact in northern Hebei province. Therefore, this is only the beginning of understanding the relationship between them, because Yangshao had contact with all the surrounding ancient cultures. The conclusion which has been drawn when comparing cultures contemporary with Yangshao is that Hongshan culture is more like Yangshao culture than other cultures, such as those on the northeast coast, the Yangzi River basin, or the northwest region. Su Bing-qi analyzed and summarized this issue.[45] According to his studies, around 4000 to 3000 BC, one branch of Yangshao, the Miaodigou type, remained in the Zhongyuan; and another branch became Hongshan culture west of the Liao river in the Liaoxi corridor north of Yanshan, that is, post-Hongshan sites represented by painted pottery decorated with dragon designs (including the scale pattern), and incised pottery. Each of these two cultures had its own antecedents, but each was stronger than other branches, and both expanded until they finally met in the northwest of Hebei province in the Daling river's upper reaches. The altar, the temple, and the cairn are the sign of this integration, showing that the meeting caused a leap in social organization. The leap was caused by the combination of these two types of economies and cultures. The center of this group is not in the northern grassland animal husbandry region, and is also far away from the Zhongyuan where agriculture is dominant; its central range is rather in the mixed region north of Yanshan, and the upper reaches of the Daling and Laoha rivers with both agriculture and animal husbandry. The natural features of this area are advantageous. The most important of these is not merely rich soil, but multiple economic components which led to prosperity.

The ancient Liaoxi region belonged to Jizhou, which included "West of East river, East of West river, North of South river,"[46] thus it covered both west and east of the Yellow river lower reaches, the whole of Shanxi and the northern part of the Yellow river in Henan province through the west of the Liao river in Bohai Bay.[47] The emperor and others often visited this area. In fact, Jizhou was regarded as the head of the Nine Prefectures because of the emperor's frequent journeys there. The time when the ancient civilization originated in Liaoxi, 3000 BC, is about the time of the early Five Emperors period. According to historic records,[48] a huge war raged in the southern part of the Zhangjiakou region, the first large war in history. As a result of this war the imperial clan united with several other clans in the north, forming the first large political power in the ancient world. The coalition then went south, providing a solid foundation for the formation of China. North China, including Liaoxi, was the area of the imperial clan's activities as well as the basis for them. Although we cannot say that the Hongshan culture is the culture of the imperial clans only, all the important archaeological discoveries of the Hongshan culture, especially those related to the cultural origins and researches of the relationship with Yangshao culture, have suggested that the historical record of the activities of the imperial clans is credible. Thus, it indicates that the Liaoxi region is a very important area to search for the origin of ancient China's civilization as well as the national culture.

(*Translated by Mingming Shan*)

NOTES

1 Hamada Kosaku and Mizuno Seiichi. *Chifeng Hongshanhou*, Archaeologia Orientalis, ser. A, No. 6. Far-Eastern Archaeology Society of Japan, (1938).

2 Survey by Torii Ryuzo of the prehistoric sites by the Yingjin river in Chifeng can be found in ibid., n. 3, p. 3.

3 J. G. Andersson. The Cave Deposit at Sha-kuo-tun [Shaguotun] in Ching-hsi [Jingxi], Fengtian. *Palaeontologia Sinica*, ser. D, No. 1, Vol. 1, Geological Survey Institute, 1923.

4 Liang Si-yong. Neolithic Pottery of the Prehistoric Sites at Xiyingcun in Shanxi. In *Liang Si-yong's Collected Archaeological Works*, pp. 1–49, Beijing: Chinese Scientific Press, 1959.

5 ibid.

6 Pei Wen-zhong. *Study of the Prehistoric Period in China*, Shanghai: Commercial Press, 1948.

7   Yin Da. On the Neolithic Sites in Hongshanhou, Chifeng. In *Chinese Neolithic Period*, Beijing: San-lian Bookstore, 1955.

8   Lu Zun-e. The Archaeological Survey at Linxi in Inner Mongolia. *Kaogu Xuebao* 1960(1): 9–23.

9   Inner Mongolia Team of the Archaeological Institute of the Chinese Academy of Social Sciences. Excavation Report of the Fuhegoumen Site of the Balin Left Banner in Inner Mongolia. *Kaogu* 1964(1): 1–5.

10 Archaeological Institute of the Chinese Academy of Social Sciences. *Archaeological Results of New China*, Beijing: Wenwu Press, 1962.

11 Huang Jun. First Collection of Ancient Jade Representations. *Wenwu* 1981(8): 58, Figure 1, which includes a pig-dragon jade.

12 Separately reported by Professor Yu Wei-chao of the Chinese Historical Museum and Professor Jiang Yi-li of Art History at Franklin and Marshall University, in *Ritual and Power: Jades of Ancient China*, ed. Elizabeth Childs-Johnson, Lancaster, PA, 1988, p.16.
    Yao Zong-yi. On Hongshan Jadeware Zhulong, Xiwei and Chenbao. *Liaohai Wenwu Congkan* 1989(1): 142–144.

13 Fang Dian-chun and Liu Bao-hua. Discovery of the Hongshan Culture Jade Tombs at Hutougou, Fuxin County in Liaoning. *Wenwu* 1984(6): 1–5.

14 Sun Shou-dao. On the Hongshan Culture Jade Dragon at Sanxingtala. *Wenwu* 1984(6): 7–10.

15 Li Gong-du. Test Excavation Report of the Chengzishan Site at Sanguandianzi in Lingyuan of Liaoning. *Kaogu* 1986(6): 497–510.

16 Wengniute Banner Cultural Center. Jade Dragon Found at Sanxingtala of the Wengniute Banner in Inner Mongolia. *Wenwu* 1984(6): 6.

17 Balinyou Banner Museum. Survey of the Nasitai Site of the Balinyou Banner in Inner Mongolia. *Kaogu* 1987(6): 507–518.

18 Sun Shou-dao and Guo Da-shun. On the Original Civilization and Dragon Origin at Rongcheng in the Liao River Valley. *Wenwu* 1984(6): 11–17.

19 Guo Da-shun and Zhang Ke-ju. Excavation Report of the Hongshan Site at Dongshanzui in Kezuo County, Liaoning. *Wenwu* 1984(11): 1–11.

20 Liaoning Provincial Institute of Cultural Archaeology. Excavation Report of the Hongshan "Goddess Temple" and Cairn Tomb Group at Niuheliang in Liaoning. *Wenwu* 1986(8): 1–17.

21 Inner Mongolia Team of the Archaeological Institute of the Chinese Academy of Social Sciences. Excavation Report of the Xinglongwa Site of Aohan Banner in Inner Mongolia. *Kaogu* 1985(10): 865–874.

22 Inner Mongolia Team of the Archaeological Institute of the Chinese Academy of Social Sciences. The Zhaobaogou Site of Aohan Banner in Inner Mongolia. *Kaogu* 1988(1): 1–6.

23 Liaoning Archaeological Institute. Test Excavation Report of the Neolithic Sites at Chahai in Fuxin. *Liaohai Wenwu Congkan* 1988(1): 11–16; *People's Daily*, October 8, 1988.

24 Liaoning Provincial Museum, Zhaowudameng Archaeological Center, and Aohan Banner Cultural Center. Discovery of Three Primary Cultures at Xiaoheyan of Aohan Banner in Liaoning. *Wenwu* 1977(12): 1–22.

25 Archaeological Institute of the Chinese Academy of Social Sciences. Archaeological Discovery and Study in New China. In *Neolithic Period of the Northern Area*, Beijing: Wenwu Press, 1984, pp. 172–180.

26 Zhangjiakou Archaeological Team. Main Results of Neolithic Archaeology in Yuxian County in 1979. *Kaogu* 1981(2): 97–105; *China Reconstructs* 1987(8): 69, lower-left figure.

27 Inner Mongolia Team of the Archaeological Institute of the Chinese Academy of Social Sciences. Excavation of the Zhizhushan Site in Chifeng. *Kaogu Xuebao* 1979(2): 215–243.

28 Inner Mongolia Team of the Archaeological Institute of the Chinese Academy of Social Sciences. The Xishuiquan Hongshan Culture Site in Chifeng. *Kaogu Xuebao* 1982(2): 183–193.

29 See note 24.

30 C14 Test Laboratory of the Archaeology Department at Beijing University, 1984. C14 Test Reports: VI, *Wenwu* 1984(4): 94; VIII, *Kaogu* 1986(7): 657.

31 See note 24.

32 See notes 15 and 20.

33 Huang Zhan-yue. Survey of the Human Sacrifice Relics in the Chinese Prehistorical Period. *Wenwu* 1987(11): 48–56.

34 Another Important Discovery of the Chinese Northern Cultural Archaeology – Neolithic Casting Mold Unearthed in Inner Mongolia. *People's Daily*, January 10, 1988, p. 3.
"Su Bing-qi," *People's Daily*, No. 2, 1988, pp.12–15.

35 *Jiangzhai: the Report of the Excavation of a Neolithic Site*, Illustration 106 (CVI), 1, 2, Beijing: Wenwu Press, 1988, p. 148.
Gansu Provincial Museum. *Thirty Years of Cultural Archaeological Work*, Beijing: Wenwu Press, 1979, pp. 141–142.
Shanxi Team of the Archaeological Institute of the Chinese Academy of Social Sciences and Linfen Area Cultural Center. Pottery First Found at Taosi in Xiangfen of Shanxi. *Kaogu* 1984(12): 1069–1071.
Luoyang Excavation Team of the Archaeological Institute of the Chinese Academy of Social Sciences, 1965. Excavation Report of the Erlitou Site at Yanshi in Henan. *Kaogu* 1965(5): 215–224.
Metallurgy History Group of the Beijing Steel Institute. Elementary Study of the Chinese Early-period Bronzes. *Kaogu Xuebao* 1981(4): 287–301.

36 See note 23.

37 See note 21.

38 See notes 9 and 25.

39 See note 22. Also Hebei Provincial Archaeological Management Center. Neolithic Site Survey and Excavation at Anxingzhuang in Qianan, Hebei Province. In *Collected Archaeological Papers*, 1984(4): 96–110.

40 See note 3.

41 Zhaowudameng Cultural Archaeological Center in Inner Mongolia. Neolithic Tombs at Shiyang Shihushan in Zhaowudameng, Inner Mongolia. *Kaogu* 1963(10): 523–524.

42 See note 21.

43 Guo Da-shun. A Post-Hongshan Culture Phase at Danangou. In *Collected Archaeological Cultural Papers* II, Beijing: Wenwu Press, 1989.

44 Akiyama Shingo. "Great Remains in the World" (in the section on Great Chinese Remains), Japanese Discussion Society, 1988, p. 24.

45 Su Bing-qi. The Rose and the Dragon. *China Reconstructs* 1987(8): 79.

46 Kong Ying-da, Yugong, Zhengyi.

47 "Yi-zhou." In *Ci Hai* (Encyclopedia), 1979 edition, p. 302, Shanghai: Shanghai Dictionary Publishing House.
Gu Jie-gang. Notes on Yugong. In *Selections from Ancient Chinese Geographic Works*, Vol. 1, Beijing: Scientific Press, 1959.

48 *Shan Hai Jing*. "Da Huang. Bei Jin." Yuan Ke, "Shan Hai Jing Jiao Zu," Shanghai: Shanghai Publishing House, 1980, p. 430.

2

THE HOUWA SITE AND RELATED ISSUES

Xu Yu-lin

EDITOR'S INTRODUCTION

Houwa is an important Neolithic site near Dandong on the North Korean border which has been virtually unreported outside of China. The human and animal heads, made of both pottery and carved stone, are particularly unusual and intriguing. Many of the heads are grotesque, and as Xu Yu-lin indicates, they may be representations of the supernatural. Others, however, may be simply portraits. The function and meaning of these heads remain to be explained.

The site has two major levels, of which the lower level is the main focus of the chapter. The author describes each layer, and then compares them. He finds that the two are related but different phases of the same culture. Differences are found in house floors (round in the lower layer and square in the upper), in the decorative techniques on pottery (more incising is found in the upper layer), and in changes in stone tools.

Xu compares Houwa with other known cultures of the same time period in the region. Most of the sites are in the southern part of the Liaodong peninsula, but Xinle, near Shenyang, is also included. The comparable layers of these sites have straight-sided pottery vessels with incised and impressed patterns on the exterior. The lower layer of Xiaozhushan has pottery closely similar to Houwa, but with differences in decorative detail and in vessel shapes. Another difference is that the stone tool industry is largely chipped at Xiaozhushan and polished at Lower Houwa. The lower layer of Xinle is also related, but is not identical to Houwa. Lower Xinle includes tripod bowls and objects made of jet which are not found at Houwa. Compared with Hongshan (which is later), Lower Houwa lacks painted pottery and microliths. Thus, each of these is seen to represent a different but related culture.

Interesting comparisons are made between the Liaodong peninsula and Shandong as well as Korea. The two Chinese peninsulas jutting into the Yellow Sea and defining Bohai Bay are seen as particularly close, with influences passing both ways. Earlier levels of Liaodong sites such as

Guojiacun and Wujiacun as well as Lower Xiaozhushan have straight-sided vessels with various kinds of impressing and incising. The influence of Longshan on later Neolithic cultures in the Liaodong peninsula is particularly notable in the addition of tripods, pedestals, black pottery, and painted pottery. Xu sees the Chulmun pottery of Korea as related to the straight-sided incised jars of Liaodong, but his examples from the southeast coast of Korea are less apt than sites such as Kungsanni and Amsadong near the central west coast would have been, since these are closer to Houwa in distance and in pottery types.

Four further issues engage Xu's attention: steatite net weights, the meaning of the figurines, canoe-shaped pottery, and variations in sea level. The first is an interesting functional argument about the use of a particular artifact, the second looks at the figurines in detail, the third is an argument about boats based on the shape of some pottery vessels, and the fourth a discussion of the implications for sea-level changes of various features of sites. These various issues enrich our understanding of the Houwa site.

S. M. N.

Until recently little work had been done on Neolithic archaeology in the Liaodong peninsula. Because the artifacts discovered were mostly surface-collected, the cultural contents and nature of the sites were not clear. Since 1976, in the southern Liaodong peninsula, particularly around the city of Dalian, such important sites as Guojiacun in Lushun, Xiaozhushan, Wujiacun on Guanglu island, and Shangmashi on Dachang island, have been discovered and excavated. These sites established the continuous development of Neolithic culture in this region. For example, Xiaozhushan Lower, Middle and Upper cultures can each be divided into Early, Middle and Late phases. The discovery of these cultures has allowed us to systematize Neolithic archaeology in the southern Liaodong peninsula, and has clarified its cultural nature and its chronology.

Since 1981, with the expansion of general archaeological surveys, several Neolithic sites have been found on the northern Yellow Sea coast of the Liaodong peninsula. The discovery of the Houwa site, with cultural layers representing superimposed stages, especially forwarded the effort to systematize the Neolithic. Lower Houwa is similar to but not identical with Lower Xiaozhushan culture, because Lower Houwa has some unique features. The artifacts unearthed from Upper Houwa appear to belong to a previously unknown culture. This chapter introduces and discusses the discovery and excavation of the Houwa site, the cultural features of Upper and Lower Houwa cultures, and the relationship between these cultures and adjacent ones as well as some related issues.

DISCOVERY AND EXCAVATION OF THE HOUWA SITE

Houwa is located on a low flat mound in eastern Houwacun, in Sanjiazi village, Majiadian town, Donggou county, Liaoning province. The middle part of the northern mound is lower than the rest, so that the whole platform is in the shape of the letter Y. The whole mound is 170 m long from south to north and 100 m wide from east to west, covering an area of 17,000m². The east and west parts of the mound are concave, and the northern part is shallow and flat. The site deposits are concentrated in the western part of the mound. Some 500 m north, an ancient river ran from west to east, but it is now reutilized for irrigation channels. The Yellow Sea coast lies 15 km to the south. On the flat field near the slope and top of Shuangshan and Shifenshan, 7 or 8 km west and southwest, other Neolithic sites of different time periods have been registered.

In the fall of 1981, the Cultural Archaelogical Survey Team of Dandong city discovered the Houwa site while engaged in general archaeological surveys. In order to probe the layers of the site and its cultural nature, they made a test excavation with an area of 12m².[1] In 1983 and 1984, an archaeological team led by the Liaoning Provincial Museum and including members of the Dandong Cultural Archaeological Bureau, Donggou County Cultural Archaeological Bureau, and others, began excavating an area of 1,800m² of the Houwa site. The discoveries included 43 house floors, 20 hearths, 1,600 or so tools, about 400 restorable pots, and several finely carved artifacts. It proved to be a Neolithic site of an early date with comparatively rich artifacts.[2]

Generally speaking, the depth of the cultural accumulation at Houwa is about 1 m or so, and it is 2 m at the deepest. Four layers were discerned. The first layer from the top is the plow zone, and the second and third are of black and black-brown earth. The artifacts excavated from these layers are similar, and together they are designated as Upper Houwa. The fourth layer is yellow, and constitutes Lower Houwa. The remains of Lower and Upper Houwa cultures are new types not previously discovered in the Liaodong peninsula.

CULTURAL FEATURES OF LOWER HOUWA

Thirty-one densely packed house floors have been discovered. Both round and square house floors were found, varying in size. The larger floors are square, around 7 m in width and length, while the smaller ones are round, with a diameter of 3 to 4 m or so. They are subterranean, and the walls are simply the native soil (Figure 2.1). Some house floors were dug into the floors below. Post holes were found in the wall footings. Inside the house, stones lined round or square hearths. Some floors contained pottery jars, the original cooking vessels. The hearths have a burned layer as well as a

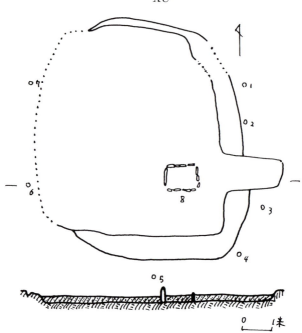

Figure 2.1 Plan of house floor, T24, Lower Houwa

supportive earth layer of 20 to 40 cm. Eighteen ash-pits were found, most of which are basin-shaped, with a diameter of 3 to 4 m or so, about 1 m deep. Some ash-pits contained large amounts of potsherds. These pits might have been used first for storage pits, and later reused as ash-pits.

The pottery vessels are mainly sandy reddish-brown and blackish-brown clay, containing steatite temper (Figure 2.2, Figure 2.3). They were hand-made, fired at high temperature. Both impressed and incised designs occur, but impressed ware is more common. Among the impressed designs, mat patterns are the most frequent, next are the impressed Z patterns, net patterns, Y-shaped bands, and horizontal lines. The impressed mat patterns mainly consist of from five to eleven slanting parallel lines, crossed by other parallel lines. The lines are sharp at one end, but at the other end they have a triangular or round shape, like matchsticks. The incised patterns include mat, net, herringbone, vertical and horizontal lines. Usually a band composed of three or four parallel lines was formed below the mouth, and below the band patterns such as mat, net, herringbone or combinations of these covered the rest of the vessel. Symmetrical vertical handles are found near the top of jars with and without necks. The shapes of the pottery include straight-walled jars, necked jars, bowls, cups, ladles, and boat-shaped vessels. Straight-walled jars are the most common shape.

The jars occur in several shapes: direct rims and straight sides with flat

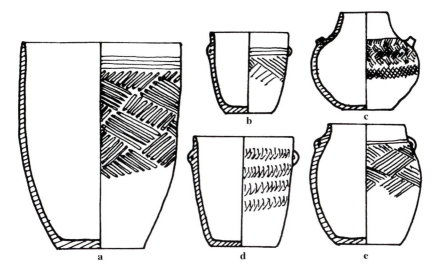

Figure 2.2 Pottery from Lower Houwa: a) large beaker; b) small beaker; c) necked jar; d) medium-sized pot; e) curved wall pot [all 1/6]

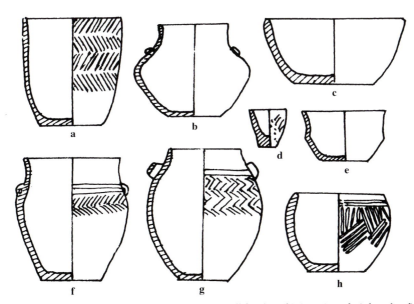

Figure 2.3 Pottery from Lower Houwa: a) small beaker; b) jar; c) and e) bowls; d) cup; f) necked jar; g) globular jar; h) pot [all 1/4]

bases; straight mouths and curved bodies with flat bases; and constricted mouths and curved bodies with flat bases. Below the edge of the mouth symmetrical vertical handles are usually found. Necked jars have small mouths, short shoulders, curved bodies and flat bases, some of which have symmetrical handles on the shoulder, vertically pierced. Bowls are characterized by straight mouths, slightly curved sides, and flat bases. A few have globular sides and flat bases. Some of the bowls have incised patterns. Cups have straight mouths, cylindrical bodies and flat bases, with incised patterns on some of the body. These vessels are small, in general 4 cm high. Ladles have a handle which may be flat or round, and points upwards. The bowl is oval. Shallow, round disks are polished on the edges. They are made from sherds from broken jars. Canoe-shaped vessels have oval mouths, direct rims, and curved sides. The whole vessel is shaped like a dugout canoe.

The stone tools include saddle querns, round grinding stones, long jade axes with curved blades, narrow and long jade adzes, flat willow-leaf-shaped arrowheads, steatite net weights, pestles, whetstones, stone balls, and chipped waisted hoes. Pottery net weights with notches at each end and pottery spindle whorls are also found.

Ornamental artifacts include stone rings, stone weights, fish designs incised on steatite (Figure 2.4), pottery toys, and small balls. Many figurines in the shape of human heads and animals, carved on steatite or molded of clay, are an interesting characteristic of the site (Figure 2.5, Figure 2.6, Figure 2.7).

Production tools include many slabs with grinding stones, stone axes, stone hoes and other agricultural tools; a great many pottery vessels for daily tasks; densely packed houses which overlap or break into each other; elaborate hand-made tools; and decorative handicrafts. These facts suggest that the people who lived in Houwa in the Neolithic were sedentary. Agriculture provided the subsistence base along with hunting and fishing.

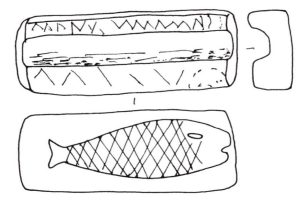

Figure 2.4 Net weight with fish design

Figure 2.5 Steatite carved figures: a) human and bird; b) head and torso;
c) humanoid pendant

However, the pottery vessels have very simple shapes, and production tools are primitive, suggesting an early date.

Similarities between Lower Houwa and Lower Xiaozhushan are many, especially vessels with impressed net patterns. In addition, the impressed Z patterns from Houwa are in horizontal lines but vertically impressed, resembling those of the Lower Xinle culture. Thus, we hypothesize that the date of Lower Houwa is close to both Lower Xinle and Lower Xiaozhushan. The Beijing University Archaeology Laboratory has calculated a C14 date for Lower Houwa of 5600 ± 110 BP; the calibrated date is 4350~4040 or 4370~4159 BCE [BK-84002].[3]

Straight-sided pots with impressed mat patterns typical of Lower Houwa have also been discovered in other sites, e.g. Shihuiyao cave in Huangtukan town, Donggou county; Shuangshan, Xidaguang in Majiadian county; and Yanjiashan, in Dongjiashan town, north of the Yellow Sea coast in the Liaodong peninsula. At the Zhouliweizi site in Yongdian village, Kuandian county, impressed Z patterns like Lower Houwa were also found. Given these similar sites, the cultural remains of the Lower Houwa culture are mainly distributed along the Yellow Sea coast east of the Dayang river in

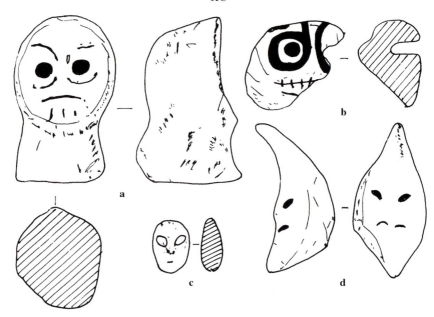

Figure 2.6 Human and animal pottery figurines from Lower Houwa: a(–c) humans; d) animal

the vicinity of Dandong. To the north the culture extends to the Pushi river in the Yalu basin. Thus, Lower Houwa is one of the earliest Neolithic cultures which has been discovered so far in the Liaodong region.

CULTURAL FEATURES OF UPPER HOUWA

Twelve houses which can be attributed to Upper Houwa have been excavated to date. They are almost all square with rounded corners, and subterranean (Figure 2.8). The houses vary in size. The largest one excavated is about 8 m long and 6 m wide. The bare earth serves as walls. The interior is comparatively flat, but near the walls yellow earth was added. Four post holes formed a pattern in the center of the house. The smallest house is about 3 by 4 m, also with four post holes in the center. The entrance faces south, with one step. The hearth is near the door. It is square and shallow, with burned earth inside. In some of the houses, two-stepped ledges were found along one wall. Most of the artifacts were distributed near the walls.

The pottery is made of coarse sandy clay mixed with steatite, baked at comparatively low temperatures (Figure 2.9). The vessel walls are thin, made by coiling. The majority are sandy reddish and dark-brown vessels, with reddish-brown and black ranking next. The patterns are mainly incised, with horizontal lines dominant. Other patterns include herringbone, net,

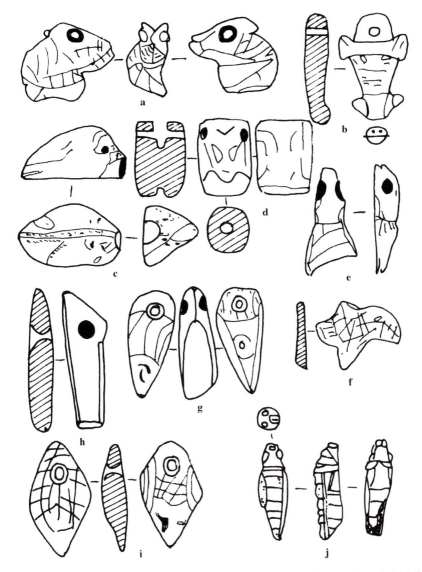

Figure 2.7 Animal figurines from Lower Houwa: a)–c) pigs; d) tiger; e) and g) bird; f) eagle; h) and i) fish; j) insect [f) 1/2, the others 1/1]

pine needles, and punctates. Compound patterns made of horizontal lines and punctates applied with awls are also found. The common features of the pottery shapes are tall sides and flat bases, mostly including beakers, jars, and bowls. Beakers have large open mouths, high walls, and small flat bases. Horizontal lines are incised on the upper part of the body and dots

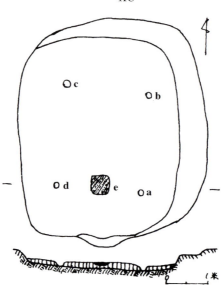

Figure 2.8 Plan of house, T16, Upper Houwa: a)–d) post holes; e) hearth

applied with awls near the bottom. Another type of jar has a small flat rim, cyclindrical body, and small flat base. Incised slanting lines and net lines are found on the body. Most jars are made with straight mouths and shoulders, globular sides, and small flat bases. They are generally small in size. Some of the bodies are undecorated, while others have punctates on the neck and the shoulder. Bowls have straight mouths, tall sides, and small flat bases.

Production tools include polished rectangular stone slabs, round grinding stones, long stone axes, flat, willow-leaf-shaped stone arrowheads with double blades and ridges, chipped stone balls, and potsherd net weights with double notches. Pottery net weights and stone balls outnumber the other tools. Decorative works of art include small rings and stone weights. Human head and animal figurines of clay are particularly notable (Figure 2.10).

In Upper Houwa, production tools mainly include various kinds of fishing and hunting equipment, and the houses are comparatively dispersed. The pottery-making technique, tools, and decorative works of art are less well developed than those of Lower Houwa. This suggests that the inhabitants of Upper Houwa engaged in fishing and hunting as the main economy, but with agriculture and animal husbandry in addition. Judging from the stratigraphy, the date must be later than Lower Houwa, but production tools such as chipped stone balls, pebble net weights, potsherd net weights and potsherd spindle whorls are all simple and primitive. With regard to everyday pottery, the wide-mouthed cylindrical beakers incised with horizontal lines are similar to those of Lower Xiaozhushan. The small flat-rimmed jars with straight collars from Upper

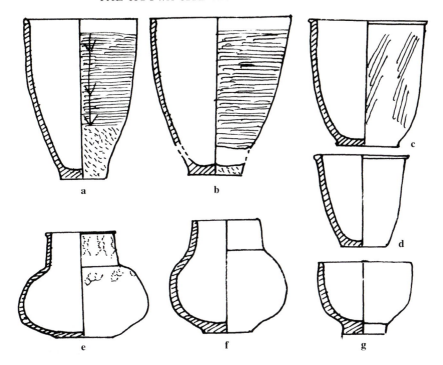

Figure 2.9 Pottery from Upper Houwa: a) and b) beakers; c) and d) beakers with lip; e) and f) necked gars; g) bowl [all 1/4]

Houwa are later than those in the other Neolithic sites along the Yellow Sea coast of the Liaodong peninsula. The C14 date from Upper Houwa obtained by the Beijing University Archaeology Laboratory is BC 2515, BC 2390, the calibrated date is close to BC 3091~2897 [4].

Several nearby sites bear a strong resemblance to Upper Houwa; for example, the Fairy cave at Xiaogushan, Haicheng county; the Water cave at Xiejiaweizi in Benxi county; Dongweizi and Shanjiaodong at Niandianxiang; Gouliweizi at Yongdian Xiang, Kuandian county; and the Lizigou cave at Zhangjiapuzi in Niumiaowu county. Pottery vessels with wide mouths and cylindrical walls having incised horizontal lines are found in all these sites. Thus the cultural remains of Upper Houwa are mainly distributed in the vicinity of Anshan, Dandong, and Benxi.

THE RELATIONSHIP BETWEEN UPPER AND LOWER HOUWA CULTURES

The excavated artifacts of Upper and Lower Houwa have many similarities. For example, there is the quality of the pottery, which is hand-made, mostly

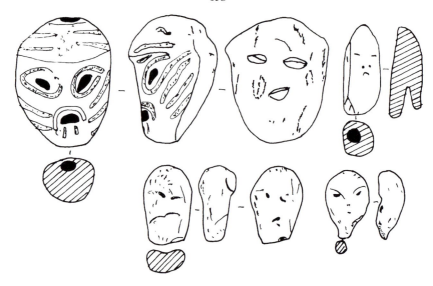

Figure 2.10 Pottery figurines from Upper Houwa

sandy red-brown and red with steatite temper; the vessel shapes including cylindrical pots, jars, and bowls; the incised patterns; and the fact that potsherd spindle whorls and pottery human-head figurines are found in both layers. These commonalities suggest that there is a close relationship between them, and that they both belong to the same cultural system.

However, there are also notable differences between them. For example, in the lower layer, the houses are mostly round, whereas the upper layer has square house floors. In the lower layer the pottery is baked at a higher temperature, contains more steatite temper, and is thicker, whereas the upper layer pottery was fired at lower temperatures, and is sandier, with less steatite and thinner walls. The patterns from the lower layer are mostly impressed mat and rocker-stamping, with very few vessels having incised lines. In the upper layer there are mainly incised horizontal lines, herringbone, net, and slanting line and dot patterns. The shapes of the pottery in the lower layer include mainly straight-mouthed cylindrical pots, small-mouthed tall pots, tall jars with small mouths and short collars, short flat-based bowls with straight mouths, cups, and ladles. In the upper layer the main vessels are the wide open-mouthed and small flat-rimmed cylindrical pots, straight-rimmed and globular jars, and high bowls. Production tools in the lower layer are mainly grinding slabs, grinding stones, stone hoes, stone adzes, and potsherd spindle whorls, whereas in the upper layer stone balls, stone and pottery net weights, and stone arrowheads predominate. Characteristic decorative works of art from the lower layer are the steatite-carved human face and animal figures, whereas from the upper layer, pottery human face figurines as well as stone rings and stone weights are found. The differences between the upper and lower layers suggest that these cultural systems are not contemporaneous, rather they indicate different stages of development and change.

LOWER HOUWA'S RELATIONSHIP WITH NEIGHBORING CULTURES

Lower Houwa and Lower Xiaozhushan Culture in southern Liaoning

There is a close link between the remains of Lower Houwa and Lower Xiaozhushan. The quality of the pottery as well as the techniques of manufacture and decoration are quite similar in both places. Both contain steatite, both have impressed mat patterns and rocker-stamping, and the main shape of the pottery in both places is the straight-mouthed cylindrical jar. These commonalities indicate that they belong to the same cultural system.

However, differences between the remains of Lower Houwa and Lower Xiaozhushan must be noted. For example, the patterns on the pottery in Houwa include impressed horizontal lines, impressed and incised herringbone and net designs, which are rarely found at Xiaozhushan. Pottery shapes found in Houwa include jars, bowls, cups, plates, ladles, and canoe-shaped vessels, which are never found in Xiaozhushan. In terms of production tools, in Houwa there are mainly polished stone axes, adzes, and arrowheads, as well as elaborate steatite-carved handicrafts, whereas in Xiaozhushan most of the stone tools are chipped, and the steatite-carved handicrafts found at Houwa are not present. These differences might be due to regional or temporal variations, but they probably belong to the same cultural system.

Lower Houwa and Lower Xinle

Both of these sites contain straight-mouthed cylindrical pots with impressed Z patterns, and the lines which make up the Z patterns are vertically impressed, as if the horizontal Z strokes have been upended. This similarity suggests that the two sites are related. However, there are also important differences between them. For example, the straight-mouthed cylindrical pots from Xinle are much deeper, there is a band below the rim and the pottery shapes include slanting-mouthed pots and tripod bowls, as well as jet products, which are not found in Lower Houwa. The shorter straight-mouthed cylindrical pots from Houwa were largely decorated with impressed mat patterns and composite lines, which are not found in Xinle.

Thus, we suggest that the remains of Lower Houwa and Lower Xinle should be considered as two different cultural systems with two different cultural types. The Lower Xinle culture is mainly distributed in the areas around Shenyang and Fushun.

Lower Houwa and Hongshan in western Liaoning

Lower Houwa and Hongshan (see Chapter 1) have cylindrical pots with rocker-stamped patterns, which might suggest that they are similar in date, but important differences are found. The rocker-stamping in Hongshan is more variable, with vertical zigzags as well as horizontal ones. Painted vessels and microliths are also found in the Hongshan culture, both of which are rare in Lower Houwa.

From the analysis above, the Neolithic cultures in Liaoning can be divided into three regions: the Liaodong peninsula, the Shenyang region, and Liaoxi (western Liaoning). Each of the three regions has its own cultural system, although contacts between them took place, and cultural features from other regions were added, promoting local cultural developments and transitions.

CULTURAL RELATIONSHIPS BETWEEN THE LIAODONG, SHANDONG, AND KOREAN PENINSULAS

Liaodong and Shandong

Geographically speaking, the Liaodong and Shandong peninsulas are close. Geologists believe that they were once joined, making Bohai Bay a closed inner lake. Fossils of Pleistocene mammoth and woolly rhinoceros were discovered in Bohai Bay, and on Changdao off the Shandong peninsula, Neolithic sites were discovered. These facts suggest that in the Quaternary some part of the Bohai region was still land inhabited by ancient humans and animals, and these two peninsulas were contiguous in ancient times. Judging from the archaeological data, the people from these two peninsulas had economic contacts very early. Neolithic sites in the Liaodong peninsula such as Lower Guojiacun, Middle Xiaozhushan, Wujiacun, and others were affected by the Dawenkou and Longshan cultures of Shandong. For example, footed basins, footed jars, solid-legged pitchers, tripod goblets and other pottery shapes common in the Dawenkou culture have been excavated in Liaodong. From Upper Xiaozhushan, eggshell black pottery, tripod vessels with round legs, plates on tripods with legs shaped like flat chisels, pitchers supported on bag-shaped tripod legs with high crotches, and engraved pedestals were excavated, all typical of the Longshan culture in Shandong.

The Neolithic in the Shandong peninsula, especially the Jiaodong region, was also affected by the Neolithic culture in the Liaodong peninsula. For instance, at Baishi village in Yantai, Zijishan in Penglai, Daheishandao Beizhuang in Chang island, and elsewhere, straight-mouthed cylindrical pots with incised horizontal lines, pine-needle designs, and net patterns similar to Middle Xiaozhushan were found. At Zhaogezhuang in Chengguanxiang, Xiping county, there are pots with Z patterns in horizontal lines but vertically impressed. These are all typical patterns of the Neolithic of the Liaodong peninsula. Based on the details noted above, the Neolithic cultures of the Liaodong and Shandong peninsulas can be said to be closely related, and must have mutually affected each other. However, in terms of influence, the Shandong peninsula had more impact upon Liaodong in the Neolithic than the other way around.

In the past the Liaodong peninsula Neolithic culture was sometimes referred to as "Dawenkou culture" and "Shandong Longshan culture," but this classification is no longer thought to be appropriate. While it is true that the two peninsulas had close links in the Neolithic, they cannot be considered to be identical. Each of these two cultures has its own features. In particular the dominant impressed and incised straight-mouthd pots in the Liaodong peninsula, make it impossible to classify the Liaodong Neolithic generally as "Dawenkou culture" or "Shandong Longshan culture."

Liaodong and Korea

Similarly, the Liaodong and Korean peninsulas are geographically contiguous, and in ancient times there were close cultural contacts. As far as current knowledge provides, at such sites as Sinamni in Ulsan, Tongsam-dong in Pusan, and Tadaep'o in Tongnae, all sites in Kyongsang Nam Do, South Korea, the straight-mouthed cylindrical pots with impressed mat designs like those found in Lower Xiaozhushan and Lower Houwa were also unearthed.[5] In North Korea, from the Misongni cave in Ilchu, Pyongan Puk Do, there are impressed mat designs and Z patterns.[6] At Sopohang, Unggi-gun, Hamgyong Puk Do, incised horizontal lines on the straight-mouthed pots are similar to Middle Xiaozhushan. A kind of double-hook pattern (in Korea called the spiral pattern) is also found at Sopohang, which is very similar to a pattern from Middle Xiaozhushan and Zijishan, Penglai, in Shandong.[7] I think that these suggest a close relationship in the Neolithic between the Liaodong and Korean peninsulas. However, the Neolithic culture in the Korean peninsula has its own features. The incised pottery in eastern Korea contains more pine-needle designs, and in the Kungsan site in Onch'on, Pyongan Nam Do, round-bottomed vessels are predominant. Thus, there are both similarities and differences between the two cultures. Each has its own distinctive features.

In sum, the three peninsulas mentioned above, the Liaodong, Shandong, and Korean peninsulas, have influences and close relationships among them in the Neolithic, but there are important differences as well. They cannot be classified as belonging to the same culture on the basis of these relationships, rather they should be regarded as different cultures.

In addition, it can be seen that at the Russian site of Zaisanovka in Peter the Great Bay near Vladivostok, there are also straight-mouthed cylindrical pots with incised patterns similar to Middle Xiaozhushan, as well as pots with spirals from Lower Yujiacun in southern Liaoning.[8] Thus, there might be a relationship in the Neolithic between the Liaodong peninsula and the coastal region of Siberia. In the eastern parts of Jilin and Heilongjiang provinces, incised pottery was unearthed in great numbers from some Neolithic sites, as well. Whether the channel for the relationship was by land from eastern Jilin and eastern Heilongjiang provinces and then to the coast of Vladivostok, or by sea from Korea along the Japan Sea coast and then to Vladivostok, remains unknown. The relationship between other incised pottery and that of the Liaodong peninsula remains an important issue in the Neolithic of the Dongbei region, and requires further study.

RELATED ISSUES

Steatite net weights

In Lower Houwa, many grooved tools made of steatite were excavated. Some are long and thin, averaging 7.5 cm long, 2.5 cm wide, and 1.5 cm thick. Some are rectangular, about 6.2 cm long, 3.5 cm wide, and 1.2 cm thick. Round specimens with a diameter of 6 cm and 1.5 cm thick were also found. Double-grooved and single-grooved examples were found, and even a few with three grooves. The grooves vary from 0.7 to 1 cm wide and 0.3 to 0.7 cm deep. Long grooved tools made of pottery and potsherds were also found. Similar grooved tools made of steatite have been found at sites such as Lower Xinle, Lower Xiaozhushan and elsewhere. In some reports they are regarded as stones to polish bone tools, and are called "grooved polishing stones." I suggest that this designation should be reconsidered. Grooved stones for polishing bone implements have been found from Houwa and other Neolithic sites, but those polishing stones are larger in size, of no particular shape, and the grooves vary in depth and width. Generally the ends of the grooves are narrower than the middle, because the polishing tool moved more in the middle.

The grooved tools in question are made of steatite and are small but very regular in size. The width and depth dimensions of the groove are the same and it does not appear to have been made with a polishing tool. Those made from clay and potsherds have an especially specific shape, and do not appear to have been used for polishing. Incised net patterns and fish patterns were noted on the grooved tools made of steatite and clay in Lower Houwa. These patterns suggest a relationship to fishing. I once investigated fishing villages on several areas of Chang island and Dalu island in Donggou county near the Yellow Sea coast and discovered that people at present still use long net weights made of steatite with grooves on one or both sides, decorated with fishing patterns. The interior of the groove is exactly the size of the fishing cord. According to fishermen, this type of net weight has many advantages. One of them is that the slipperiness of the steatite means it does not get stuck on rocks. Thus, I suggest that these artifacts are net weights.

Sculpted figurines

From both the upper and the lower layers of Houwa, many figurines were unearthed. They are a unique characteristic of the Houwa site. These figurines are made of both steatite and clay, but steatite figurines are more common (Figure 2.11). The artifacts are carved or molded on one or both sides, and include depictions of human faces and animals. The

Figure 2.11 Pottery figurine from Lower Houwa

Figure 2.12 Animal head from Lower Houwa

animals include pigs (Figure 2.12), fish, birds, insects, and birds with heads turned back.

The human heads provide information about the primitive people of ancient China and their clothing. Two particularly interesting human face carvings are made of steatite. One is half a torso. It has hair on the head, deep eyes, and a big mouth, and on the body an incised pattern represents clothing (Figure 2.13). The other is a head wearing a turban. The face is shallow, with the teeth exposed (Figure 2.14). Of the six pottery human heads which were found, one has clear facial features, incised with two crescent eyes and a mouth. It has a human face on one side and a monkey's on the other (Figure 2.15). Another has round eyes (Figure 2.16).

So far only one other stone sculpture of a human face in the Neolithic in China has been found, at Yuanyangchi in Yongchang county, Gansu province.[9] Thus, this steatite carving from Houwa is one of the earliest in China.

Regarding the human head and animal sculptures from Neolithic sites, various interpretations and explanations have been offered. Some think that the figures are related to religion, representing either gods or goddesses; some think they indicate ancestor worship or clan totems; others think they are works of art, merely for decoration. I suggest that they cannot be generalized, but rather each example should be analyzed separately. With regard to the head and face sculptures from Houwa, some are small with a natural expression. These are not mysterious or supernatural, nor do they

Figure 2.13 Head and torso steatite carving from Lower Houwa

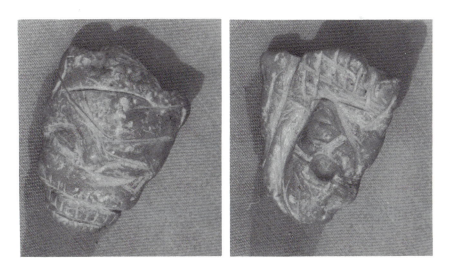

Figure 2.14 Steatite carving with human face on one side, bird on other, from Lower Houwa

Figure 2.15 Two-faced figurine from Upper Houwa

Figure 2.16 Round-eyed figurine from Lower Houwa

have abstract patterns; they appear to represent the faces of the people at that time. These were used as ornaments. However, other human face sculptures look very serious, with deep eyes and big open mouths showing the teeth. It is likely that these are related to the ancient religion, and were some kind of god figures, perhaps for the worshipping of ancestors.

Canoe-shaped pottery

At Houwa several sherds from canoe-shaped vessels were unearthed, and a complete specimen of a canoe-shaped vessel was excavated from the lower layer (Figure 2.17). The complete vessel is of sandy red clay containing steatite temper, made in the shape of a long oval. The two ends are curved. It is 13 cm long, the widest part at the middle is 7 cm across, and it is 4 cm high. It is called canoe-shaped pottery for the obvious reason that the shape resembles a dugout canoe.

This shape of pottery has been found also at Guojiacun[10] in Dalian and Wujiacun[11] on Guanglu island in Changhai county along the Yellow Sea coast in the Liaodong peninsula. The fact that these vessels are made in the shape of a dugout canoe, indicates that canoes or boats already existed. The discovery of such pottery is of great help in studying the origin of the canoe or boat in ancient China.

The origin of the canoe in ancient China can be traced not only from the canoe-shaped pottery along the Yellow Sea coast in the Liaodong peninsula, but also from other locations throughout China. For instance, at Hemudu in Zhejiang province, wooden oars and canoe-shaped pottery were found, at Wuxingqian, Shanyang a wooden oar was found, and a painted boat-shaped jar was also found at Beishouling in Baoji, Shanxi province.[12] All these discoveries suggest that six to seven thousand years ago the inhabitants in ancient China had already begun using canoes or boats, and that the earliest type of boat was the dugout canoe.

Among the Neolithic sites along the Yellow Sea coast in the Liaodong peninsula, the earlier canoe-shaped pottery from Houwa is small with a rounded base; the later canoe-shaped vessels from Wujiacun and Guojiacun have narrow bodies with flat bases. This indicates that at different times in the Neolithic the dugout canoe varied in shape.

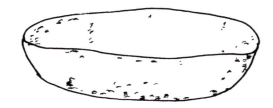

Figure 2.17 Canoe-shaped pottery vessel from Lower Houwa

Dugout canoes were used mostly for fishing in ancient times. From Guojiacun, comparatively large net weights as well as bones of large marine creatures – whales and sharks – were found. Thus we see that in the ancient time people fished not only close to shore but also in distant oceans. This type of fishing activity might have been practiced collectively with people in several dugout canoes.

Dugout canoes were also used as a means of transportation on the sea in ancient times. As noted above, some types of pottery from Dawenkou and Longshan in Shandong were found in the Liaodong peninsula, and some types from Lower and Middle Xiaozhushan on the Liaodong peninsula were found in the Jiaodong region of Shandong. These discoveries indicate that six to seven thousand years ago people had economic exchanges between the Liaodong and Shandong peninsulas. The typical tool of the southeastern coast of China in the Neolithic, the stepped adze, was also found in other regions and islands in the Pacific such as the Philippines and Polynesia, which also suggests that the ancient Chinese had economic contacts with people in the Pacific at that time. In fact, dugout canoes became the means of transportation over the sea for such exchange. Therefore dugout canoes were used not only for shore sailing, but also for ocean travel in ancient times.

The Issue of Sea Inundation

The majority of sites in the range of four to five thousand years old along the Yellow Sea coast in the Liaodong peninsula were located in flat fields and mounds near the sea coast, and other sites are located on the terraces near comparatively low and flat fields. These sites include Guojiacun, Baigangzi, Dapanjia, Guandimiaopu in Dalian; Tasitun in Xinjin county; Qinghuagong on Dachangshan island in Changhai county; Wujiacun, Xiaozhushan, and Wangtongli Chagang on Guanglu island; Shapaozi and Liqiangtun on Zhangzi island; Dantuozi and Wangtuozi; Dagang and Houwa in Donggou county, and others. Later sites of four to three thousand years ago, that is, late Neolithic to early Bronze Age, are mostly located on comparatively higher terraces or even several hundred meters higher on the tops of hills. They include Liaotieshan, Lieshishan, Xiaomupangshan, Chengshan, and Shuangtuozi in Dalian; Shiguoshan, Wunzishan, Dadingshan, Guangtushan, Liaoshishan, Shuangshan in Dongguo county; and others. Why did the ancient people leave their low land and move to the hills? The geological and archaeological data suggest that in this period great changes occurred along the Yellow Sea coast in the Liaodong peninsula, that is, the land was submerged by the sea.

The scale of the sea inundation has been studied by investigating the shell bank unearthed from Wangtuozi in Dongguo county as well as the layers of the Dantuozi site in Xinjin county. Sea-shell banks provide excellent data for studying the change from sea to land, that is, the submergence of the land.

A shell midden of four thousand years ago or so was unearthed near Wangtuozi in Dongguo county. It is currently about 15 km from the sea,[13] indicating that the sea water invaded some 15 km of the land at the time of the site. Other evidence is that Dantuozi in Xinjin county lies about 10 m above sea level, but on top of the cultural layer alluvium is found, containing young shells attached to rocks.[14] This suggests that the site was inundated by water, and the level of the water was about 10 m higher than the present.

CONCLUSION

In sum, the discovery of Houwa is important for understanding Liaoning as well as all of northeastern China in the Neolithic. It is useful for studying the chronology and the regions of the Neolithic in Liaoning and northeastern China; it is valuable for understanding the relationship of primitive societies between the Liaodong peninsula, the Shandong peninsula, the Korean peninsula, and coastal Siberia; and it is of great significance for studying economy, art, religion, sea transportation, ancient geography, and climate in ancient China.

(Translated by Mingming Shan)

NOTES

1 Cultural Archaeological Survey Team of Dandong City. Survey and Test Excavation Report of the Neolithic Sites at Donggou. *Kaogu* 1984(1): 21–36.
2 Anonymous. Neolithic Sites at Houwa in Donggou. *Kaogu Annual* 1985: 123.
3 Anonymous. *C14 Dates of China's Archaeology, 1965–1991,* Beijing: Wenwu Publishing House, 1992, p.15.
4 ibid.
5 Arimitsu Kyoichi. *The Kushimemon Pottery of Korea,* Publications of the Department of Archaeology, Kyoto University, Vol.III, 1962.
   Choe Tong-jung. Comb-pattern Sherds Unearthed at Sosaengsok, Ulsangun, Kyongsang Nam Do, Korea. *Kokogaku Zasshi* 1985 (26, 6): 382.
6 Kim Yong-gan. Interim Report of the Excavations of the Cave Site at Misongni. *Munhwa Yusan* 1961(1): 45–57.
7 Archaeological Institute, North Korean Academy of Social Sciences. *Basics of Korean Archaeology,* 1983.
8 T. N. Andreev. Remains of 2000 to 1000 BC Found along Peter the Great Bay and Nearby Islands. *Kaogu Xuebao* 1958(4): 27.
9 Archaeological Team of the Gansu Provincial Museum and Survey Team of the Wu-wei Area. Excavation of Neolithic Tombs at Yuanyangchi in Yongchang. *Kaogu* 1974(5): 229.
10 Xu Yu-lin and Su Xiao-xing. On the Neolithic Sites at Guojiacun. *Liaoning University Journal* 1980(1): 43–46, 287–329.

Liaoning Provincial Museum and Lushun Museum. Excavation Report of the Guojiacun Site in Lushun. *Kaogu Xuebao* 1984(3): 287-329.

11 Dongbei Kaogu Yanjiu. Unpublished reports on Wujiacun.

12 Xu Yu-lin. The Origin and Development of China's Ancient Canoes and Boats, Based on Findings of Canoe-Shaped Pottery in the Liaodong Peninsula and along the Yellow Sea Coast. *Liaohai Wenwu Xuekan* 1986(1): 57–65.

13 Laboratory of Quaternary Palynology and Laboratory of Radiocarbon, Kweiyang Institute of Geochemistry, Academia Sinica. Development of Natural Environment in the Southern Part of Liaoning Province During the Last 10,000 Years. *Scientia Sinica* 1978 (21, 4): 516–532.

14 Hamada Kosaku. *P'i-Tzu-Wo*, Tokyo: the Far-Eastern Archaeological Society, 1929.

3

RECENT NEOLITHIC DISCOVERIES IN JILIN PROVINCE

Liu Zhen-hua

EDITOR'S INTRODUCTION

Distinguishing between true Neolithic sites and Bronze Age sites without bronze has led to major strides in understanding the Neolithic of Jilin province. With this distinction, what seemed to be an impossible jumble has been turned into a pattern. In this chapter, Liu Zhen-hua discusses six excavated sites in different parts of Jilin province, and considers their cultural affiliations, their temporal placement, and their subsistence bases. He also distinguishes each Neolithic manifestation from the Bronze Age sites nearby. The sites range in age from the fifth to the third millennium BCE. Some interesting characteristics of these sites include the use of obsidian in the east, the common find of spindle whorls and small clay figurines. Obsidian is obtainable in the Changbai mountains (Paektusan in Korean) on the current border with North Korea, but was not widely traded. The creation of small heads of humans and animals is a feature that links Jilin to Liaoning, especially the Houwa site. Spindle whorls imply raw material to spin, but whether it was derived from a plant such as hemp or an animal such as sheep or double-coated dogs is unknown.

The first two sites, Daliudaogou and Jingu, are both in the Yanbian Autonomous Region, but they are quite different. Daliudaogou has the only tent-like feature reported here. Abundant obsidian flakes and impressed, incised and plain potsherds were found in association with the possible tent floor. Later house floors at the same site also contained some obsidian tools, and pottery vessels were found in a variety of shapes including some with handles. A kiln was also excavated. The Jingu site shares its location with a Bronze Age settlement described in Chapter 7. The Neolithic site has obsidian tools in adddition to bone, shell, and even birch bark artifacts. The pottery includes spindle whorls. Houses are semi-subterranean with post holes. The site has three C14 dates, all in the middle of the third millennium BCE. Liu suggests that the differences between these sites are ethnic (cultural) rather than temporal.

Zuojiashan is an important site north of Changchun, closely related to Lower Xinle and other Liaoning sites. A carved jade object may be a forerunner of the Hongshan "pig-dragon." The site is divided into three phases, of which the first is dated about 5000 BCE and the third around 3000 BCE. All the phases included settled farmers.

Xiduanliangshan is near the Liaoning border. It is divided into two phases. Stone entranceways to houses are found in the late phase, and the simpler geometric line designs of the early period gave way to hatched diamonds and triangles.

The Yaojingzi site is on slightly higher land between the basins of the Liao and the Songhua rivers, in an area of sand dunes and marshes, but no large rivers. Both dwelling floors and burials were found. Jade pendants and tubular jade beads are interesting discoveries. Many bone and shell tools were found. It is perhaps not surprising, given the sandy and marshy soil, that the houses were not dug into the ground, but were built on the surface with clay floors and ridged edges. Microliths in composite tools are common. Harpoons and fish-hooks, as well as abundant fish bones in the site, show that much of the subsistence base was supplied by fish. Animal bones include cattle, horse, and dog, with one ox bone dated to the third millennium BCE. It would be important to know the age of the horse bone, but this was not reported.

Finally, the Bashan cemetery, in northwestern Jilin province, is also in a sand dune, with a rich array of burial objects. Two of the richest graves had multiple interments, four in one and two in the other. Both included juveniles. Most of the grave goods were stone, shell, or bone tools.

Liu concludes by comparing the sub-regions within Jilin province and pointing out their similarities and differences.

S. M. N.

The recent discoveries discussed in this chapter represent a major achievement of Neolithic archaeology in Jilin province. Formal excavations of these sites began in the 1970s and the work has gradually expanded, until in the 1980s the general appearance of the Neolithic in Jilin began to be understood. Prior to this, some Bronze Age sites were misinterpreted as Neolithic remains because stone implements are common in the Bronze Age in this area, but bronze implements are few. This error began prior to World War II. In the 1960s, when scattered Neolithic remains were found during a surface survey in the suburbs of Jilin, the error was corrected preliminarily through comparison and reappraisal of the sites.[1] In the early 1970s, in Daliudaogou of Huichun county, in the eastern part of Jilin province, a new Neolithic site was discovered and excavated. Based on the excavated materials, and with reference to survey information from several other locations, the division of the archaeological discoveries into

Neolithic and Bronze Age in the whole province was established.[2] Following this insight, over the past ten years many Neolithic sites have been located within the province, and about ten sites have been excavated. In this article I present six excavated sites in order to introduce the major achievements and discuss them (Figure 3.1).

THE DALIUDAOGOU SITE IN HUICHUN COUNTY

Huichun county is located near the easternmost point of Jilin province, on the north bank of the lower reaches of the Tumen river. The Huichun river, a major tributary of the Tumen river, runs from northeast to southwest within the county. At the middle reach of the Huichun river the Daliudaogou river enters from the northwest. An isolated mound about 20 m high is found at the confluence of the two rivers. The site is located on the relatively flat summit of the mound between the two rivers.

The site was discovered in 1972, and in the same year test excavations were begun. In the following year it was formally excavated. The total exposed area is about 415m,[2] in which both early and late period remains were found (Figure 3.2).

The early period is represented by feature 72L1, located at the southeast corner on top of the mound. It is a tent-like dwelling floor without clear boundaries, with an area of burned earth at the center about 1m in diameter. The artifacts found in this feature are mainly chipped stone spears, stone arrowheads, and net weights made of tuff, as well as many obsidian flakes. Most of the obsidian flakes were not retouched, but a few of them bear use marks. The pottery was all broken, fired at low temperature. Sandy reddish-brown and sandy brown sherds were found. The former are mainly plain; the latter are mostly decorated with incised and impressed patterns. The incisions include parallel slanting lines, date-pit-shaped indentations, and herringbone; the impressions consist of dense impressed dots in horizontal lines. The shapes of the vessels include small straight-rimmed jars, two types of bowls, and cups, with very few large vessels.

The late period is represented by six house floors as well as a kiln. These features are located at the top of the northwest corner of the mound, which is about a hundred meters away from feature 72L1. The six houses are all shallow pits. The plans have three shapes: square, rectangular and irregularly round. Most of the houses are 0.3–0.5 m deep; the length of the rectangle is about 7 m, and the width 5 m or so. The square house is about 4 m on each side, while the irregular round house is much smaller. In the first two types of house floors there are post holes in the four corners which are not consistent in size and shape; the irregular round houses have round post holes at the center of the dwelling floor. None of the houses has

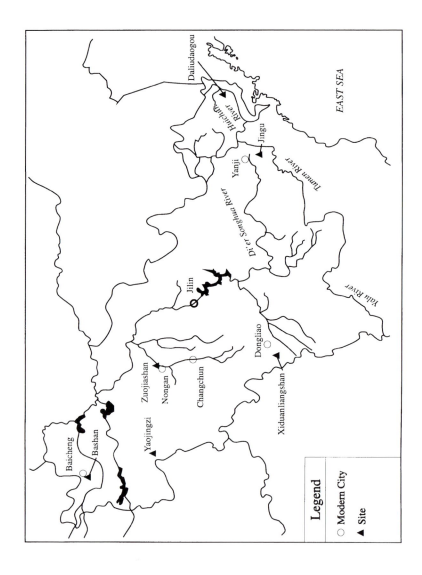

Figure 3.1 Locations of sites described in Chapter 3

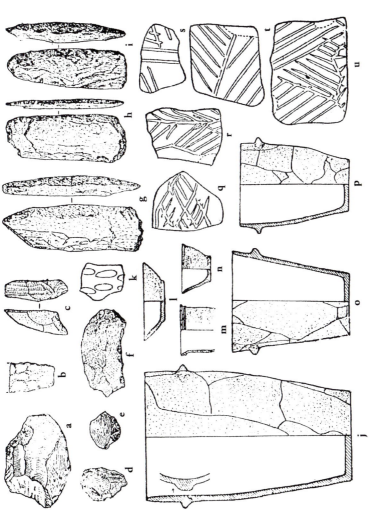

Figure 3.2 Pottery and stone tools from the Daliudaogou site: a) scraper; b) and c) microliths; d)–f) obsidian tools; g) and h) stone hoes; i) stone spear point; j) and l)–p) pottery vessels; k) and q)–u) potsherds with designs. [a) and i) 1/4; b)–f), k), q)–u), 1/2; g) and h), 1/6; j) and l)–p) 1/8]

a stone-built hearth; only ashes were found. No entrances were noted in the pit walls.

A kiln for firing pottery is labelled 72Y1. First a pit was dug into the ground, and then a semicircular hole was dug horizontally in the west wall. There is no kiln grate; the oxidation method was used. The horizontal pit in the west wall was shielded from the wind coming from southwest and northwest. At the bottom of the kiln large amounts of charcoal and ash were found, along with a single sherd of red-brown pottery.

Within and around the house floors, chipped stone axes, stone hoes, stone spears, stone arrowheads, and a large number of irregular stone flakes of tuff were excavated. Also choppers, scrapers, and net weights made of large flakes or cores were found. A large stone slab was discovered. The small chipped stone implements include obsidian scrapers, pointed tools, and some irregular utilized flakes. A few microliths were made of flint and rhyolite. A uniformly shaped stone core, which was flaked from the pointed end rather than the wide end, represents an unusual manufacturing technique. Tools commonly made of flint and rhyolite are scrapers and tools on blades. Bone tools are unknown, with the exception of one bone awl.

In terms of the pottery, a few vessels were made of reddish clay, and the rest of them were sandy reddish-brown and brown pottery similar to that unearthed from 72Y1. The sandy pottery from this site contains less sand in the clay, which does not appear to have been added purposely. It might have been originally in the clay itself. These hand-made pottery vessels were all fired at low temperature and polished. Their color was quite red when first taken out of the ground. They are markedly different from the pottery of the Bronze Age in the same area, in that the latter always has a pale yellow tone. The pottery shapes are simple. They are mostly large-mouthed, flat-based pots, including straight-walled cylindrical urns, jars, cups, with extended rims, bowls and plates. There are two kinds of vessel handles: lug-shaped and tongue-shaped. Columnar handles like those from the Bronze Age are not found. Most of the sherds are plain. The few with patterns include incised mat, pine-needle, parallel herringbone, and bow-string patterns, with a few cases of impressed and incised shallow indented dots.

The two levels of Daliudaogou belong to the same archaeological culture. The economy in the early period included mainly gathering, fishing and hunting; the late period was characterized by settled agriculture, although fishing, hunting and gathering were still important supplements. The location of the site, in the mountains and near rivers, made it very convenient to gather wild plants and fruits, hunt animals, and fish, and the advantages of foraging were not totally replaced by incipient agriculture.

The characteristics of Daliudaogou include shallow house floors without stone-paved hearths, chipped stone tools made mainly of tuff, flaked obsidian microliths, hand-made sandy red-brown and clayey pale red pottery urns, jars, bowls, and cups, some of which are decorated. Compared with the typical Bronze Age remains such as polished stone tools, sandy plain brown pottery *dou* (pedestal vessels) and *zeng* (rice steamers), the differences are evident. In particular, the manufacture of stone tools is remarkably primitive at Daliudaogou. During the excavation, no evidence of the use of metal tools was found. It is clearly a new Neolithic culture in the eastern part of Jilin province. The earliest carbon date of the charcoal unearthed from Daliudaogou is 2220 ± 75 BP (ZK–0282), the latest is 2130 ± 100 BP (ZK–0281).[3] The excavators believe that these carbon dates are too late, so that they are not applicable. They argue that, as this site is located in the forest, rotten leaves and logs covered the ground prior to the excavation. The deposit layers are quite thin, and easily mixed with the large amount of humus and the roots of grass and trees under the ground. In addition there is the consideration of ancient forest fires. It is hypothesized that an appropriate date would be around 3500 to 1800 BCE.[4]

THE JINGU SITE IN LONGJING COUNTY

Longjing county is another part of eastern Jilin province. It is located on the left bank of the middle reaches of the Tumen river. The Longgang range – a branch of the Changbai range – extends into the southern part of its territory. The Jingu site is on the northern ridge of the Longgang range. A branch of the Hailan river (a tributary of the Tumen) runs beside it. The Neolithic site is on the western side of a modern reservoir, on a hill running from south to north, 30 to 50 m above the adjacent ground. On the western side the Wudao creek flows toward the north. The hill is surrounded on the east, west and south by mountains, with only the northern side extending toward the open valley. The Jingu Neolithic site is located on the northern part of this hill, and to the south Bronze Age sites and burials were located.

The site was discovered in 1979, when test excavations were carried out. In 1980, another excavation took place. The two excavations cover 300m². Within an area of 17 m from east to west and 35 m from south to north, six house floors were unearthed. Among these six houses, F2 is square, with a small area, and the rest are all rectangular, with an area of 24–36m². F3 is 6.1 m long from south to north and 4.1 m from east to west, and the pit wall is 0.7 m deep. Since it was built into the hill slope, it is fan-shaped. The east wall is the highest, while there is no wall on the west side. However, in the middle part of the west side there was an area of hard ground, 1.4 m wide, connecting the inside with the outside, which is assumed to be the doorway. Nine post holes were found in the house, with diameters of 10–25 cm. They are not arranged in a regular pattern. Near the north end of the east wall a round burned-earth area has a diameter of about 50 cm. No stones surround it, but it can nevertheless be identified as a hearth. Another example is F5. Its depth is 0.8 m, and its area is similar to F3. The doorway is also in the west. A difference, however, is that another doorway in the south faces F6. A burned hearth of 40 cm diameter lies in the house a little west of center. Four post holes were found, one in the northeast corner, and the other three slightly east of center, also without regularity. An important discovery was four human skeletons found in the northern area of the dwelling floor. The skeletons were all male: an aged man, a middle-aged man, a youth, and a juvenile. It is hypothesized that there might have been a sudden disaster, burying them in the fallen house.

About 350 artifacts, made of stone, pottery, bone, antler, teeth, shell, and birch bark, were found (Figure 3.3). The chipped tools include stone hoes; grinding stones and slabs are pecked. Flaked tools include conical cores, utilized flakes, spear-shaped tools and projectile points, pointed tools, and scrapers, while axes, adzes, chisels, and arrowheads were polished. Most of the pressure-flaked tools are obsidian; the chipped and polished tools are made from andesite, and the pecked from sandstone. Jade pendant ornaments were also found. The remainder of the artifacts are bone awls, needles, antler pickaxes, ornaments made from wild boar tusks, shell containers, and shell ornaments (pendants and rings).

The clay vessels are hand-made, mostly sandy brown, with a few sandy dark grey sherds, which were fired at low temperature. Most of the pots are decorated. The dominant technique is incision, with patterns of herring-bone, parallel slanting lines, dotted lines, rectangular spirals, etc. The patterns are usually placed on the middle or upper side wall of the vessels (some of them even go to the rim), but the lower zone was left undecorated. The pottery shapes include tall undecorated urns with contracted mouths; wide-mouthed cylindrical pots with straight walls; tall wide-mouthed jars; tall basins with wide everted mouths; contracted bowls, some with a false ring-foot; shallow or deep bowls with wide everted mouths; straight-mouthed and curved-walled cups; disk-shaped pottery lids; and pottery spindle whorls in both the pierced conical and flat bead shapes.

Sea-shells and birch bark are particularly important materials. Birch-bark artifacts were excavated from F3, but unfortunately they were too damaged for the shape to be identifiable.

Differences between the artifacts and features of this site and those of the Bronze Age in the same area are great. The Bronze Age is represented by polished stone tools of various shapes, and pottery vessels such as undecorated *dou* [pedestals] and *zeng* [rice steamers]. During the excavation process, no evidence of the use of metal tools was seen, indicating that the sites are Neolithic.

However, compared with Daliudaogou which is just a few dozen kilometers away, there are also many differences. There are many polished stone tools in this site but very few in Daliudaogou; most of the pottery

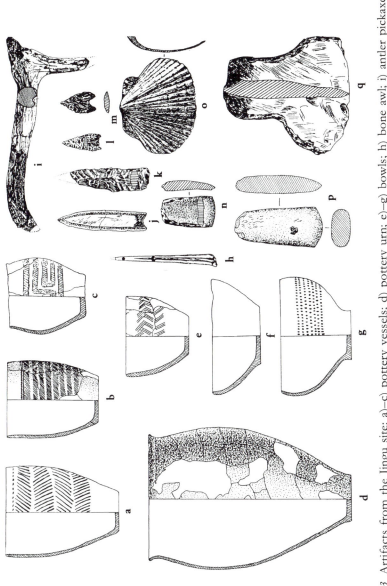

Figure 3.3 Artifacts from the Jingu site: a)–c) pottery vessels; d) pottery urn; e)–g) bowls; h) bone awl; i) antler pickaxe; j) polished stone projectile point; k)–m) obsidian projectile points; n) stone adze; o) shell tool; p) polished stone axe; q) large stone axe [a)–c), e)–h), n)–q) 1/3; d) 2/15; i) 4/15; j)–m) 2/3]

vessels were decorated with patterns, whereas few are found in the other site; very few pottery vessels have handles here, whereas those in Daliudaogou have lug handles or short tongue-like handles; the pots in Jingu have in different degrees curved walls, whereas those in Daliudaogou are quite straight; and although the pots in both sites are flat-based, some of the pots at Jingu have a pseudo ring-foot, whereas at Daliudaogou they do not. Regarding the houses, the shallow pits in Jingu are fan-shaped, with doorways and irregular post holes, which is not the case in Daliudaoguo. Thus, although both sites are Neolithic, they do not belong to the same cultural type. They are separately named "Daliudaogou culture" and "Jingu culture." In regard to the distribution of the two cultures, the former is mostly scattered in the lower reaches of the Tumen river; the latter in the upper reaches. In Yanji city and Long county, relics similar to Jingu have been found. Excavations at the Jingu site suggest that the inhabitants already led a relatively stable and sedentary agricultural life. The level of cultural development in general is higher than that of Daliudaogou. There are two C14 dates from this site: 4465 $\pm$ 100 and 4340 $\pm$ 100. The calibrated date is 3094 ~ 2890 BCE [ZK–0785].[5]

THE ZUOJIASHAN SITE IN NONGAN COUNTY

Nongan county is located north of Changchun city, in the central part of Jilin province, the valley of the Di'er Songhua river. The Yitong river, running from south to northeast, enters this county from the southeast and turns northeast merging at the eastern border with the Yinma river, thence pouring into the Di'er Songhua river. The whole county is flat, with little variation in elevation, as it is part of the Hongji Plain in front of the eastern hills. The Zuojiashan site, discovered in 1983, is on the second terrace on the north bank of the Yitong river, not far from the northeast boundary of the county. In 1984, an area of 400m^2 was excavated. One house floor, two burned-earth areas, and twenty ash-pits were discovered. Multiple levels of cultural deposits were found in this site. Based upon the stratigraphy, the overlapping features, and the relationships between the artifacts and features, the cultural remains of this site were divided into three phases. Within the first phase, early and late sections could be further identified.

The early part of the first phase is represented by T16(4), the fourth layer of test pit 16. The pottery is all hand-made, but the pots were smoothly polished inside and out. Sandy grey-brown pottery predominates, with some shell-tempered yellow-brown pottery and very small amounts of sandy red and sandy black pottery. The shapes are mostly cylindrical pots, with a few globular jars, bowls, and other shapes. Most of the rims are thickened with raised ridges. The joining points between the base and the walls do not have curves or edges, but instead are quite smooth, and furthermore the bases are flat. The decorative patterns begin at the rim and extend downwards, covering one-half to two-thirds of the vessel. Except for a few composite decorative bands, most of the patterns consist of the same design in several lines making up horizontal or vertical parallel bands, with a distinct separation between bands. Both impressed and incised

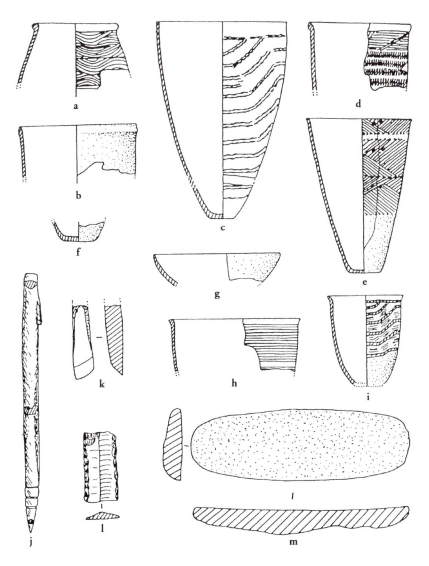

Figure 3.4 Artifacts from Zuojiashan Level 1: a) jar; b)–e) and h)–i) tall pots; f) vessel base; g) bowl; j) bone tool; k) jade burin; l) microlithic flake; m) grinding slab [a), d), g) and i) early phase; others, late phase; j) 1/2; k) and l) 1/1; others, 1/5]

patterns occur. The incised patterns include diamonds, bow-strings and parallel lines; the impressed are Z patterns, comb-Z patterns, and connected-dot lines. Another characteristic of this level is the bone shovel.

The later part of the first phase is represented by T16(3) and F1, and Hearth No. 5 can also be considered here. House No.1 is badly damaged, with unclear boundaries. Judging from eight regular post holes, the floor plan appears to be square. The entrance is in the west, about 1.5 m wide and 1.8 m long, slightly sloping. At the center of the floor a gourd-shaped hearth was 1.45 m long, 1 m wide and 0.13 m deep. The hearth opening faces south. The bottom is burned hard in a basin shape. The pottery of this phase is generally similar to the earlier pottery in terms of its overall appearance. Although the mouth is slightly flared, the walls are straighter than the earlier pots and the protruding edges on some of the rims are lower and wider than before. In addition, straight-sided and slanting-mouthed pots were found. A few cases of incised twisted lines and herringbone patterns also appear. Many stone and bone tools were found. Most of the stone tools are polished, including stone axes, small carved jade objects, grinding stones and slabs. Long, side-bladed tools are flaked. Bone tools include awls, needles, arrowheads, spears, and netting needles.

The second phase is represented by T5(3) and F1 where the deposits overlapped. There are three hearths. The amounts of sandy pottery and shell-tempered pottery are quite similar. The sandy pottery is grey-brown; the shell-tempered pottery is mainly yellow-brown and grey-brown. The manufacture is the same as the first phase. Except for bowls, most of the vessels are straight-sided jars. The joining section at the base of the jar is arch-like. Most of them are straight-mouthed jars, without a noticeable ridge outside the rim. The characteristics of the pattern distribution upon the vessel are that there are undecorated spaces below the rim and near the base. Both incised and impressed patterns occur. The impressions and incisions are mainly Z designs (rocker-stamping). A few cases of triangles filled with parallel slanting lines also occur, along with comb-Z, wave, and raised patterns. Different designs making parallel horizontal bands on the same vessel are quite varied. The stone tools include polished axes, adzes, spears, arrowheads, and a dragon-like ring carved from white stone. Furthermore, there are pecked stone grinding slabs and chipped stone arrowheads and drills. Awls, needles, chisels, and daggers comprise the bone artifacts. Shell earrings, sawn antler, and bone pieces incised with parallel lines were also found (Figure 3.5).

The third phase is represented by T16(2) and T5(2). Sixteen hearths and two areas of burned earth belong to this phase. Near the burned area of T7 there are some post holes, which are badly damaged. T13 contains a thick burned layer and some burned lumps of earth, which is hypothesized to have been a kiln for firing pottery.

Striking differences between this and the first two phases can be noted.

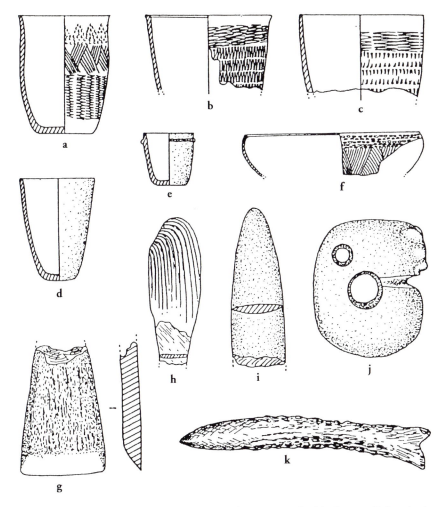

Figure 3.5 Artifacts from Zuojiashan Level 2: a)–e) cylindrical pots; f) bowl; g) stone adze; h) shell tool; i) stone point; j) jade pendant; k) bone fish lure [g) and j), 1/1; h), i) and k) 1/2; the others, 1/5]

The commonest pottery is shell-tempered and yellow-brown, followed by grey-brown shell-tempered pottery. There is little sand-tempered pottery. All the vessels are hand-made, and rather roughly manufactured. Neither the exterior nor the interior of the pots is polished, and they were baked at low temperature. Most of the pots are straight-mouthed, very few are wide-mouthed, and the rims were not thickened. The join between the wall and the base is definite. Some pots have indented bases. The base is larger than those of the first two phases. Most of the pottery is plain, with very little decoration. The decorative patterns, when they exist, cover less of the pot, from about one-fourth to one-half of the vessel, starting from the rim. The lower part of the vessel is plain. There are raised, incised, and rocker-stamped patterns. The common patterns were made in horizontal rows, with either a single pattern repeated or varied patterns, often grouped in sections. The incising includes herringbone, triangles filled with slanting parallel lines, net patterns and Z patterns; the impressed includes fish-scale-like punctates, fingernail impressions, and decorated rims. Vessel shapes include tall jars, bowls, cups, slanting-mouthed vessels, funnels and pedestals, spindle whorls, and some crude pottery figurines resembling human heads, bird heads, and animal heads.

Most of the stone tools are polished, but a few are chipped or flaked. The stone materials used include sandstone, shale, marble, gneiss, mudstone, granite, and flint. Stone tools include axes, pestles, hammers, grinding slabs, hand stones, gravers, choppers, spears, arrowheads and pointed objects. Antler tools include knives, awls, arrowheads, chisels, spears, daggers, shovels, dart-tips, netting needles, and handles for composite tools which were inlaid with microlithic flakes. Some bone pieces were also found incised with herringbone, parallel slanting lines, and saw-tooth patterns. A few shell tools were found as well (Figure 3.6).

Through these brief discussions of the relics and artifacts of Zuojiashan, it can be seen that the differences between the three phases are relatively large. A C14 date from the late first phase is 6100 ± 80 [BK 85061], the second phase does not have testable samples, and the third phase C14 date is 4375 ± 80 [BK 85060]. Therefore the first phase is 4936~4773 BCE; the last 2921~2703 BCE.[6] The relatively large difference between the third phase and the first two phases is related to the lapse in time between them. In terms of the cultural affiliation of the third phase, two different views are expressed in the research papers available: (1) they might belong to different cultural categories; (2) the first two belong to the same culture in different developmental stages, but the third one belongs to a totally different culture. We think it inappropriate to classify the three phases into three different cultures, because the first two phases have an obvious inherent similarity, so that they should be regarded as the same culture but in different stages. In terms of the third-phase remains, although they show differences compared with the first phase, they do not lack commonalities with the second phase; particularly the patterns of incised designs are linked. In regard to several new factors which appeared in the third phase, they might have been influenced by other cultures. It is also possible that the intermediary stage between the second and the third phases has not yet been found, although a sudden change cannot be excluded. Until abundant reference materials are available, the second view is preferable. As to the economy, the people of all three phases no

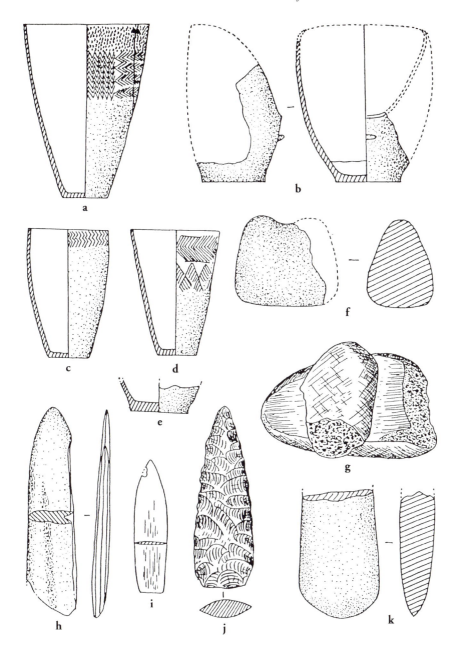

Figure 3.6 Artifacts from Zuojiashan Level 3: a), c) and d) cylindrical pots; b) slant-mouthed pot; e) pottery base; f) pottery stand; g) grinding slab and roller; h) bone knife-handle; i) stone projectile point; j) flaked stone point; k) stone axe [a)–d) 1/5; e) and f) 1/3; g) and k) 1/2; the others, 1/1]

doubt were settled farmers, who supplemented their fare with fishing and hunting.

THE XIDUANLIANGSHAN SITE IN DONGFENG COUNTY

Dongfeng county is located in the south central section of Jilin province, bordering Xifeng county, Liaoning in the southwest. This region is part of the low hilly land of central Jilin. The Hadaling mountain range extends along its west border from northeast to southwest and its south end is known as Sahaling. The East Liao river originates from the western slope, and all the tributaries to the Di'er Songhua river's upper reaches rise from the eastern slope. The Mei river, originating from the south of the county, is one of these.

The site is located on a hill of Xiduanliang, 50 m above the north bank of the upper Mei river and about 50 m from the river. The site was excavated in 1986 and 1987. A total of 534m^2 was exposed. Three house floors and six hearths were found. Based upon the stratified deposits, the relationship of overlapping strata, and the analysis of artifacts, the remains can be divided into early and late periods.

The early period is represented by F3, T4, and T22. F3 is a round, subterranean dwelling floor. The diameter is about 6 m or so. As the pit was dug into sloping terrain, it is deeper in the south and shallower in the north. The south wall is 0.75 m and the north 0.50 m. The entrance is in the northeast, with three steps. The entry is 1.35 m long and 0.76 m wide. At the center of the house there is an oval hearth, 0.85 by 0.5 m. The pottery belonging to this period is mostly sandy, and the majority is red-brown, followed by yellow-brown, and black-brown, with a small number of black sherds. Over half have incised and impressed patterns. These include incised patterns such as bow-string, pine-needle, wave, banded-line, rectangular spirals, diamonds, dots, and comb-Z. Some of the pottery contains a composite of several patterns. In terms of pottery types and shapes, there are cylindrical pots with straight mouths, contracted mouths, wide-flared mouths, and open-mouths; tall pots; bowls with straight-mouths, wide-flared and open mouths; and oval-sectioned spindle whorls. Most of the stone tools are chipped, with some polished stone tools and a few pressure-flaked stone tools. The chipped stone tools include choppers, hammerstones, pointed tools, scrapers, knives, and stone axes. The polished stone implements are axes, knives, chisels, and arrowheads; the pecked stone utensils include grinding slabs, grinding stones, and whetstones. There are a few large pressure-flaked scrapers (Figure 3.7).

The late period is represented by F1, F2, and T11. F1 is badly damaged. Its entrance is in the north, constructed with two layers of pebbles. F2 is

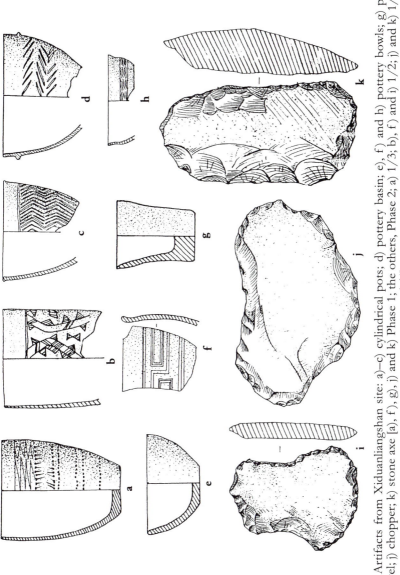

Figure 3.7 Artifacts from Xiduanliangshan site: a)–c) cylindrical pots; d) pottery basin; e), f) and h) pottery bowls; g) pottery cup; i) stone shovel; j) chopper; k) stone axe [a), f), g), j) and k) Phase 1; the others, Phase 2; a) 1/3; b), f) and i) 1/2; j) and k) 1/1; the others, 1/4]

round and subterranean. The diameter is 3.20–3.30 m and the depth 0.75 m. The entrance, which is damaged, is in the northeast. It is 0.99 m. wide, but the length is not known. Approximately in the south of the floor there is a hearth built with six stones of different sizes. The plan is round, with a diameter of about 1.20 m. The pottery is hand-made, but a few rims were processed on turntables. They are all sandy-tempered, mainly dark-brown, but also some yellow-brown and a few red-brown and black. Most of the interior walls are black. The decorative patterns include herringbone, bow-string, parallel slanting lines, criss-cross parallel lines, vertical lines, double-line net patterns, multi-line diamonds, triangular patterns filled with parallel slanting lines, vertical bands, and Z patterns. The diamond patterns are made of abutting zigzags. Shapes include cylindrical pots with various mouth forms – straight, everted, and contracted; bowls, basins, and small cups have the same variety. There are various handle shapes such as tongue, lug, and ring-like.

Disk-shaped and scalloped spindle whorls were found, along with simple pottery figurines of human heads and goose heads.

Flaked stone tools were no longer made. The chipped stone tools include hammerstones, knives, stone balls, stone axes, stone shovels, hoes, and net weights. Polished tools include stone axes, arrowheads, adzes, and chisels, and jade chisels. Pecked stone slabs and hand stones were also found.

With regard to the similarities between early and late periods, the floors are all circular, with entranceways but no post holes; pottery is mainly made of sandy brown clay without shell temper; the decorative patterns are impressed and incised, and the shapes are cylindrical vessels and bowls; and stone tools are mostly large chipped stone tools, with a great number of polished tools and a small number of flaked stone tools. No bone or shell tools were found. Compared with the Neolithic remains in eastern, northern, and central Jilin province, there are important differences. This is therefore a culture with specific features distributed in south central Jilin province. Given the archaeological discoveries, the economy appears to be based on farming. There are many large chipped and polished tools for cutting trees and tilling the earth, polished slabs and grinding stones, but very few flaked stone tools and net weights, and no stone spears. This indicates that although fishing and hunting were practiced, they played a secondary role, and were not an important supplement to the daily diet.

Differences between the early and late periods mainly lie in the following: 1) in the late period, the houses began to have stone entrances and stone-lined hearths; 2) the sandy pottery disappeared in the late period, and the red-brown pottery was replaced by black-brown. The decorative patterns of the early period, such as composite patterns made up of incised or impressed zigzags, impressed comb-dots, and incised diamonds, disappeared in the late period and were replaced by incised geometric patterns such as herringbones, double-line diamonds, and triangles filled with parallel slanting lines. Tall pots disappeared in the late period, but pottery basins, pottery cups, and scalloped-edge spindle whorls, various kinds of vessel handles, indented-base pots and pseudo ring-feet made their appearance. As to stone tools, the few flaked stone tools seen in the early period disappeared in the late period, and the technique of making chipped stone tools made some progress. Some of the tools are flaked across the entire face. The polished stone tools began to include long stone adzes. In particular, the chipped stone tools with narrowed waist or stem for hafting should be noted. This type of artifact is quite common in Bronze Age remains in the south and southeast part of central Jilin. The origin of this artifact has been established here in southern Jilin.

During the excavation of the site, testable carbonized samples were not found, so that relative dating must be used to estimate its date. Cylindrical pots of the early period, in terms of their shapes and decorative patterns, are similar to the big-mouthed pots of Type I at Xishuiquan which belongs to the Hongshan culture in western Liaoning. Xishuiquan is earlier than Dongshanzui (both belong to the Hongshan culture), which has C14 dates of 4895 ± 70 and 4760 ± 70 [BK 82079].[7] The cylindrical pots with composite zigzag patterns of the first period here are like the Zuojiashan second period in terms of decorative patterns and shapes of vessels. The radiocarbon date for the late Zuojiashan Period I, is 6100 ± 80. With reference to these data, Xiduanliangshan Period I calibrated at 4936~4773 BCE [BK 85061]. In the late period, the pottery incised or rocker-stamped with herringbones, parallel lines, double-line net patterns, and triangles filled with parallel lines was very common, which is very much like the remains of Lower Guojiacun and Wujiacun in the Liaodong peninsula. The carbon dates for Wujiacun are 4830 ± 100 and 4690 ± 100 [BK 78064],[8] and Lower Guojiacun has dates of 5015 ± 100 and 4870 ± 100 [ZK–0414].[9] Thus, Xiduanliangshan Period II is probably around 5000 BP, or from the end of the fourth millennium to the early half of the third millennium BCE.

THE YAOJINGZI SITE IN CHANGLING COUNTY

Changling county is located in western Jilin province, between the Shuangliao Plain in the south and the Song-Nen plain in the north, and it is included in the Hongji hills of the Song-Liao watershed. It is a land of rolling hills without large rivers. Within its boundary are many sand dunes and marshes. Yaojingzi village is in the northwest of this county. In the south there is a large marsh, and a long sand dune 20 m high extends from southwest to northeast. The site, 80 × 1000 m, is at the southwest end of this sand dune, surrounded by flat grassland and cultivated land. In 1986, the middle section of the site was divided into four excavation areas, designated A, B, C, and D. The total excavated area is 550m². Seven house floors, one hearth, and two burials were excavated, and 115 artifacts were unearthed in addition to 91 artifacts collected from the surface. The cultural deposits are thin and uncomplicated. Because there are no overlapping floors at this site, the excavators did not pursue chronological studies.

F3 and F2 are good examples of house floors. F3 is rectangular with round corners. The dwelling floor was covered with yellow-white sticky earth and around this a ridge 6–10 cm wide and 4–6 cm high was built with the same kind of sticky earth. The entrance is at the east end of the south wall. The house is orientated 195 degrees. It is 4.56 m long from east to west and 3.84 m wide from south to north. Near the center of the house there is a sub-rectangular hearth 18 cm deep, 85 cm long from south to north, and 80 cm from east to west. F2 is oval; its diameter is 3.2 east-west and 3 m south-north, 180 degrees in its orientation. The ridge along the side is 6–8 cm wide and 8–10 cm high. The entrance is in the middle of the south side. Six irregular post-holes of varying sizes were found along the edge of the dwelling floor. A hearth, slightly east of center, was rectangular with rounded corners, 59 cm × 56 cm and 14.5 cm deep.

The graves are rectangular vertical earth-pits. M1 is 205 degrees in direction and 1.40 m long, 0.65 m wide and 0.61 m deep. It is a single extended supine burial of an adult female. Burial objects include four tubular stone beads. M2 is 200 degrees in its orientation. The burial pit is 1.75 m long, and 0.90 m wide. It is a single secondary burial of a male adult without any burial objects.

Through both excavation and surface collection 119 stone tools were obtained, 68 of which are flaked stone tools, 35 polished and the rest pecked and chipped. The flaked stone tools have round, flat, and indented bases, or stems, there are also narrow waisted shapes, stemmed stone arrowheads, faceted spears, and scrapers of long, round and rounded tip, cutting tools, pointed tools, flake and blade cores. The polished stone tools include long single-blade axes, short-bodied rhomboid axes, long adzes, leaf-shaped arrowheads and pierced heavy stones. Pecked stone tools include grinding slabs and hand stones, and hammerstones are chipped. There are also polished tubular stone beads, hemispherical stone ornaments, and other items. Six jade objects deserve particular attention: a semicircular jade object with an oval section, a flaked jade pendant found with three tubular jade beads, and a leaf-shaped jade arrowhead.

Bone tools abound. Fifty-seven examples were obtained, including bone spears, arrowheads, daggers, awls, chisels, darts, knife-handles (used for inlaid flakes), bone ornaments, antler spears, wild-boar-tusk knives, etc. There are five shell tools, as well as shell daggers and ornaments.

All the pottery is hand-made. Both sand and shell temper appear, but sand temper is more common. The dominant sandy pottery is brown, followed by dark-brownish and black, with a few yellow-brown and red.

The sand-tempered pottery is baked at higher temperatures than shell-tempered pottery. Many of the sherds contain drilled holes, which may have been used for hanging, or perhaps for repair. Few handles were found; they were pierced lug handles or vertical curved handles. Very few sherds are plain, but rather they are decorated with various patterns in several ways (Figure 3.8). In general, the sandy sherds are incised with geometric designs consisting of parallel lines, triangles, or wavy lines. Impressed patterns include bow-string, zigzag, dotted parallel lines, net, rectangular spirals, mat, and band filled with parallel slanting lines. Composite patterns consist of the patterns noted above, making bands with geometric or irregular patterns on pots.

The shell-tempered pottery includes pinched raised ribbons, some of which are indented with short incised lines or impressed nail designs or fingertip patterns. Incised patterns include parallel short slanting lines and pine-needle. Impressed designs were made with cord marks and dots.

Because most of the pottery samples collected or unearthed are sherds and few vessels could be restored, it is very difficult to reconstruct the shapes of the vessels. It seems that the sand-tempered pottery includes cylindrical pots, most of which have everted rims, although some have straight mouths and a few have constricted mouths. Some pottery rims were thickened. There are also bowls with slightly contracted mouths and thickened rims as well as small cups. On a few potsherds vertical curved handles are seen. Shell-tempered pottery includes cylindrical pots with or without thickened rims. The largest number are straight-mouthed, with a small number of constricted mouths and only a few everted mouths. There are wide-mouthed bowls and also spindle whorls made of potsherds. A pottery paddle was found decorated with squares. The patterns made by this paddle would be raised squares, but during the excavation, no such sherds were found.

A typical feature of this site is the round or sub-rectangular houses which are not subterranean but instead surrounded by ridges. Perhaps the houses were a kind of tent structure built on the ground. Flaked stone tools are most common, with very few large chipped stone tools and many bone tools; the dominant pottery is sandy brown and shell-tempered grey pottery. There are varieties of decorative patterns and techniques, and there are also many composite patterns. Some sherds have pierced holes. Thus, compared with the Neolithic remains in east and central Jilin province, it is a new kind of archaeological culture. There are many flaked microliths with a variety of stone arrowheads and spears; as well as harpoons, fish hooks, knives, and sword-handles of bone. Many fish bones were excavated, along with shells and animal bones. Thus, fishing seems to have played a dominant role in their economy. Since some polished stone tools, grinding stones and slabs were unearthed also, the existence of farming is suggested. Animal bones identified include ox, horse, dog,

Figure 3.8 Rubbings of pottery patterns from the Yaojingzi site: a)–c) zigzag patterns; d) comb-zigzag pattern; e) twisted-cord pattern; f) comb pattern; g) cord lines; h) combined-dot lines; i) and k) incised lines; j) print on the pottery bottom; l) square dot line; m) incised lines n) and o) incised lines

and others, thus there is also animal husbandry. This kind of economic life is suitable to the natural environment of the site: sand dune, marsh, and grassland.

The artifacts on this site are very complicated, which might be due to its geographical location as well as its contents, which cover a long span. For instance, the raised band designs on the pottery and the pierced holes in it are related to the remains of the northern Song-Nen Plain (see Chapter 8). Wide-band zigzags and comb-dotted zigzags are commonly seen in the Liaohe plain to the south. Extra thickness of cylindrical pot rims, smooth joins between the lower wall and the base bottom, and the large area of patterns on the pottery are all signs of an early date in central Jilin. However, some of the cylindrical pots are wide and short; these are slightly different. Although there are also zigzag patterns, they are few. There are also many composite patterns, and plain cylindrical pots, which seem to be later. In sum, the Yaojingzi site seems to have had a very long time span. The ox bone unearthed from AT2(1) (the first layer of test pit 2 in area A) is dated by C14 to 4726 ± 79 BP.[10] We think that the site falls between the fourth and third millennia BCE. However, this does not exclude the possibility that some parts might be earlier.

THE BASHAN CEMETERY IN BAICHENG CITY

Baicheng city is on the left bank of the Tao'er river, a tributary of the Nenjiang river in northwest Jilin province. Bashan, located 5 km from the western suburbs of Baicheng, is a stable sand dune 150 m long east-west and 60 m wide north-south. The cemetery is in the dune. In 1984 when it was discovered, it was already damaged by removal of the top layer in the expansion of a shooting range. In the same year, part of the cemetery was excavated. The total area of the excavation is 554m^2. Five graves contained 267 burial objects. In addition, some artifacts were surface-collected, which might be either from the damaged tombs or remains contemporary with the graves (Figure 3.9).

Five graves are rectangular earth-pits without any lining. Due to damage to the top level, the remaining pits are only 0.15 to 0.40 m deep. The graves were placed in a row, roughly facing west, oriented about 250 to 330 degrees. The skeletons are all extended and supine. M1 and M4 are multiple burials and the rest are single burials. There are greater numbers of burial objects in the multiple burials – over 100 artifacts; for single burials, only 2–14 artifacts were included. For example, M1 is a damaged tomb containing four skeletons, two being female adults and two children. M4 is 2.6 m long and 1.3 m wide, containing two people: on the left a male of about 16 years old, facing left; at the right a female of 11 years old or so. Burial objects were placed along the head and thigh and below the feet. The 126 artifacts include shell, bone, and stone tools. M5 contains a male adult

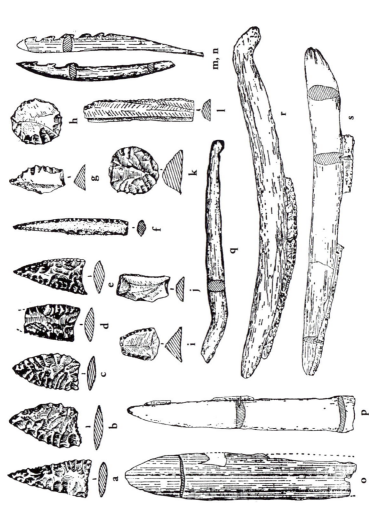

Figure 3.9 Artifacts from the Bashan cemetery: a)–f) stone projectile points; g) stone drill; h) and k) round scrapers; i) scraper with cruved edge; j) short scraper with single edge; l) long scraper with single edge; m) and n) bone fishing dart; o) bone knife with stone insets; p) bone knife with stone insets; r) and s) bone knives with stone insets [a)–k) 7/10; l) ????; m)–o) and q) 1/2; p), r) and s) 2/5]

about 55 years old, with only 11 burial objects. The pit measures 2.4 × 0.8 m. A shell and a stone-bladed knife with bone handle were placed at the head, and at the foot flaked stone tools such as scrapers and pointed implements were found. M2 is 1.8 m long and 0.7 – 0.75 m wide. A female adult about 40 years old had few burial objects. A shell was placed on her chest, and between her femurs there was a long stone flake. Judging from the facts that the two sexes were buried together, that single burial exists, and that great differences in numbers of burial objects between the tombs were found, it is suggested that tha site date from the late stage of matriarchal clan society.

The burial objects from these tombs can be divided into artifacts of stone, bone, and shell. Polished stone tools include only two stone hammers with holes. The rest (170) are flaked stone artifacts, such as conical cores, flakes, arrowheads, scrapers, pointed tools, carving tools, etc. There are 61 bone tools, such as awls, knives, daggers, shovels, fishing darts, hairpins, needles for crocheting and netting, tubular beads, and tooth pendants. Particularly notable are three stone-bladed knives with bone handles and one stone-bladed short dagger with a bone handle. These were all made with slots in the bone handles for inserting stone blades. Shell artifacts include ornaments and containers for drinking and eating. Surface collections include potsherds which are hand-made and plain. There are two kinds of pottery: sandy red-brown pottery, baked at high temperature and well polished; and shell-tempered yellow-brown pottery, baked at low temperature, not as well polished as the former. As no pottery was found during the excavation of the graves, it is difficult to judge whether these collected potsherds belong to the same period as the burials.

Such artifacts as flaked stone arrowheads with both straight and indented bases, bone harpoons, and stone-bladed knives with bone handles are quite similar to those from the Ang'angxi Neolithic of the Nenjiang valley in Heilongjiang province, but the shapes of the artifacts differ, suggesting that the two are identical in terms of age but differ in cultural attributes.[11] The human bones from M1 and M4 were tested and the dates are 4870 ± 80 and 4730 ± 80 [ZK–1375];[12] the calibrated date is 3634~3374 BCE. The shapes of the artifacts also indicate that these tombs are remains from around 3000 BCE. The economy was centered on fishing and hunting, along with farming, because there were polished stone tools among the burial objects and several polished stone axes in the collected artifacts.

DISCUSSION

Judging from the area of the sites and the burials excavated, Neolithic culture extends over the whole province, suggesting a certain representativeness. In regard to the geographic distribution of the Neolithic sites in Jilin Province and through excavation in combination with surveys, some regularities can be noted. Sites were usually located along or near rivers and marshes. In the east and central regions, they are often on low mounds or platforms, and in the west on sand dunes. This is related to the convenience of fetching water, production, life and defense. Thus, the locations were purposefully selected.

Most of the remains from the six sites which have been excavated date to around the fourth and third millennia BCE, except for a few which date to the fifth millennium. Although these remains are in different developmental stages, and played different roles in the whole economy, farming existed in all of them, especially in the central and eastern regions. In the eastern and south-central regions, there are a great many cutting and tilling tools chipped from large stone flakes and regularly shaped specialized tools such as stone axes and hoes, which were used for farming on hills; whereas in the west and north-central regions many bone tools, shell tools, and flaked microliths are found. This is related to the location in sand dunes and grassland and near marshes and rivers where fishing and hunting of grassland animals were practiced. In the east, there are obsidian microliths and chipped stone spears, net weights, and so forth, because there are more forests and streams in the valley where excellent fishing and hunting are found. Moreover, judging from the excavated animal bones, it is in the west that large domesticated animals such as ox and horse appeared earlier. Dwellings in the central and eastern regions are mostly subterranean. Post holes are not in rows and probably the houses were still huts. In the west where the dwelling floors are oval or rectangular with round corners surrounded with low earth ridges, dwellings might have been tents. This seems to be related to fishing, hunting and animal husbandry and to a shortage of wood and stone. All these indicate that natural geographic environments have had a great impact upon the production and lives of the early Neolithic people.

During the period of the fourth to third millennia BCE, Neolithic cultures were at different levels of development over various parts of Jilin province. Comparatively speaking, the Song-Liao Plain in the center was more developed, and next were the sand dunes and marshlands in the west. This is demonstrated by the manufacturing skills of production tools and living utensils, and is particularly reflected in jade ornaments; for instance, the elaborate dragon-like and fish-like rings. In addition, the techniques and varieties of patterns on the pottery are rich, indicating that the material and spiritual life had reached a relatively high level, which was not surpassed in the eastern mountainous regions. In terms of the two Neolithic cultures, found in the eastern area, the level of Daliudaogou is lower than Jingu where there are well-polished stone tools, whereas in Daliudaogou there are no polished tools, but roughly chipped tools dominate. The pottery is baked at low temperature and the manufacturing technique is rough, with simple shapes of vessels and no ornamentation. However, the two sites are not far from each other. The remains of Daliudaogou are not earlier than Jingu. With regard to the imbalance of the development between the two cultures which are close to each other, we think that it should be approached from the perspective of different cultures belonging to different ethnic groups. According to later historic records, the related ancient nationalities or communities are Sushen, Yilou, Yuezhu, and others. The nationality records in southwest regions of China show that there are also regions where mountains and valleys are close together, and it is quite possible that different ethnic groups were mingled. So, when dealing with the imbalance of the two cultures, we should approach the issue from this perspective.

Three points regarding Neolithic remains in Jilin province should be emphasized. First, compared with the Bronze Age, the cultural features of Neolithic archaeology in Jilin province include dominantly large chipped stone tools and flaked microliths, while in the Bronze Age polished stone tools increased in east and central regions and also in the west where processing became more skilled and elaborate, so that the shapes of tools became more regularized. In the Neolithic, the pottery was all decorated on the surface, especially in the central and western regions. In the Bronze Age, pottery became plain in central and eastern regions and in the west, although some plain pottery also is found, complicated geometric designs consisting of comb-dots and animal-like patterns developed. Some vessels were painted inside and out in red.

Second, the commonalities of the sites in Neolithic Jilin are that most of the sites (except Daliudaogou) have polished stone tools, the pottery is almost all sandy brown, baked at low temperature, and most has incised straight-line geometric patterns. However, there are important differences among regions and cultures. For instance, the large chipped stone tools were common in the east and central south, the flaked stone tools in the west and central north, while in the eastern region obsidian microlithic artifacts were found. Bone and shell tools are particularly developed in the west and north-central regions. Pottery in the east has patterns including incised vertical lines, herringbone, pine-needle, and rectangular spirals, but composite patterns are rarely seen. In the central and western regions, in addition to incised patterns, there are also many impressed and rocker-stamped patterns and in the west there are raised patterns, while composite patterns became more and more frequent. People began to repair the pottery. In terms of the dwelling sites, the houses in Jingu have connected ditch-like channels, and in Yaojingzi the houses are not subterranean but tent-like. Summing up the features of the artifacts and the relics, there are large differences between eastern and western regions when seen as far ends, but the central part is more or less neutral, transitional and comprehensive.

Third, in regard to the relationship between the Neolithic culture of Jilin and other places, it is obvious that the impressed zigzag patterns, which were quite common in the fourth millennium BCE, existed also in Liaoning, southeastern Inner Mongolia, Hebei and elsewhere at the same time or a little earlier. According to the published data, impressed zigzag patterns appeared earliest in those places. Another example is the manufacture and use of jadeware, especially the jade dragon-like and fish-like objects, which are very similar to those in the previously mentioned regions. This suggests that the Neolithic culture of central and western Jilin is closely linked to the south. In terms of the characteristics of the incised and impressed straight-line geometric patterns and composite patterns which were common all over the province in the third millennium BCE, they were prevalent south of this province as well. In Jilin province, based upon the information available, this type of pattern existed earlier in the central region than in the west, suggesting that the eastern area was influenced either from the central and western regions or from the south beyond the province. To the west of Jilin province, raised patterns and rocker-stamping on the pottery were very common decorative techniques. These traits are frequently found along the Nenjiang valley in Heilongjiang province and further north, so that Jilin and the west may be closely related.

The above discussions are based upon the six excavated sites and with reference to surface surveys. It should be recognized that the archaeological cultural types within Jilin province were probably not limited to this degree, so that our understanding is very limited also. In particular, the current findings are mostly dated in the fourth and early third millennia BCE. They are not in the category of early Neolithic, for which excavated sites are minimal. To understand the relationships of developmental and transitional origins and system types relies upon future work and the current knowledge needs to be redefined with new knowledge.

(Translated by Peng Ke and Du Jie)

NOTES

1   Zhang Zhong-pei. Cultural Types of Ancient Sites in Jilin City. *Jilin University Social Science Journal* 1963(1): 69–75.
2   Liu Zhen-hua. Several Neolithic Remains in Ancient Cultures of Jilin Province. *Bowugwan Yanjiusuo* (Museum Research) 1982(1): 73–82.
3   Dates reported in *Kaogu* 1978(4): 284–285.
4   Liu Zhen-hua. Excavation Summary of the Daliudaogou Site, Huichun County, Jilin Province. Archives of the Jilin Provincial Archaeological Research Institute, 1974.
5   Yanbian Museum. *Concise Edition of Yanbian Relics*, pp.16–20, Beijing: Yanbian People's Press, 1988.
    Brief Report on the Clearance of the Jingu Neolithic Site at Langjing in Jilin. *Beifang Wenwu* 1991(1): 3–9.
6   *Kaogu Xuebao* 1989(2): 209.
7   ibid.
8   *Kaogu* 1979(1): 89.

9   ibid.

10 *Bowugwan Yanjiusuo* (Museum Research) 1990(3): 58.

11 Liang Si-yong. Prehistoric Sites at Angangxi. In *Liang Si-yong's Collected Archaeological Works*, Beijing: Chinese Scientific Press, 1959.

12 *Kaogu* 1988(12): 1084.

4

THE NEOLITHIC IN HEILONGJIANG PROVINCE

Tan Ying-jie, Sun Xiu-ren, Zhao Hong-guang,
and Gan Zhi-geng

EDITOR'S INTRODUCTION

The Neolithic in Heilongjiang shares several characteristics with that of Jilin. In both regions archaeologists needed to distinguish true Neolithic sites from Bronze Age sites without bronze before progress could be made. Neolithic sites are thinly spread (as far as is now known) in both provinces. Both have pottery with incised and impressed geometric markings. Sites in Heilongjiang are found in the same kinds of locations as in Jilin. It is clear that the two provinces make a continuous region, so that it is artificial to divide the archaeology according to these administrative units.

In Heilongjiang, however, the group of Neolithic sites at Ang'angxi has long been known and published in the west. In addition, some surveys have revealed new sites in Heilongjiang. Sites on the eastern edge of the province, including Yinggeling and Shihuichang, are in a drainage that empties into the Japan Sea near Vladivostok, sharing characteristics with sites around Peter the Great Bay. Yinggeling is a hilltop site with five layers. The lower level has flat-based pottery vessels with simple shapes. Antler hoes were found, similar to those found in the shell mound of Kungsanni in western Korea. The upper layer features lively figurines of pigs and dogs. While the stone tools of the lower level are mostly chipped, in the upper stratum they are almost all polished. Obsidian is found, relating these sites to those of eastern Jilin and northeastern Korea around the Tumen river. Many kinds of bone tools were found, including spoons and hairpins, along with shell knives in semi-lunar shape. Birch-bark artifacts were also found, again echoing eastern Jilin sites. Stone-walled houses were excavated. Shihuichang is on the Mudan river in a mountainous region, surrounded by other sites. Stone walls outlined the houses here as well.

The Yabuli-Beishachang culture, found in the southeastern part of Heilongjiang province, is believed to belong to early Neolithic times. The pottery is quite simple, with geometric designs. The only excavated house floor has an oval basin-shaped hearth.

The Ang'angxi culture is in sand dunes, like the sites of western Jilin

118

province. A notable characteristic is the amount of cryptocrystalline raw material, such as flint, jasper, and agate, which was finely pressure-flaked into tools, especially projectile points of several types. A female burial with a spear and a dart is an interesting discovery, interpreted as a woman hunter.

The Sanjiang Plain region includes the Xiaonanshan and Xinkailiu sites. Xiaonanshan overlooks the Ussuri river. It is a single component site, and the pottery has simple shapes, either plain or incised or impressed. Xinkailiu is on the banks of Xinkai lake [Lake Khanka], a large lake partly in eastern Heilongjiang and partly in Russian Siberia. Pottery is decorated all over, with diamond-shaped patterns, and has flat bases. Xinkailiu is more like coastal Siberian sites than those of interior Heilongjiang. An interesting feature of the site is a series of pits with whole fish skeletons, which apparently were for storage of fish. Many bone tools were found. Graves include both primary and secondary burials, with the secondary burials attached to the primary ones.

Microliths are common in the Neolithic throughout Heilongjiang province, but they are associated with several different types of pottery. The authors conclude the chapter by describing the distributions of the various types of sites.

S. M. N.

DISCOVERIES AND ANALYSES

As early as the end of the 1920s a report on the Neolithic discoveries in Heilongjiang had been completed. At the beginning of the 1930s, the reknowned Chinese archaeologist Liang Si-yong excavated and surveyed in the dunes at Wufu point in Ang'angxi, Qiqihaer, laying the foundation for Neolithic studies in the northern areas of China. Large-scale scientific archaeological excavation and survey began after the foundation of the People's Republic of China. Archaeologists in Heilongjiang have discovered a great many archaeological sites since 1949. Many reports and summaries appeared, but before the 1970s, the study of the local archaeology was at the stage of mere data accumulation. Knowledge of the cultural characteristics of the numerous Neolithic sites reported was limited, since sites had not been excavated on a large scale.

Another problem was that, because ceramic production in these areas remained at the manual stage for a long time, all sites with hand-made pottery were considered to belong to the Neolithic age. It was difficult to discover and attach the proper importance to bronze workshops, found in the Bronze Age sites in this area, where only small bronze implements were made. At the same time the finding of bronzeware accompanying abundant stone and bone implements, along with the limitation in documentary data and traditional lore, resulted in many Bronze Age sites not being recognized as such. After further fieldwork and research, many cultures have been moved from the category of Neolithic into the Bronze Age, because they include bronze-casting technology in addition to common stone implements. Some of these cultures even belong to the Iron Age. The solving of these problems means that the characteristics of the real Neolithic cultures in Heilongjiang are becoming clarified.

In a recent general survey of archaeological sites many new Neolithic sites were discovered, which have not yet been excavated. After the 1970s, following the excavations in Xiaonanshan and Xinkailiu, more and more archaeological research has been accomplished and published. However, there are still many exploratory questions concerning the Neolithic in Heilongjiang, such as the cultural context, distribution, mutual relationships, developmental stages, and the division into areas, systems and types, which need to be answered. Although the data are limited, a brief introduction can be made.

NATURAL SURROUNDINGS AND SITE CHARACTERISTICS

The distribution of Neolithic sites is basically in keeping with the natural geographic divisions in Heilongjiang (Figure 4.1). This province is a relatively integrated natural geographic region with vast territory and varied topography such as lofty mountains, undulating hills, and wide, rich plains. The terrain is high in the north, northwest and southeast, and low in the northeast and southwest regions. It is basically made up of three large mountain chains and three large plains. The Greater Xingan mountains dominate the northwest, and the Lesser Xingan mountains rise in the north. The Zhangguangcai, Laoye and Wanda mountains are found in the southeast.

The Mudan river runs between the Laoye and Zhangguangcai ridges, finally emptying into the Songhua river in the Song-Nen Plain. The latter is in the southwest, surrounded by the Great Xingan range in the west, Lesser Xingan range in the north, the Zhangguangcai mountains in the east and the Song-Liao watershed in the south. The Song-Nen Plain is linked to the Sanjiang Plain by the Songhua [Sungari] valley. It has undulating terrain, well-developed rivers, and vast flood plains. There are dunes, marshes, and many surviving ancient lakes and springs. The Songhua river runs through the Song-Nen and Sanjiang Plains and finally empties into the Heilongjiang river.

The Sanjiang Plain, located in the eastern part of Heilongjiang province, was created by the alluviation of three rivers, the Heilong [Amur], the Songhua and the Ussuri. It is surrounded by Xiaoxing Anling in the west, the Ussuri river in the east, the Heilongjiang river in the north and Xinkai lake in the south. The Wanda mountains lie across the Sanjiang Plain

Figure 4.1 Locations of Neolithic sites in Heilongjiang province

from west to east and divide the plain into two parts, south and north. The Sanjiang Plain, one of China's largest marshlands, is vast, rich, and well watered. Its average elevation is 80–100 m, but it is less than 50 m along the rivers. On the shallows and marshlands of the plain, besides the 10–20 m-high star-shaped isolated hills, there are also some ridges of sand dunes.

The terrain suggests that the prehistoric cultural relics in the Heilongjiang area should appear mainly in the Song-Nen Plain, the Sanjiang Plain, and the valleys of the Mudan and Suifen rivers. The locations of recently discovered Neolithic sites in Heilongjiang can be summarized into several types; that is, dunes and hillocks, terraces along the rivers, mounds beside the lakes, hillocks at the foot of the mountains, or valleys in the mountains. The villages are usually 10–20 m higher than the river-bed. Vast water areas

121

and rich aquatic products are present on the plains, dense forests in the mountains, lush waterweeds at the foot of the mountains, abundant animal and plant resources, and convenient conditions for drawing water and catching fish. This varied ecological environment supplied favorable conditions for collecting, hunting, fishing and extensive cultivation. Villages at that stage began to assume different sizes, with large sites of about 10,000–20,000m^2, and small ones varying from several thousand to only several hundred square meters. The area of the semi-subterranean rectangular house is generally 25m^2. The ancient people lived a sedentary village life with small clan units.

THE VALLEYS OF THE MUDAN AND SUIFEN RIVERS

The Mudan and Suifen run through the hilly land in the southeast part of Heilongjiang province among which there are large or small basins. The Suifen river, rising in Jilin province, runs through Dongning county, enters Siberia and finally empties into the Sea of Japan near Vladivostok. It is the only river in this province which is not included in the Heilongjiang basin, but empties into the sea alone.

As to the prehistoric cultures of this area, the Russian archaeologist V. V. Ponosov in 1931 surveyed along Jingbo lake and the nearby Mudanjiang area, collected some stone and ceramic implements, and wrote a report.[1] In 1939 (during Japan's invasion of China), the Japanese archaeologist Okuda Naosaka also surveyed the Jingbo lake area and excavated some sites along the lake, such as Jingmingshui, Yaolingzi, and Nanhu.[2] In 1958, 1959 and 1960, the Heilongjiang Provincial Museum surveyed these areas three times. So far, there are only two excavated sites in the Mudanjiang valley, Yinggeling in the southern part of Jingbo lake in Ningan county, and the Shihuichang site in the eastern part of Dongjing town of Ningan county.

The Yinggeling site

In 1963, the Yinggeling site was largely destroyed by lake erosion. During that summer, the Heilongjiang Provincial Museum excavated the site, and later published several reports and articles.[3]

Yinggeling, a hillfort stretching east to west, lies on the bank of the southern part of Jingbo lake. With its western point entering the lake, it is surrounded by water on three sides in flood season. About a hundred meters north of the hillock, a river called Songyihe runs east-west and empties into the lake, while about three hundred meters southeast of the hillock, a mountain spring called Fangshengou pours into the lake. Part of the site has eroded into the lake, leaving a ragged bluff. A cultivated slope 50–200 m wide is topped by a thick oak forest. Many features and artifacts can be seen eroding from a layer in the bluff which is 2–5 m above the water. Since the site is continually eroded and denuded year after year, sherds and stone implements are often found on the lake-bed near the cliff when the lake recedes.

The excavated area of Yinggeling is about 100m^2 and is divided into upper and lower cultural layers. Four house floors have been found, but all are incomplete due to erosion. Among the four dwellings, F1, F2 and an ash-pit (H1) belong to the upper cultural layer, while F3 and F4 belong to the lower layer. Along with the houses, a group of artifacts was unearthed.

The stratigraphy of Yinggeling can be divided into five layers from top to bottom. The relations between these five layers were clarified during the excavation. The fourth and fifth layers are assigned to the lower culture, before the Shang dynasty, the second and third belong to the upper cultural layers which are included in the later period cultures (during Shang and Zhou). The first layer contained no cultural material. Charcoal and birch bark found in F1 were dated to 3025 ± 90 [ZK–0089] (the calibrated date is 1310~1008 BCE) and 2985 ± 120 years [ZK–0088] (calibrated to 1300~920 BCE). This indicates that the upper cultural layer belongs to the time range of Shang and Zhou in the Central Plain. The lower cultural layer is thin and has few artifacts, indicating that social differentiation was not great and the settlement was not permanent. The artifacts of the upper cultural layer are rich and the cultural features are clear.

Lower Yinggeling

The pottery of the lower layer of Yinggeling is characterized by red-brown sand-tempered ceramics, with a few coarse grey ceramics. Most of the vessels are broken. The decorative patterns include slanting parallel lines, A-shaped dotted lines, comb-impressed lines, W-shaped lines, and many varieties of dotted-line patterns in bands.

The ceramic shapes of the lower layer are very simple. All are flat-bottomed wares including jars, bowls, and cups which are incomplete. Jars can be divided into those with straight mouths and vertical walls and those with constricted necks and open mouths. The former are decorated with A-shaped lines or slanting parallel lines under the edges of the mouths. The lines are deeply incised. Some appear short and thick, like pine needles. The latter are yellow-brown ceramics decorated by dotted lines below the rims and on the shoulders. The only small ceramics are spindle whorls in three types: some are trapezoidal, others have a central raised area, and the third group are bead-shaped, in longitudinal section.

Among the stone implements of the lower layer of Yinggeling, chipped stone implements are common, while polished stone tools are rare. Hoes and axes are the two most common tools. Chipped stone hoes have three variants: those with convex tops, short tangs and slanting shoulders; those with long tangs and wide edges (Figure 4.2a); and those with constricted waists, triangular tops and one side with unchipped cortex, which are roughed-out implements. The chipped stone axes can be divided into four types: those that are rectangular with rounded corners and four edges chipped thin; those shaped like flat rectangles, with wide waists and thin and blunt convex blades; those with stepped, narrow tips and flat and straight blades; and the fourth group, small rectangular implements with raised backs and flat handles. The polished stone axes are narrow, long and regular, with narrow handles, flat tops, ace-shaped blades, and cortex remaining on the bodies which are little polished or only blade-polished.

Other excavation reports mention chipped stone implements including shouldered hoes, constricted-waist hoes, disk-shaped implements, and axes which are narrow in the upper parts, wide in the lower parts, and raised in the middle parts, with two thin sides, convex blades, and trapezoidal flat and straight blades. These are included with the lower layer because of their technology and shape.

Bone needles (Figure 4.2b) and antler hoes are the only bone and horn implements in the lower cultural layer of Yinggeling. Antler hoes were found on the floor of F4. The top of the antler was rubbed to a rounded point, and a rectangular socket was cut in the middle section, piercing a hole on each side of the socket in order to consolidate the handle by driving in a peg. It is the first antler digging implement discovered among the Neolithic relics of Heilongjiang.

The only building remains of the lower layer are two houses, numbered F3 and F4 in the reports. They are both semi-subterranean buildings, with the west walls eroded by the lake. Rooms of the houses are rectangular with rounded corners. The natural black soil comprises the pit floors and walls. The dwellings are different sizes: the east wall of F3 is 5.9 m long while the incomplete south wall is 3.2 m long; F4 is 6 m in length and 2–2.7 m in incomplete width. Therefore the house floors were no less than 25m^2. When the pit was finished, post holes were dug for wall and roof support. For example, F3 had 7 incomplete post holes in the east, north and south walls, with the diameter 10–16 cm and the depth 24–28 cm. Stone blocks were set closely at the foot of the east wall with soil filling in the gaps. The floor is the natural soil surface which was compressed by year-round activities to a flat and fine floor 5 cm in depth. An oval stone ring 0.9–1.1 m in diameter, was found in the middle of the house at the same level as the floor. The hearth is very solid, with red burned soil on the outside and black-red burned soil on the inside, and some carbon cinders in the burned soil. F4 has 23 incomplete post holes in the east, south and north with the diameter 10–17 cm and the depth 10–31 cm. The entry area is not known. It is estimated that the door was in the west or southwest part of the house. It is therefore quite possible that the entry was eroded by the lake.

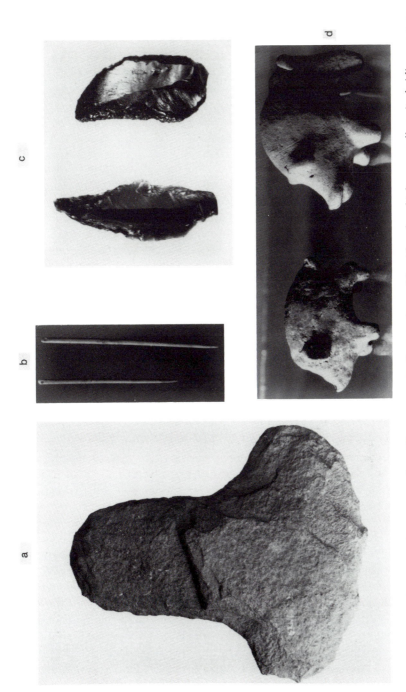

Figure 4.2 Excavated artifacts from Yinggeling, Ningan county: a) stone hoe with wide edge; b) bone needles; c) obsidian scrapers; d) clay pigs

Upper Yinggeling

Originally it was reported that the upper and lower cultural layers of Yinggeling were both Neolithic cultural accumulations, with no direct successive relations between them. The pottery of the upper layer is characterized by dark-grey sand-tempered sherds, with a few black clayey sherds. Most of the potsherds have plain or polished surfaces with limited and simple decorations including irregular lines of large trellis design on the body and zigzag borders around the mouth. The majority of the pottery pieces were hand-made, and heavily burned.

Pottery figurines are a characteristic of the upper layer of Yinggeling. The lifelike animals in various postures are distinctive and could be considered original works of art (Figure 4.2d). They were made of sand-tempered brown clay with variegated color and black-brown spots. The ceramics were well fired and quite solid, with obvious fingermarks. They are mainly pigs and dogs. The pig figurines are quite varied – some are standing with thin bodies, high backs, and projecting mouths, some are walking with slightly projecting snouts, erect ears, eyes made with pointed implements, and tails attached to the buttocks; some are running with slightly projecting mouths, erect ears, bent-upwards tail, and pedaling back legs. There is one small pottery pig with round body, closed mouth, high back, only two legs, no eyes and no tail. Although it was made by slightly processing a clay ball, the result is simple but vivid. Some of the pigs were only sketchily molded with no eyes, ears, mouths, or noses. The large pigs are complete with long necks, erect ears, pointed mouths, and curling tails on the buttocks. The small pigs have incomplete heads and long necks, curly tails, protruding front legs, and are oinking. These original works of art were made by the prehistoric people after observing the animals for a long time. They are not only art masterpieces but also data for studying early animal-keeping, that is, the domestication process from wild boars to pigs.

The stone implements of Upper Yinggeling are quite well made. Polished stone implements are the most common, followed by flaked tools. Pressure-flaked implements made of obsidian are important examples of this type (Figure 4.2c). Polished stone implements include axes, adzes, spears, and arrowheads. Stone axes are finely polished with rectangular plan and convex blade. Adzes are long, flat, and finely polished all over. Spears had sharp double-edged blades. Polished arrowheads are fine, and can be divided into five groups: triangular concave-based, triangular flat-based, willow-leaf-shaped, leaf-shaped with rhomboid cross-section, and long-narrow body with flute.

All the pressure-flaked implements were made of obsidian. The flaked arrowhead has two types: one sharp and finely flaked with triangular concave base and long or short triangular body; and one thin with a flat base. The flaked spearhead had a stem and an indefinite ridge. The long scrapers can be divided into large and small with long, narrow body, convex top, raised back and edge retouch. Short scrapers had wide and regular flaking around the edges, thick narrow backs, and raised backs with cortex surfaces. The majority of scrapers are made of flakes with irregular shapes, some triangular, some rectangular, and some slightly retouched on the edge.

The bone implements of the upper layer of Yinggeling include needles, awls, hairpins, spoons, and chisels. The bone needles are divided into three groups: finely polished with curved body and an eye; square or round cross-section and thick end with a slit; and roughly made of fish bone with holes in the ends. All the bone awls are made of animal long-bones with only the working end polished. There are two kinds: one made by splitting the long-bone and polishing one end; the other made by retaining the joint of bone, polishing the whole tool, making a hole on one side, and polishing the blade flat and pointed. Bone hairpins are also made of polished long-bones. Bone spoons are made of animal ribs and are flat with an elliptical hole on one end and the other end polished. One bone chisel has a rectangular cross-section and an incomplete blade.

Tooth and shell implements were also found. An arrowhead was made by cutting down and polishing the pointed tip of a wild boar tusk. It has a triangular flat bottom and the tooth enamel can still be seen. Tooth knives were made by splitting a wild boar's tusk into two parts and then polishing them. The shell knife has a half-moon shape with two holes drilled in it.

Birch-bark artifacts are characteristic of Upper Yinggeling, but it is unknown exactly what they were. They were found on the floor of houses F1 and F2, in curls or slices. The "knobs" on the implements can still be seen clearly. The original investigator inferred that these pieces of birch bark were either used as household utensils or spread on the roof for cover, like tiles.

There are only two remains of dwellings (numbered F1 and F2 in the original report) found in Upper Yinggeling. They are both semi-subterranean buildings. The single room at this stage was constructed like those of the lower layer. The only new technology was building stone walls. For example, F1 is a rectangular semi-subterranean house. Soil filled the cracks in the stone walls, which remained to 0.7–0.9 meters high. The construction method was to lay one stone upon another. The stone wall is 25 cm in width and the sizes of the stones are variable, from 27 × 16 cm to 5 × 6 cm. Five to six layers of large stones were first laid as a base, upon which about 14 layers of small stones were erected. The wooden posts in the pit bottom were reinforced with stone. The east wall is complete, 5.4 m in length. The west wall is missing, while the incomplete north and south walls are each about 1 m long. There are 18 incomplete post holes in two rows near the east wall, with 10 holes outside the east wall and 8 inside. The distance between holes is 50 cm. The diameter of the holes is 10–20 cm and the depth is 15–65 cm. The holes outside the wall are large and deep.

There was a great deal of carbonized wood on the floor, whose incomplete length was 20–50 cm and diameter 12 cm. The pieces lay in the east-west or southeast direction with the flattened birch bark. The fact that the wooden poles in the walls were carbonized indicates that the house was destroyed by fire.

Most of F2 was washed away by the lake. Most of the east wall and part of the south wall were left. The east wall is made of earth and the incomplete length is 4.6 m, while the south wall is made of stones; a fragment 1.43 m long and 0.73 m wide is left. The building method of the walls is the same as F1. The floor was not processed. There are 17 incomplete post holes. The holes near the east wall are divided into two rows in the north-south direction, and the holes near the south wall are also in two rows whose diameter is 8–14 cm and length 13–19 cm. Carbonized wood lay on the floor south to north. The largest piece is 70 cm in length and 7 cm in diameter. This house was also destroyed by fire.

The Lower Shihuichang culture[4]

Lower Shihuichang is a late Neolithic culture which is distributed over the mountainous area of the middle reaches of the Mudan river. The Shihuichang site is located on the delta of the confluence of the Mudan and Muleng rivers, 2 km from the northeast edge of Shihuichang hamlet, Changdong village, Ningan county, Heilongjiang province. The elevation of the delta is 280 m and the relative altitude of the delta above the river is 12 m. To the northeast of the site and opposite the river is Sandaoliangzi village, while at a distance of about 4 km to the west is the Niuchang site, and about 5 km to the southwest is the site of Dongkang.

Shihuichang is in the northeast corner of the alluvial basin in Dongjing city on the upper and middle reaches of the Mudan river. The Mudan runs west to east through the northern part of the site, while the Muleng river comes from the southeast and empties into the Mudan in the eastern part of the delta. On the north are the Zhangguangcai mountains, while the middle section of the Laoye mountain range lies southeast of the right bank of the Muleng river.

The central portion of the Shihuichang site was destroyed by digging clay for bricks, leaving a crescentic ragged cliff of 400 m long on which the site is located. The excavation area is 140m^2, in which four houses and twelve ash-pits were found. The excavators divided this area into three cultural periods, Upper, Middle, and Lower, based on stratigraphic study of the site.

The archaeological units of the lower cultural layer are F3, F4, F4a, and F5a. The relics belong to the Neolithic. The ceramics of the lower layer culture of Shihuichang are mostly ash-brown and yellow-brown, followed by red-brown pottery (Figure 4.3). All the ceramics are hand-made. Since they were baked at low temperature, the surface color of the vessels is

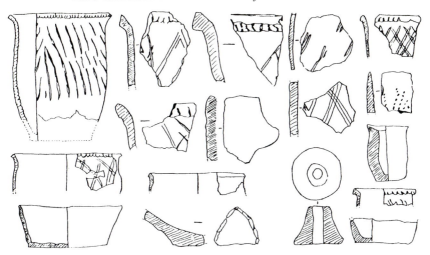

Figure 4.3 Pottery from Shihuichang

uneven. There is coarse sand in the clay and the tempering materials are irregular. The shapes are unstandardized and the surface is slightly polished. Most of the ceramics are incomplete and fragmentary. Household utensils include only jars, basins, bowls, and cups. The jar is the most common. It usually has an open mouth, slightly curved walls and a flat base, while basins have open mouths and big flat bases. Besides the vessels with plain surfaces, there are many with decorative patterns, such as single lines, parallel lines, and rough geometric figures made of parallel lines. Some of the ceramics are also decorated with impressed dotted lines, usually on the pots. The decorations are placed from the edge of the mouth to the lower part of the vessel wall. The individual lines of the decoration are thick, short, and deep, and the parallel lines are thin, long, and shallow, while the grouped parallel lines are even thinner and closer if there are many lines in one group. The various designs are made by different techniques, that is, parallel lines are made with a comb-like implement, while the single line was made with a round-edged tool. Most of the vessels have thickened lips with triangular cross-section. The raised part is indented into a ribbon shape by the same implement. The effect is like appliqué but the technique is different. Pressed dotted lines, which appear only rarely, were made with tubular implements.

The stone implements of Lower Shihuichang include axes, spades, wedges, grinding slabs, and grinding stones, of which the large polished round-bladed stone spade and the rectangular flat stone spade are the most characteristic. The methods of manufacturing the stone implements include chipping, pecking, and polishing. Sometimes these three methods were used on the same tool, that is, chipping the blank, pecking it into the desired shape, and finally polishing the blade or whole body.

Among the building remains of Lower Shihuichang, only two houses (F3 and F4) were found, but both were damaged. They were semi-subterranean with square or rectangular plan. F3 is square, created by digging into the natural black soil. On the south side there is a stone wall whose inside surface is flat and straight. Yellow soil fills in the gaps between stones. The stone wall stretches to the east and then turns to the north near the broken cliff, indicating that this was a semi-subterranean building. No stone hearth, post holes or doorway were found in the floor, which was burned. The incomplete room is 3.2 m long, 2.5 m wide, and 0.4 m deep. The incomplete wall is 0.6 m high and 0.8 m wide.

The Lower Shihuichang culture is late Neolithic, in the later half of the third millennium BCE. Its relative age is between Lower and Upper Yinggeling.

The Yabuli-Beishachang culture[5]

The Yabuli-Beishachang culture is a newly discovered Neolithic culture which is located in the southeastern mountains. The town of Yabuli is located in Shangzhi county. The Suibin railway runs through the town, and the Mayan river flows through it from east to west, then turns to the north, and finally empties in the Songhua river. Thirty km to the east is the main range of the Zhangguangcai mountains.

The Beishachang site is on a hillock 1.5 km northeast of Yabuli town. To the north and west of the site are low mountains and hills, while to the southeast is a long narrow plain. The Mayan river runs 2 km to the south of the site. Due to sand-quarrying, an eroded bluff 20 m high was formed in the eastern and southeastern parts of the site. The majority of the site was destroyed by removing the sand, and only a limited area remains. The land has not been cultivated recently, but to the west of the site, a hill rises gradually to planted coniferous forest. Eight square test pits (each 5 × 5 m) were excavated. The total area was 200m^2. One house floor was found.

At Beishachang, yellow-brown pottery is in the majority, while red-brown and ash-brown sherds are few (Figure 4.4). The ceramics are tempered with fine sand, lightly fired, hand-made and of loose texture. Most of the ceramic decorations are impressed cord and comb lines, while some dotted lines, impressed lines, and incised lines also appear. These decorative patterns may occur alone or with two patterns together to form a compound figure or a decorative range of geometric design. Some plain ceramic pieces were also found. The mouth edge is usually decorated with cord impressions while the lower wall has a geometric design of cord marking or comb marking. Many vessels are flat-bottomed, but some have solid round feet. The shapes of ceramics are very simple. Only jars and bowls are found.

The stone implements of Beishachang are divided into chipped and

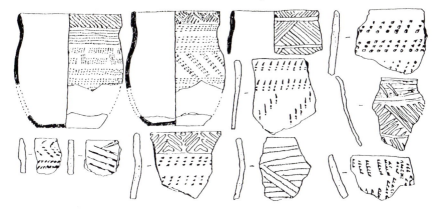

Figure 4.4 Pottery from Beishachang

polished tools (Figure 4.5). On the floor of F1 were some chipped constricted-waist stone plows and polished stone arrowheads, grinding slabs and hand stones. There are only two scrapers, which were made on flakes. The stone arrowheads had willow-leaf shapes and were made on very thin flakes. There were also rarer implements and ornaments, such as a long stone axe with a convex blade finely polished all over, a polished stone shovel with holes in it, stone adze and jade chisel, jade adze, and jade pendant.

The only house-floor found in the Beishachang site, was in the eastern section of the excavated area near the bluff. The east wall was severed by the eroded cliff while the other three walls are well preserved. This is a semi-subterranean building in rectangular shape. It is 3.4 m long east-west, 3.3 m wide, and 0.2–0.25 m deep. The entry faces south, and there is a long doorway divided into two steps, each 0.85 m long, which are high in the south and low in the north. The first step is 5 cm higher than the floor and is flat. The second step is 5 cm higher than the first one but it gradually rises to the south. The entry is 0.9 m wide on the north end and 0.7 m wide on the south end. The floor was not processed, but looks solid because of being trampled. The hearth is north of center. It has an oval surface, burned into a solid, thick red-brown layer. It is on the same level as the floor, containing much ash. No post holes were found. Stone tools and ceramics lay on the house floor. The pottery consists of jars and bowls. The stone implements include stone plows, arrowheads, grinding slabs, and hand stones.

The excavation report assigns the Yabuli-Beishachang type to the early Neolithic. It is a new cultural type.

131

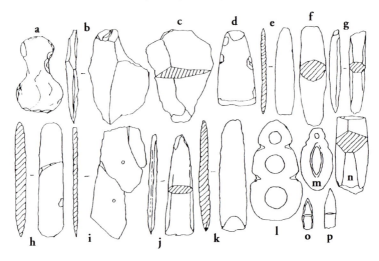

Figure 4.5 Stone artifacts from Beishachang: a) stone hoe; b) and c) scrapers; d) stone adze; e) grinding stone; f) grinding bar; g) jade chizel; h) stone axe; i) stone shovel; j) jade adze; k) grinding stone; l) and m) jade ornaments; n)–p) stone arrowheads

THE SONG-NEN PLAIN

The main Neolithic culture of the Song-Nen Plain is the Angangxi culture. Angangxi is 25 km to the southeast of Qiqihaer. The site occupies four sand dunes to the south of Wufu station, 4 km west of Angangxi.

In the early 1930s, Liang Si-yong, a pioneer Chinese archaeologist, surveyed and excavated this area, which is now well known in archaeological circles.[6] Similar cultural relics were also surveyed and excavated after the foundation of the People's Republic of China. Before and after this, Russian[7,8] and Japanese[9] archaeologists also came here for survey and excavation. The remains of this culture are distributed along the Nenjiang valley, with Angangxi at the center.[10,11,12]

The ceramic characteristics of Angangxi cultures are as follows. The clays contained fine sand and limited shell temper. The color is mottled and is usually grey-brown. It can be divided into four color groups: grey-brown, yellow-brown, light grey, and dark grey. The grey-brown ceramics are usually plain, although some have designs of irregular triangular shapes, incised lines and fingernail marks. Some of the yellow-brown pottery was fired at high temperature and contained a grey core, while the others were high-fired with light color and fine texture. In addition to the designs noted above, there are also stab-and-drag lines on some of the yellow-brown clay ceramics. The grey ceramics have a few, simple shapes, such as basins, bowls, and pots. Some of the bowls have pouring edges. Most of the pots are cylindrical or have a small mouth and globular walls, while some have round bottoms. There is a thick round or square everted lip around the mouth decorated with saw-tooth or dotted lines. The decorations are mostly made with raised lines, but there are also incised irregular triangles, stab-and-drag, and small rectangular combed lines.

The major production tools of the Angangxi culture are made of stone, which can be divided into three types according to technology: flaked, chipped, and polished (Figure 4.6). Having many types, various shapes and great quantity, the flaked stone implements are the most common of these three types, and could be called the most important Neolithic production tools in this area. Raw materials are mainly jasper, agate, and flint. During their long development, the ancient people accumulated much experience in making stone implements and knew the characteristics of the stone materials thoroughly. Using pressure-flaking skillfully, they produced small fine stone implements, making all the implements according to established patterns.

Among the pressure-flaked stone implements, the projectile point is most common. The majority were made in two sizes. There are four shapes: those with flat bases, with round bases, with indented bases, and with stems. Some of the stone projectile points with flat bases are long, some have three sides of similar length, while the others have big, thick and wide bodies with diamond cross-sections. Some of the stone projectile points with round bases have long and thick bodies with blunt blades and diamond cross-sections while others have wide bodies with convex sides. The arrowhead with an indented base is the most common (Figure 4.6a–d). Besides being finely pressure-flaked all over, it also has finely retouched serrations on the sides, and diamond cross-sections. These arrowheads were finely made and represent a high level of manufacturing technology of pressure-flaked implements. The stone arrowhead with a stem has a long body, a diamond cross-section, and a long wide end which is completely edge-retouched.

A few willow-leaf-shaped spearheads were also found. They are large, with bifacial flaking. They were attached to a shaft to throw at wild animals. They can be divided into three types: those with round bases, those with indented bases, and those with stems.

There are four types of pointed implements: round points, flat points, triangular points, and curved points. The round-pointed implements have round or diamond cross-sections and mostly have shoulders. Some have long sharp points, two shoulders, and short, wide, flat bodies which are flaked completely (Figure 4.6e); others have short points and long bodies and are flaked only on one side. There are also a few triangular pointed implements made by flaking the edges. Most of them have no shoulders and have only one pointed end.

Scrapers were made by pressure-flaking and were processed on only one

Figure 4.6 Stone artifacts from Angangxi: a)–d) stone projectile points; e) stone drill; f), h) and i) Stone scrapers; g) stone knife

side (Figure 4.6f, h, i). They can be divided into four types according to the shapes: rounded-top, small round, notched, and backed.

Some knives were made by completely flaking the edges of a blade (Figure 4.6g). Some have one slanting side and one straight side while others have convex or rounded blades. Core knives were made by flaking an oval blade core into an arc-shaped blade. Microliths were carefully flaked for use as inlays in composite cutting tools. Many flakes have traces of use, while some were resharpened. There are also blades. A few chipped or polished stone implements were also found.

Production tools are mainly flaked stone and bone for fishing and hunting. One of the characteristics of the Angangxi culture is the large number of implements which were found in excavations. Harpoons with a single row of hooks are characteristic. Fish bones and animal bones, which are common among the artifacts, indicate that the ancient people made their living mainly by fishing and hunting. In the excavation of a male grave at Angangxi, some fishing and hunting implements were found, such as bone spearheads, bone harpoons, and bone knife-handles, which shows that the ancient people were engaged in hunting and fishing. In a female burial, implements included an indented base spear, a round-based dart and knives, which indicates that ancient women also sometimes hunted.

Because flaked stone implements were the commonest and most important production implements, and because ceramic technology lagged behind and there were no metal implements, this culture is assigned to the earlier Neolithic stage. Angangxi culture is very similar to Xinkailiu culture in age and cultural content.

THE SANJIANG PLAIN

Archaeological work in the Sanjiang Plain began in the 1970s. The main Neolithic cultural relics of this area are the Xiaonanshan site and the Xinkailiu culture.

The Xiaonanshan site

Xiaonan mountain is located in the southern part of Raohe county. It overlooks the left bank of the Ussuri river with an elevation of 106 m. It is a raised highland running north-south, with the south end high and precipitous, while the north end is low and gentle. The local people generally call the south end of the ridge Dananshan and the north end Xiaonanshan. The site is in an orchard between two hills, on the east bank of the river, 25 m above the river surface.

The Xiaonanshan site was first excavated in 1971.[13] It is obviously a single component site. The stratigraphy is very simple – the second layer beneath the plow zone is the Neolithic cultural layer. Under the second

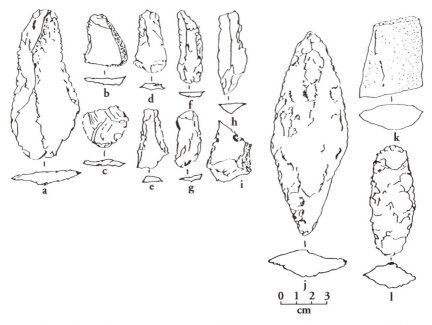

Figure 4.7 Artifacts from Xiaonanshan, Raohe county: a)–c) scrapers; d)–j) flakes; k)–l) stone spears

layer, traces of living floors and a group of stone implements were found, but among the collected ceramics, in addition to potsherds, there is only one restorable jar.

Among the ceramics of Xiaonanshan, only coarse sand-tempered red pottery occurs. It is tempered with large quartz grains, and is low-fired and friable. The joins come apart easily. All the ceramics are hand-made, and traces of hand-molding can still be found on some vessels. Most of the ceramics have plain surfaces. The decorations include square lines, incised lines, combed lines, horizontal lines, and wavy lines. The shapes are only jars and bowls. Jars have straight slanting sides, constricted mouths, cylindrical shapes, and serrated rims. The bowls usually have open mouths and slanting or straight walls, with no decorations.

The stone implements of Xiaonanshan are mainly made of jasper, agate, crystal, flint, slate, sandstone, and diabase (Figure 4.7). The polished stone implements include axes and projectile points, while the chipped tools include spears, arrowheads, scrapers, and pointed implements. Most of the stone artifacts are chipped. Some of the implements and utensils are similar to those of the Xinkailiu culture; for example, laurel-leafed projectile points, sword-shaped projectile points, long projectile points with stems, and round-end scrapers with tangs.

136

Figure 4.8 Ceramic vessel from Xinkailiu, Mishan county

Since the ceramic shapes and decorations are very simple, pots and flat-bottomed jars, and the production tools include only stone implements, most of which were chipped, it can be concluded that the Xiaonanshan site is Neolithic, later than the Xinkailiu culture. No traces of metal implements or imitation metal implements were found.

The Xinkailiu site

The Xinkailiu site is located on the bank of Xinkai lake in Mishan county of Heilongjiang province. The site area is 240,000m^2. In 1972, two cultural layers were exposed in excavation by the Heilongjiang Provincial Museum.[14] The two layers belong to different developmental stages of the same culture and the ages are not far apart. Thirty-two graves and ten fish storage pits were also found.

The Xinkailiu ceramics (Figure 4.8) are mostly grey-brown and sand-tempered, with some yellow-brown sand-tempered ones. Red pottery is very rare, usually decorated with multiple patterns, from the mouth down to the middle of the wall or even all over the exterior surface. Some ceramic

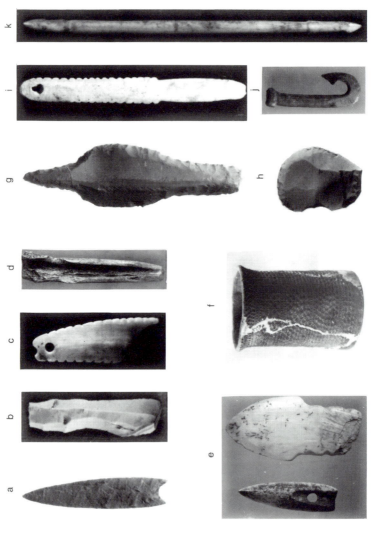

Figure 4.9 Artifacts from Xinkailiu, Mishan county: a) stone projectile point; b) scraper; c) tooth ornament; d) bone chisel; e) projectile points made from tusk; f) cylindrical bar; g) tanged point; h) bone spatula; i) scraper; j) bone fish-hook; k) bone fishing dart

jars are decorated with incised and dotted lines around the mouth. The designs include fish-scale figures, diamond lines, combed lines, short diamond lines, small rectangles, parallel square lines, and net figures. Among these the fish-scale figures and diamond lines are the most characteristic. All the ceramics were hand-made by coiling and scraping. There are few vessel shapes – only jars and bowls. Most of the jars are wider at the top and narrower toward the base, gradually turning into flat or indented bases. Variations of mouth shapes include straight, constricted, and everted mouths and those with thickened lips. There are also cylindrical jars, which are mainly tall, with wide mouths and flat bottoms (Figure 4.9f).

Most of the Xinkailiu stone implements are microliths. Large chipped or polished stone implements are rare. The flaked implements include arrowheads, points, scrapers (Figure 4.9b, i), leaf-shaped blades, flakes, and cores. There are various stone projectile points. Shapes include laurel-leaf with round bases, willow-leaf with indented bases (Figure 4.9a), and those with a stem (Figure 4.9g). There are also burins and round-end scrapers with tangs which are characteristic of the site. The laurel-leaf projectile points are flaked on both sides. They are believed to have been inserted into handles to make composite tools. Polished stone implements include axes, chisels, grinding stones, arrowheads. They are coarse – some even contain some cortex while others are polished only on the blades. Thick and heavy polished stone axes with one raised side and a semicircular cross-section are a local trait.

A large quantity of bone, antler and tooth implements is another characteristic of the Xinkailiu culture. There are harpoons, fish spears, fish-hooks, spearheads, arrowheads, knife-handles, spoons, awls, and needles (Figure 4.9d-e, j-k), among which the harpoons, fish spears, and spearheads are the most characteristic. Bone knife-handles were used to inlay stone blades.

Ten fish storage pits found in Xinkailiu had two shapes – round and oval. The round ones are 0.6 m in diameter and 0.6 m in depth while the oval ones are 0.85 m from south to north, 1 m from east to west, and 0.6 m in depth. Fish bones were stacked in the pits, including articulated skeletons. It is assumed that the ancient people stored whole fish in these pits and covered them with soil. Such traces are rare in the Chinese Neolithic.

Among the Xinkailiu graves, only two vertical-pit graves lack burial goods. Burial methods include both primary and secondary burials. There are 11 primary burials and 18 secondary. The former are all single graves, and most were extended and supine. The graves are rectangular with irregular orientations. Pottery vessels were placed beside the heads and other funerary articles either by the heads or along the sides of the bodies. The burial goods are mainly projectile points, adzes, chisels, harpoons, fish spears and spearheads. Most of the secondary graves are square with round corners and contain only one body, but there are some with two to four

Figure 4.10 Bone carving of eagle head from Xinkailiu

bodies. The bodies were laid in rows but in different directions. Most grave goods were limited to jars and projectile points, although a bone carving of an eagle head was found (Figure 4.10).

Among these graves, some of the secondary burials are attached to a nearby primary grave. For example, M3 and M5, M31 and M29, M20 and M26 have obvious attached relationships. In addition to the main burial, M7 has 4 secondary burials. The primary burials are all males, each with a large quantity of funerary goods. M3, M6 and M7 contain the greatest quantity of grave goods, mainly ceramics and stone, bone, and antler implements, some of which are unfinished. The secondary burials are both male or female. It is presumed that the males of the primary graves occupied high standing in the clan or family. Among the 32 graves, all were in the second layer except M18, which was in the third layer.

The implements and utensils of Xinkailiu culture have their own characteristics, and are unrelated to other Neolithic cultures. The age of the M5 bones of the upper layer is 5430 ± 90, calibrated to 4239~3995 BCE (4130 BC) [ZK–0424].[15]

SUMMARY

The above data suggest that Heilongjiang in the Neolithic should be divided into three large regions. For quite a while, because of poor data, many later sites or graves were mistaken for Neolithic cultures, which held

140

up the exploration of real Neolithic cultures. Now according to the material of the confirmed Neolithic cultures of important sites, such as Xinkailiu, Xiaonanshan, Lower Yinggeling, Upper Yinggeling, Lower Shihuichang, and Angangxi, the Neolithic cultural characteristics can be summarized.

Almost all the Heilongjiang Neolithic sites have flaked stone implements as the main production tools. The Yinggeling obsidian implements are flaked but the stone material is unusual. Some metamorphic stone tools and chipped stone hoes were also found there. Such discoveries correct the mistaken view that only pastoralists/horse-riders on the grasslands developed flaked stone implements. This is an important supplement to the distribution area of flaked stone implements, joining the known flaked stone tools to the north of the Heilong river and east of the Ussuri river to the maritime region of Siberia.

The distribution of sites with flaked stone implements in Heilongjiang is quite irregular. Many sites with a great quantity of flaked stone are concentrated in the middle reaches of the Songhua and Nen rivers, indicating that fishing and hunting supplied the major subsistence, which continued to be very important even after the development of animal husbandry. In other areas, sites are limited, possibly indicating the later appearance of agriculture.

Various Neolithic cultures in Heilongjiang not only have different pottery, but also different shapes of flaked stone implements, or even if the shapes are the same, the proportions of implements are different. Each type has its own characteristic tools and vessels.

It has been shown that the Angangxi and Xinkailiu cultures are both located in forest, grassland and lake areas rich in fish and animals. Their geographical surroundings and fishing implements, fish storage pits near houses, and even the clan cemeteries, all indicate that the ancient people lived here for a long time, leaving a vivid picture of fishing and hunting. In the long history of Heilongjiang province, there must have been very many ancient people living by fishing and hunting on the Song-Nen and Sanjiang Plains. They accelerated the early exploration and historical development of the Heilongjiang area.

Among the Neolithic cultures of China's northeast, there is a widespread occurrence of microliths which belong to different cultures and different times. They should be given different names. Pressure-flaked stone implements are distributed widely in every continent of the world. They appeared in the late Paleolithic period and became prevalent in the Mesolithic and Neolithic periods. Over the middle and lower reaches of the Yellow river from the late Paleolithic to the Mesolithic period, pressure-flaked stone implements were extremely common, but few continued to be made in the Neolithic period. The assemblages containing pressure-flaked stone implements in China are distributed over the northern area from Heilongjiang to Xinjiang as well as in the regions of Tibet, Yunnan, and Guangdong. The materials and shapes of pressure-flaked implements and assemblages were used over a long span of time in the northern area.

The differences among the pottery types of the various areas are quite obvious. Therefore the method of generalizing about "Microlithic culture" or differentiating different types under this formulation does not reflect historic reality and the mutual influence of different ages, areas, and cultures, which represent different ethnic groups. The development of widespread fieldwork, finely differentiating and naming the different cultures according to typical sites, is one of the new objects of regional archaeological studies.

Other sites similar to Angangxi are extensively distributed over the Song-Nen Plain, concentrating on the bank of the Nenjiang where there are more than a hundred sites. Wufu, Moguqi, Erlasu, and Hongqi Yingzi in the Angangxi area are the most characteristic site groups. Remains of Angangxi culture type are rarely found in the lower reaches of the Nen river or on the left bank of the upper and middle reaches of the Songhua river. The Qingkenpao site in Anda county to the north of the Songhua river is an example of an Angangxi cultural site on the Song-Nen Plain. The newly surveyed Shajiajyao site in Saqing also belongs to the Angangxi culture. The sites of Beigangzi in Zhenlai Tantu, Hougang in Baolitun, Xigangzi and Yonghetun in Da'an, Ao-baoshan, Dongshantun, and Zouderen, are typical examples, similar to Angangxi in the southwest part of Song-Nen Plain. The Huangshan site in Harbin, on the right bank of the middle reaches of the Songhua river, includes artifacts of different periods, among which some also belong to the Angangxi culture. It can be predicted that more assemblages belonging to the Angangxi culture will be found in the lower reaches of the Nen river and the middle reaches of the Songhua river in the future.

It should be pointed out that the Angangxi culture had a long developmental process, and the sites with flaked stone implements as the major production tools were formed over a long time span. The surface artifacts belong to different periods and have regional differences. Eventually we will be able to differentiate periods of the Angangxi culture.

The Xinkailiu culture has its own characteristics and distribution. The recent survey enlarges its range. Although the sites have many common characteristics, they also have some individual traits, regional differences, and different developmental periods. For example, the Daobeishan site in Jixi and the Wufenglang site in Yilan are two regional types probably at the same stage as the Xinkailiu culture or a bit later.

There are still some blank spots and uncertainties about the Neolithic cultures in the upper and middle reaches of the Mudan river, the upper reaches of the Heilong river, and the upper and middle reaches of the Ussuri river over the eastern mountain land. The developmental order cannot be systematized completely.

Among the upper and lower layers of Yinggeling, Lower Shihuichang, and the Yabuli-Beishachang type, there are both common and individual characteristics which formed the different cultural types. Together they make up the various features of the Neolithic periods of the southeastern mountain land. Chipped knives, shouldered stone hoes, large stone spades, grinding stones, and many chipped stone implements were the main production tools in Upper Yinggeling, Lower Shihuichang, and the Yabuli-Beishachang type. Their common characteristics reflect the forest-mountain area. They appear to be a kind of forest agricultural culture.

There are similar buildings, that is, semi-subterranean houses, in the Lower Shihuichang and the Upper Yinggeling. The ancient residents built complete or partial stone walls around the house pit not only to reinforce the walls against collapse, but also to increase the strength of the walls to support the roof, and to make the house moisture-proof and more pleasant to live in. Compared to the inhabitants of Lower Yinggeling, they created new building technology. The small semi-subterranean houses made full use of the excavated space, and the enclosing walls are very solid. The hearth in the middle of the house was important for keeping warm. Once the semi-subterranean house was invented, with its special structure and shapes, it was quickly and widely adopted. The improvement of building technology was the crystallization of the wisdom of the ancient people in the process of adapting to the natural surroundings and climate.

In the sites of Lower Shihuichang, Xiangshui in Ningan[16] and Tundong in Xi'an, the same or similar lined sherds and rim sherds are found. According to survey data, Lower Shihuichang culture mainly is found on both banks of the middle reaches of the Mudan river and the upper reaches of the Muleng river. Concerning the Lower Yinggeling, the Upper Yinggeling, and the Yabuli-Beishachang types, their distribution range and cultural origin are one of the problems to be solved by regional archaeologists.

(Translated by Peng Ke and Du Jie)

NOTES

1 V. V. Ponosov. Prehistoric Cultures in Eastern Manchuria. *Academia Sinica* 1938(3, 2): 337.
2 Okuda Naosaka. Survey Report of Prehistory on the Jingbo Lake Shore. *Academia Sinica* 1940(4, 2): 274.
3 Cultural Archaeological Team of Heilongjiang Province. Yinggeling Site at Ningan in Heilongjiang. *Kaogu* 1981(6): 481.
4 Archaeological Management Center of Mudanjiang City. The Shihuichang Site at Ningan. *Beifang Wenwu* 1990(2): 3.
5 Archaeological Research Institute of the Heilongjiang Province. Clearance Report of the Neolithic Site at Yabuli in the Shangzhi County of Heilongjiang Province. *Beifang Wenwu* 1988(1): 2.
6 Liang Si-yong. Prehistoric Sites at Angangxi. In *Liang Si-yong's Collected Archaeological Works*, Beijing: Chinese Scientific Press, 1959.

7 A. S. Lukashkin. Survey of the Neolithic Site near the Qiqihaer Train Station. *Vestnik Manchzhurii* 1934(3): 135.

8 V. S. Makrov. New Data on the Neolithic Culture near Angangxi. *Harbin Natural Science and Ethnological Journal* 1950(4): 8–17.

9 Okuda Naosaka. Microlithic Layer Found at Angangxi in Northern Manchuria. *Anthropological Journal*, 1945(59, 2): 35 (Tokyo).

10 Heilongjiang Provincial Museum. Survey of Microlithic Cultural Site on the Nenjiang River Banks. *Kaogu* 1961(10): 534.

11 Heilongjiang Provincial Museum. Survey of the Angangxi Neolithic Site. *Kaogu* 1974(2): 99.

12 You Shou and Wang Yun. Archaeological Survey in the Nenjiang River and Mudanjiang Cultural Areas by Some Professors in the History Department of the Harbin Teachers' College. *Heilongjiang Daily*, August 28, 1962.

13 Heilongjiang Provincial Museum. Test Excavation Report of the Xiaonanshan Site at Jehol in Heilongjiang. *Kaogu* 1972(2): 33.

14 Cultural and Archaeological Team of Heilongjiang Province. Xinkailiu Site at Mishan. *Kaogu Xuebao* 1979(4): 491.

15 Archaeological Institute of the Chinese Academy of Social Sciences. Report on Radioactive Carbon Tested Dates: VI, *Kaogu* 1979(1): 89.

16 Cultural and Archaeological Team of Heilongjiang Province. General Archaeological Survey in the Jingbo Lake Area of Ningan County. *Heilongjiang Archaeological Journal* 1983(2): 56.

Part II

BRONZE AGE

5

LOWER XIAJIADIAN CULTURE
Guo Da-shun

EDITOR'S INTRODUCTION

Lower Xiajiadian is the term applied to a group of sites in western Liaoning, once called Chifeng Phase II. Exposed house floors and walls of several types, painted pottery in unusual colors, shapes and designs, and elaborate graves with characteristic jewelry are some of the characteristics of this culture.

Guo begins by describing the distribution and chronology of these sites, which are found both north and south of the Yan mountains. The time is now placed from Late Longshan to Early Shang, that is, 2000–1500 BCE, and is divided into three periods. Most of the pottery is quite ordinary, but different from the daily pottery of the Yellow River region. The vessel shapes include steamers, baggy-legged *li* tripods, solid-legged tripods, and jars. Ceremonial pottery includes *gui* tripod pitchers and *jue* tripod spouted wine vessels, found in matching sets in burials. Both shapes are found in Shang sites, but there the vessels are made of bronze, and in this connection it is interesting that Lower Xiajiadian vessels have rows of bumps resembling rivets. The *taotie* [monster mask] design appears among the painted patterns. Cloud patterns, thunder patterns, turtles, and dragons are also found, also resembling Shang bronzes. However, the dates indicate that the Shang is later than Lower Xiajiadian, rather than the other way around. Large numbers of pig bones were found both in dwelling sites and in burials. Cattle, sheep and deer bones are also represented.

Bronze was used for small objects, including ornaments, tools, and weapons. The bronze earring with a fan-shaped end is a notable characteristic of this culture. A pottery mold for casting bronze has also been found.

Houses differ markedly in size and complexity. The earliest dwellings are round pit houses with stepped entrances. Later houses are larger, with adobe walls and paved floors. Some houses have stone walls outside the adobe walls. Frequently there is a raised platform made of adobe bricks on one side. Surrounding earth and stone walls are grouped into several types, but they all seem to be defensive walls.

Excavated cemeteries are few, but so far those that have been excavated are rich. Dadianzi, northeast of a well-preserved dwelling site, is the most important of these. Burials are quite close together. The graves are earth-pits, with wooden coffins in most cases. The heads are oriented northwest, but males and females lie on different sides. The graves are up to 8.9 m deep. Earthen niches at the foot were filled with grave goods, such as painted pottery in sets, pig and dog bones, and lacquerware. Jade and bronze ornaments were found in the coffins, and some males had stone battle-axes.

Lower Xiajiadian is contemporaneous with the Erlitou site in the Zhongyuan. The inhabitants practiced intensive agriculture, with domesticated pigs and dogs. Guo suggests that there were not only specialized artisans, but also workshops each of which has a distinctive style. Stratification is clear in the burials. The depth of the burials is associated with the amount of burial goods and their complexity. The largest burial has two pigs and four dogs. The vessels in the deepest graves are larger and more elaborately painted. Sometimes there are multiple sets of pottery. There may be no niches or from one to three to contain the burial goods. The coffins range from mud bricks to wooden coffins 2 m high. *Gui* and *jue* are deposited only in the largest burials.

Guo argues that the Lower Xiajiadian is a local development, an outgrowth of the Hongshan culture. Transitional pottery types can be found, for example. However, Zhaobaogou is seen as another antecedent of Lower Xiajiadian. The tripod vessel has no local antecedents at all. Guo traces the appearance of tripods from Shandong and suggests a connection through the Gaotaishan culture from east of the Yiwulu mountains.

Lower Xiajiadian is followed after a pause by Upper Xiajiadian, with quite different features. Guo argues, however, that there is some continuity between them. Both have the tripod *li* as the major vessel shape. The Weiyingzi culture may be transitional between them. The *li* is widespread in the northern Bronze Age.

Finally, Guo considers the question of whether anything in the documentary record can be said to apply to the Lower Xiajiadian. He sets forth four views, and subscribes to the fourth, that Lower Xiajiadian relates to the Shang culture which arose in the Dongbei. The argument goes as follows: The character for "Yan" is found on oracle bones, therefore the state of Yan coexisted with the Shang. Furthermore, pre-Shang levels have been found at the site of Liulihe which became the capital of the Yan state. The *taotie* animal mask is traced from Lower Xiajiadian to Shang, and Guo points out the continuation of this motif in the Yan state as late as the Warring States period. He also relates the elaborate lacquerware of Liulihe to Lower Xiajiadian, as well as the *li*, and suggests that Shang *li* are also connected. Northern-style bronzeware was also found in Shang. Some osteological evidence which might uphold this view is noted as well.

Thus, Guo believes that one branch of Lower Xiajiadian became the Yan, and another the Shang.

S. M. N.

In the early 1960s, the Chinese scholar Liu Guan-min and others excavated Xiajiadian and Yaowangmiao in the suburbs of Chifeng, Inner Mongolia. An ancient bronze culture was differentiated from the other ancient cultures in northern China and named Lower Xiajiadian.[1]

Even earlier, in the beginning of this century, the remains of Lower Xiajiadian had already been noted by scholars at home and abroad. There were some publications, such as *Pi-tzu-wo*,[2] in which a group of pottery vessels collected from Xiaokulun was discussed. Xiaokulun is located between Naiman Banner in southeastern Zhelimumung, Inner Mongolia and Fuxin county in western Liaoning province. In this group of pottery there are five pottery steamers on fat tripod legs belonging to the Lower Xiajiadian culture (Figure 22: 2–4, 11, 12, ibid.). These artifacts are now stored in the Lushun Museum.

In 1936, Yawata described surveys of Lower Xiajiadian sites.[3] In 1938, Hamada and Mizuno compiled a book entitled *Chifeng Hongshanhou*. In the chapter covering the pottery from the first dwelling place at the Hongshanhou site they published a pottery *li* (Figure 21: 14, 15), cord-marked potsherds with incised patterns, and raised design potsherds with basket patterns (Plate 28: 1 and 2; Plate 25; Figure 38: 21–24) belonging to Lower Xiajiadian culture. The authors called these artifacts and another later bronze culture Chifeng Phase II.[4]

In 1943 the Chinese scholars Li Wen-xin and Dong Zhu-chen investigated the Dongbaijia site in the eastern suburbs of Chifeng, and measured the 57 house floors which were exposed. This was the first comparatively complete report on a Lower Xiajiadian site.[5]

In the 1950s and 1960s, reports on Lower Xiajiadian culture increased. In addition to the report in 1960 on Xiajiadian and the Yaowangmiao site, the most important discovery in this period occurred in 1955 at Xiaozhuanshanzi, in Haidaoyingzi, Machanggou in the Mongolian Autonomous Region of Liaoning Kelaqinzuoyi (simplified hereafter as Kezuo county, which once belonged to Lingyuan county of Jehol province). One house at this site was disturbed by a storage pit of Early Western Zhou, which became important evidence to establish the date of this culture.[6] Another important discovery was that of the Datuotou site in Tianjin Dacheng, Hebei province in 1965. This site of the Lower Xiajiadian culture can be divided into early and late units, so that the research on this culture was able to proceed farther into the discussion of different phases, and also demonstrated the distribution of this culture south of Yanshan.[7] Progress in this period also included the excavation of the

149

Changping Xuanshan site in Beijing and the discovery of Lower Xiajiadian cultural artifacts during surveys in the Chengde region in Hebei.[8]

In the period after 1970, research on Lower Xiajiadian culture made further progress. For instance, in 1972 at Fengxia in Beipiao, Liaoning, 650m^2 were excavated and 18 houses were found;[9] and in 1976, 2,200m^2 of the Shuiquan site in Jianping county, Liaoning were excavated and 120 houses were discovered;[10] in 1975–1978, 700 burials from the Dadianzi cemetery in Chifeng Aohan Banner, Inner Mongolia were excavated.[11] In 1979 at Sanguan in Wei county, Hebei province, a large number of dwelling sites and burials belonging to the Lower Xiajiadian culture were excavated.[12] Since 1979 when archaeological surveys were done in the Chaoyang and Fuxin regions in Liaoning and Aohan Banner in Inner Mongolia, about 2,000 sites belonging to the Lower Xiajiadian culture have been found.[13] All this information has provided us with a rich understanding of this culture.

DISTRIBUTION AND CHRONOLOGY

Lower Xiajiadian culture has a wide distribution. As far as we now know, its northern boundary lies at the Sharamurun river; the eastern boundary at the western foot of the Yiwulu mountains; the southern boundary reaches to the Bohai Sea and goes south of the Yanshan, entering the North China Plain. The southernmost site that is known so far is in Rongcheng county in the Juma River basin in Baoding, Hebei province. The western line lies in the Yi River basin in the Zhangjiakou region in northwestern Hebei. It is located at the ecotone where the Mongolian plateau is transitional to the North China Plain, so that it is in the center of this region, between two river basins – the middle to upper reaches of the Laoha river and the Daling river. This region is mainly hilly land without large stretches of plains, although along these two rivers and their tributaries some open land can be found. In these cases the sites are located on low platforms and hills near the rivers. In certain places the sites are distributed very densely, some even more densely than present villages.

The chronology of Xiajiadian was not easy to interpret in the beginning. As noted before, in the 1960s when the Lower Xiajiadian culture was just established, according to the stratigraphic relations of the Machanggou site, it was considered that its final date was later than Early Western Zhou and based upon the similarities of its pottery to that of the Shang dynasty, the time span was considered to be about the same as the Shang dynasty [1500–1000 BCE]. In the early 1970s, after the excavation of Fengxia in Beipiao, Liaoning, a new hypothesis was established on the basis of the typical black pottery from the lower layer of this site as well as the similarities of most pottery material and shapes to Erlitou culture, and it was suggested that its duration was from Late Longshan to Early Shang, i.e.

2000 to 1500 BCE. Upon the excavation of the Sanguan site in Zhangjiakou, Hebei, at the cultural layer of Late Lower Xiajiadian culture, the coexistence of pottery *li* of Shang Erligang and primitive potsherds was found, which further indicated that the ending date of this cultural period is no later than Upper Erligang.[14] The C14 dates have supported this conclusion. So far several C14 dates for this culture have been obtained, among which the earliest date is from Zhizhushan in Chifeng, 3965 ± 90 (calibrated at 2466~2147 BCE) [ZK–0176], the middle layer of Fengxia is 3550 ± 80, (calibrated date 1886~1681 BCE) [ZK–0153], and it is hypothesized that the lower layer of this site is about the same time as Zhizhushan. The two latest dates among this group are from the Dadianzi graves No.454 and No.759: 3390 ± 90 (calibrated date 1685~1463 BCE) [ZK–0402] and 3420 ± 85 BP (calibrated date 1735~1517 BCE) [ZK–0480] respectively.[15] Thus, the general range of Lower Xiajiadian culture date can be summarized: the earliest is before 2000 BCE and the latest is around 1500 BCE. These dates correspond to the relationships of pottery and assemblages. Since the Lower Xiajiadian culture went through a developmental process lasting more than five hundred years, it can roughly be divided into phases, and changes can be described.

Fengxia serves as a type site to define the phases of Lower Xiajiadian culture, because the southern part of this site can be clearly differentiated into three strata, representing the three phases of the site. Through the comparison of this site with others, the three periods of the Fengxia site are seen to be representative, and in addition, other sites amplify the situation with more data. The results of these comparisons indicate a division into three periods and five phases.[16]

Period I, represented by Lower Fengxia (Fengxia Period I), includes Chifeng Sifendi, Aohan Baisilongyingzi, Houses No.1 and 2 (F1 and F2), the lower level of Chifeng Zhizhushan and the lower layer of Tangshan Dachengshan. The characteristics of this period include mainly dark grey pottery, but also much typical black pottery. At Baisilongyingzi and Sifendi, there are vessels with earlier features, such as large flat-based basins, some decorated with bamboo-joint patterns as well as others joined to three fat legs, and wide-mouthed basins wholly decorated with basket patterns. Thus Period I is the earliest period of Lower Xiajiadian culture yet known.

Period II, represented by the middle layer of Fengxia, includes Chifeng Yaowangmiao Temple site, Lower Xiajiadian, Lower Nanshangen, Dacheng Datuotou (Pit No. 2 [H2]) in Chifeng, and Sanguan Phase I in Wei county, Hebei. The characteristics include mainly grey-brown pottery, an increase in red-brown pottery, and a decrease in black clay pottery. This period mostly is noted where there are thick accumulations and rich artifacts, especially pottery, so the layers can be divided into early and late periods.

Period III, represented by the Fengxia upper layer, includes the stone cist tombs of Tangshan Xiaoguanzhuang, Sanguan Phase II in Wei County, and

Dacheng Datuotou Cache Pit No.1 (H1). Its characteristics are: red-brown pottery has become dominant, with nearly pure red sandy pottery, low-fired black pottery decreases, so-called black-slip pottery appears as well as new shapes of vessels such as the short red ring-footed bowl. Bent-shouldered *li* might be later in terms of time, and could be treated as a period later than Fengxia Period III, that is, the latest period of Lower Xiajiadian.

The phases of Lower Xiajiadian still need further study since there is neither a standard variable for differentiating phases nor sufficient ideal groups of vessels. Research which has been done primarily on phases indicates:

1) that the change of Lower Xiajiadian culture from early to late is quite obvious, with its own features different from the Yellow River basin, suggesting that this culture has its own independent developmental process;

2) that south of Yanshan, the center of the distribution, the earliest period of this culture can be clarified, with obvious features of Late Longshan culture and a date before 2000 BC, whereas north of Yanshan no artifacts typical of Longshan have been discovered yet. This suggests that before 2000 BC, Lower Xiajiadian culture north of Yanshan developed parallel to Longshan culture in the Yellow River basin.

ANALYSIS OF CULTURAL FEATURES

Pottery, stone and bone tools, bronze metallurgy, houses, clusters of walled cities, and burials will be discussed in that order.

Pottery

Pottery is the most common artifact class of the Lower Xiajiadian culture (Figure 5.1). A group of special vessels has been designated as differentiating this culture. Sandy grey-brown pottery baked at low temperature accounts for 60 percent of the vessels. This kind of pottery is quite different from the grey pottery of the contemporaneous Xia and Shang dynasties in the Yellow River basin, which is high-fired and of pure quality. The pottery is constructed of coils and then wheel-finished so that the exterior and interior of the vessel have join marks at the side or base. Among the rarer pieces of black and grey pottery, the black vessels were baked at high temperature and most were processed on the potter's wheel. The exterior is well polished and finely made with regular shapes. The patterns on the pottery were mostly created with cord and incising, next come raised designs and then basket-mark designs, square designs, etc. which are commonly seen among Yellow River sites at the same time, but are quite rare in Lower Xiajiadian culture. The pottery can be classified by function into cooking pots, storage vessels, serving dishes, and eating vessels. Cooking pots comprise the largest group, although some of these

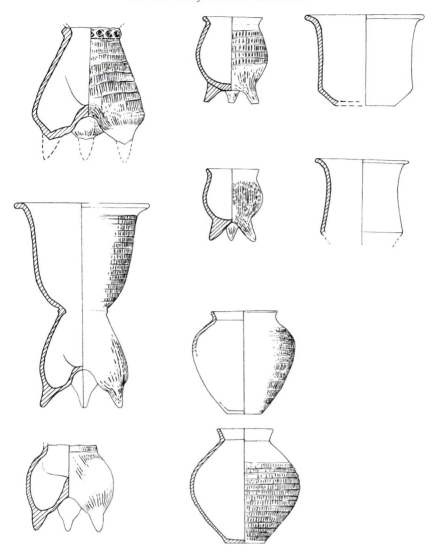

Figure 5.1 Lower Xiajiadian culture pottery

were also used as storage jars. The main shapes of the vessels are *yan* [steamers], *li* and other tripod vessels, *ding*, and jars. The *yan* is very well made of sandy grey-brown pottery, with three fat baggy legs each with a solid leg underneath, raising the vessel for better heating. The whole body is decorated with cord-marked patterns, and there are raised clay strips at the widest part. The upper part of the vessel is basin-shaped or jar-shaped, each with a pottery grate for steaming. The *yan* is usually large, the tallest is

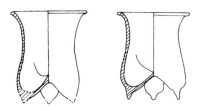

Figure 5.2 Yu-shaped *li*

about 40 cm high. Its abundance suggests that steamed food was a major part of the cuisine during the Lower Xiajiadian period. Another typical vessel is a jar-shaped tripod cooking pot, mostly made of black clay with the whole body polished, down to the lower part of the legs. The upper part is in the shape of a *yu* [tall jar], with three short legs. Because this kind of vessel is not as good for heating as *li* and *yan*, and is made of a kind of pottery not appropriate to place directly in the fire, it is polished where the leg would touch the fire. Since they are not very practical for cooking, they were mainly used for storage.

Among the funerary objects, the *yu*-shaped *li* (Figure 5.2) play a very important part. They are mostly decorated with paint on the lower part of the legs. This indicates that this kind of typical pottery from Lower Xiajiadian culture was mainly used for funerary and ceremonial purposes. *Ding* [food containers] are mostly in the shape of a deep bowl, with a big flat base and three legs in the shape of short flat adzes. They are usually not large. Cord marks and incised lines decorate the whole body, and the cord marks continue all the way down the legs. The mouth and the shoulder are very well polished and black.

Sandy clay pots were the most widely used in the Lower Xiajiadian culture. The shapes vary, but they can be roughly divided into two kinds: the big-mouthed and the medium-mouthed. The medium-mouthed pots are dominant. They have globular bodies and the join between the body and the base can be seen. The whole body is decorated with cord marks and incised patterns (Figure 5.3, left). The storage vessels are mostly huge jars. The whole height is about 1 m and the body is decorated with multiple raised lines or with cord marks and basket designs. Although these storage pots are large, the walls are quite thin and hard, baked at high temperature. The mouth and the upper body are well polished, while dozens of parallel raised strips are found on the body. The strips help to make the wall solid as well as being decorative. Since this kind of storage pot is very finely made, it suggests that at that time, storage for surplus was considered very important.

The small-mouthed jars are also decorated with cord marks. The smaller opening indicates their use for storing liquid such as water or wine. The containers include basins, jars, pedestals, and plates. The basins mostly have

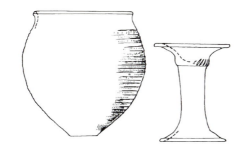

Figure 5.3 Pottery urn (left), *dou* (right)

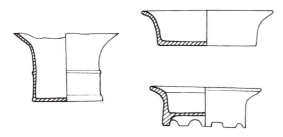

Figure 5.4 Early Lower Xiajiadian pottery

some height in the sides. The rim of the big-mouthed examples curves upward in the early pots and downward later, showing an obvious temporal change. The sides are characterized by cord marks plus incisions, and two crown-like handles. Pedestals (Figure 5.3, right) are fewer in Lower Xiajiadian culture, but have strong features. They are made of black pottery. The plate part is shallow but the stem is slim and tall, so that they might not be very practical except as ceremonial vessels. Plates have big flat bases and low sides, reminiscent of Longshan in the Yellow River basin. They are common in the remains of Early Lower Xiajiadian culture and can be considered typical of the early period (Figure 5.4). *Yu* is another typical vessel in the Lower Xiajiadian culture. The upper body is tall and straight but the lower body is short and narrow. There is a mark like a band at the join between the upper and the lower body, which is similar to banded-wall basins from Longshan.

The identifiable eating utensils include mostly small cups and bowls (Figure 5.5). The bowls are wide-mouthed, with curved slanting walls. The cups are cylindrical. The presence of *gui* [a pitcher on three legs] (Figure 5.6, right) and *jue* [a tripod wine vessel with handle and open spout] (Figure 5.6, left) constitutes an outstanding feature of Lower Xiajiadian culture, because these characteristic vessels with complex shapes are frequently found in the Yellow River basin. Along the Yangzi

155

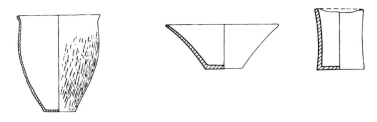

Figure 5.5 Pot (left), bowl (middle) and cup (right)

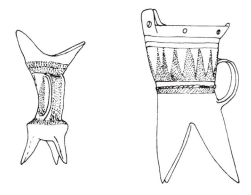

Figure 5.6 Pottery *jue* (left) and *gui* (right)

river only the *gui* is found. The *jue* is not seen there until the Shang/Zhou period, when *jue* were made of bronze. The earliest *jue* are found in the Erlitou culture, although not in great numbers. *Gui* and *jue* unearthed from graves from Lower Xiajiadian culture are in matching sets. The spout, the single handles, the distinction between the upper and the lower walls, the three tall and pointed legs as well as the flat upper wall of the *jue* are almost the same as those of Erlitou, but those from the Lower Xiajiadian culture seem to be even more elaborately made. These vessels are different from other vessels of the Xiajiadian culture in terms of the manufacturing technique and the process. The paste is very fine, as if it were washed and processed, and fired at a high temperature. The walls are thin, similar to egg shell pottery. There are spirals on the rim, the body, and the legs, indicating that the pieces were constructed on the potter's wheel before they were joined. Both *gui* and *jue* have spouts and handles. *Jue* were made in sections with an elliptical body so that it required high technique, and on the exterior very thin raised lines, comb patterns, dots, and lines of rivet decorations were employed. These two types of vessels were mostly unearthed from graves, in great numbers of matching groups. All these

Figure 5.7 Lower Xiajiadian painted pottery

traits suggest that these two types of vessels were made for high-ranking people, and used for drinking wine.

Painted pottery is a typical feature of Lower Xiajiadian culture, and also a gem of this culture (Figure 5.7). It is mainly seen in burials, but a few examples were found in houses. In 1972 when we first saw painted potsherds of this kind at Fengxia, we could hardly believe the bright colors and wonderful patterns. In 1978 when we excavated the Dadianzi cemetery in Aohan, on large numbers of painted potsherds there were animal-mask designs with eyes. This helps us to understand this culture.[17] This painted pottery is different from that of the previous period in that the later pottery is first painted and then baked so that the paint does not come off; the earlier is baked first and then painted, so that the color comes off easily. In terms of the skillful techniques as well as the mysterious patterns, they are much improved from the previous period. The paint is not merely monochrome, but uses vermilion and white as a striking contrast, painted on the exterior of the complicated shapes of vessels such as polished *li*, jars, *ding*, and *yu*, including the rim and the legs. The motifs include various kinds of cloud patterns, turtles, dragons, and animal faces.

The patterns are distributed according to the shape of the vessel. For instance, the jars are decorated on the rim, the shoulder, the sides, and the ring-foot, and the *li* is divided into three units by the legs (but there are also examples where the whole body is decorated with patterns without division). Some patterns have animal faces as the motif with cloud backgrounds, there are also cloud and thunder patterns connected together with curved, straight, and semicircular lines, forming clear-cut combinations of curved and straight lines. The overall designs are well planned and variable, making the patterns various.

The red and white colors with black background make striking contrasts, creating a mysterious impression. In addition, because the paint was applied smoothly, the pottery had to be made to a high standard. Furthermore the paint it is not simply applied to a flat surface, but to difficult surfaces like curves. The effect is clear and smooth, with varied patterns, so it must have required a special skill. Without the accumulation of long-term experience and the special demands of the society, it would not have reached such a high level, suggesting that this kind of technique could only be that of specialized artisans who passed down their knowledge from generation to generation. They could be the earliest artistic painters of China. For example, a painted pottery *lei* [wine jar] which was unearthed from a Dadianzi grave has a motif of two animal masks symmetrically placed on the shoulders, and on the sides there are animal masks and cicada patterns, with cloud patterns as the background. The whole body of the vessel was covered with paint. This is the largest pattern as well as the most complicated among the painted pottery of Lower Xiajiadian culture so far known. Another example of a painted *yu*-shaped *li* is decorated on three sides with animal mask patterns. The design was painted so that when the *li* stands on its base, it looks upside-down.

It is worth particular mention that the various motifs on the painted pottery of the Lower Xiajiadian culture are reminiscent of the patterns on

Figure 5.8 Painted pottery urn (right) and *li* (left)

the bronze vessels of the Shang dynasty (Figure 5.8). Looking closely and carefully at the fine structures and even the location of the patterns, shows that most of them are exactly the same as those of the bronze vessels of the Shang dynasty. The best example might be the similar structure between the animal mask on the painted pottery and the *taotie* [monster mask] designs on bronze vessels. In addition, fire designs, slanting thunder designs, dragon designs, etc., are found on the shoulders of the pottery *lei*; these are also dominant designs on bronzeware. Because the Lower Xiajiadian culture was followed by Shang dynasty bronzeware, the former are not the standardization of the latter, but the latter was quite mature when it appeared in the middle of the Shang dynasty. Thus, we infer that this kind of advanced painted pottery of the early northern bronze culture is not influenced by the Shang dynasty's bronze vessels, but to the contrary, it may be one of the very important origins of the Shang dynasty's bronze designs.

Stone and bone tools

A large number of stone tools were unearthed in the Lower Xiajiadian, which are mainly three types: hoes, axes, and knives (Figure 5.9), as well as various microlithic tools. The hoe is usually small in size, polished, flat and thin, and a shoulder is chipped on the upper end. The blade slants toward one side. There are also unshouldered rectangular hoes. Because this type of hoe is small and thin, it could only have been used for working porous soil, so that it might be a tool for loosening the soil and weeding. It is the most common stone tool in this culture. For instance, at Fengxia, 50 hoes were unearthed.

The axe is large, thick, and heavy. In the upper middle there is a waist for easier hafting, and the blade is thick rather than sharp. It is practical for cutting wood and digging earth. The triangular knife is edged on one side

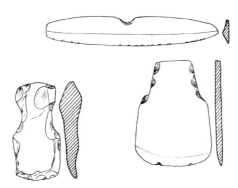

Figure 5.9 Stone tools: knife (upper), axe (left), and shovel (right)

and flat on the other. The middle part of the top has a notch for holding in the hand. The blade is not sharp, so that it might be a kind of reaping tool. Rectangular single-hole and double-hole stone knives are found as well as semi-lunar double-holed knives. The flaked tools are mostly scrapers, but there are also arrowheads and awls, which are made of cryptocrystalline stone such as flint and chert, with the whole body finely processed. In addition, finely ground, small stone adzes, triangular arrowheads, grinding stones, and stone axes are found.

Bone tools are common; for example, bone shovels made of pig scapulae, as well as knives, saws, and needles made of bone. Many bone arrowheads are found, some of them triangular, others cylindrical with a triangular or rounded point. At both dwelling sites and burials a large number of pig bones were found. A custom of burying whole pigs and dogs was followed. Over half of the 800 burials at Dadianzi have pig bones, identified as large domesticated pigs. There are also bones of cattle, sheep and deer. The carbonized grains from Fengxia which have been identified by the Genetic Institute of the Chinese Academy of Sciences, include two kinds of millet, broomcorn millet and foxtail millet. The tools of all kinds, the animal bones and the grains mentioned above suggest that Lower Xiajiadian culture had a relatively advanced hoe-farming agriculture, which stressed careful attention to farming and raising livestock. The people lived a stable and sedentary life.

Bronze metallurgy

The bronze-casting industry of Lower Xiajiadian had developed to a certain level. The archaeological findings include the following.

At the dwelling sites and burials bronze earrings, rings, and awls are found. There are many earrings with bronze wire fashioned into an oval ring, with one end cast into an expanded flat piece like a spread fan, so that this is called a "trumpet-shaped bronze earring."

A bronze arrowhead and a dagger-axe were also found. The bronze arrowhead was unearthed at Dacheng Dufengtou in Hebei province, and the bronze dagger-axe at Xiangshuiyingzi in Jin county, Liaoning province. The bronze dagger-axe has the handle and body cast together. It is long and straight, and the tip of the short handle thrusts outward like a hook. Its shape is very much like one from Erlitou, which is considered to be the earliest shape. The handle is flat and rounded, decorated with connected beads along with slanting triangles. A bronze attachment for a stone battle-axe was also found, which was fixed by the upper and lower ends to a wooden handle.[18]

A pottery mold for casting bronze was found at Sifendi in Chifeng, Inner Mongolia (Figure 5.10). It is of grey pottery with smoothed cord marks with the same characteristics as the pottery designs from Lower Xiajiadian

160

Figure 5.10 Clay mold excavated at Sifendi, Chifeng

culture. It is one part of a composite mold. The cross-section is almost oval, and the dimensions are 2.4, 3.4 and 0.7 cm. A mark for joining the composite mold is made at both sides. A funnel-shaped casting hole runs all the way through the body. The cast artifact may be a decorative object. At the lower left of the mold surface there is a round hole for reinforcement when the molding was put together. It seems to be the major section of a two-piece mold. This is the only pottery mold found so far in Lower Xiajiadian culture, and it is also one of the earliest pottery molds known so far in China.[19]

Related to bronze-casting, among the pottery of Lower Xiajiadian culture, imitation bronze rivets were used as decorations. The shapes most commonly so decorated are *gui* and *jue*. At the joins of these two vessels there are lines of imitation rivets for the purpose of reinforcement. This led us to hypothesize that the making of these special shapes might not be the direct product of pottery-making technique, but that instead when these shapes were made, the bronze pieces were hammered and then joined together, so that lines of rivet decoration reflect the historically changing process of the pottery imitation of bronze.[20]

From the examples which have been cited above, it seems that the fact that large bronze vessels have not been found as yet among Lower Xiajiadian sites suggests that bronze might have been mostly used for ornaments, ritual items, and attachments, so that it is still the preliminary stage of the Bronze Age. However, the use of the composite mold and the inner mold also indicates that the main procedures and technology of bronze-casting were known and the basic conditions for making bronze vessels were present. On the basis of this fact, we call Lower Xiajiadian culture the Early Northern Bronze Age.

Settlements and houses

Over a thousand settlements of Lower Xiajiadian culture have been surveyed and some have been excavated. Most of these settlements consist

161

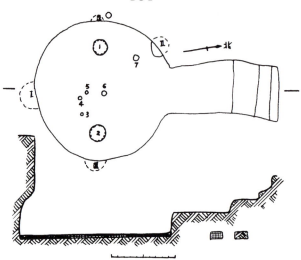

Figure 5.11 Pit house at Sifendi, Chifeng

of clusters of houses which fortunately are well preserved. This helps us to understand the features and other characteristics.

In the settlements the houses are quite dense; for instance, at Fengxia within the excavated area there are a great many houses. In general, dwellings can be classified into the following types. The pit house is seen only at Sifendi in Chifeng. It is mostly round, small in size, with the diameter generally between 3 and 4 m. The entrance is long and slanting and there is also a niche. A drainage ditch was dug near the house. The dwelling floor was coated with mud mixed with straw, and in the floor there are two symmetrical post holes. For example, House No. 2 is round, with a diameter of 2.2 to 2.3 m, and it is 1.8 m deep with the door opening in the north (Figure 5.11). There is a stepped doorway of 1.6 m long and 0.7–0.9 m wide, with four steps. In the four walls of the pit house there are niches, with the biggest and widest niche facing the doorway. In the east and west side of the floor there are large post holes. The one on the east side is 0.27 m in diameter and 0.31 m deep; the one on the west side 0.3 m in diameter and 0.29 m deep. On the sides and the bottom of the post holes a layer of potsherds was placed. Because Sifendi is an early site of this culture, it is hypothesized that this kind of pit house is the earliest.[21]

Semi-subterranean houses are the commonest type, found in most sites. The plan view is mainly round, but the largest houses are square with rounded corners. The walls are mostly built with sun-dried mud-bricks. People already knew how to line up bricks in the advanced arrangement of alternating bricks in rows. The mud-bricks are almost regular, about 20 cm long, 18 cm wide, and 10 cm thick. The dwelling floors are paved in two ways, either with mud mixed with burned straw or with lime. There are also floors paved with mud and straw and then with lime. Some of the dwelling floors have several layers. One has six layers, the top of which is baked. The lime floor is white and smooth, about 0.3 cm thick, which is paved all the way to the lower part of the interior walls and the doorways. On the dwelling floor near the wall an earth platform was usually built with mud-bricks. The post holes are generally found in the east and the west, filled with rocks topped by earth and potsherds, rammed to make a firm post foundation. Some post foundations protrude above the dwelling floor. In the center of the house there is a round burned area, which is commonly described as the hearth, and beside the burned place a pottery jar is usually found, which might have been used for storing kindling. The entrance, located in the southern wall, is narrow inside but wide outside, with a threshold. The mud-brick wall is very thick, and outside the mud wall a stone wall was constructed. Some stone walls have one layer and others two layers, and sometimes there is a distance between the stone and the mud walls, forming a space called "the courtyard type." Beyond the stone walls there are stone pavements or other attached constructions. Some of the large houses have a small room at the side. Layers of floors in which a new floor was laid without disturbing a former one are occasionally seen at the same location. There is one with five floors together which is over 2 m thick. The sites of this culture were formed on flat land, building up a mound, reflecting a sedentary life at that time, continuous and stable to a certain degree.

There are differences between houses in size and in quality of features, which are obvious within the same site. At Fengxia, for instance, the largest house (No.12) is a square double-room house located in the southeastern part of the site (Figure 5.12). The main room was large and square. At the middle of the southern wall a small square room was attached. A semi-circular pavement is connected to the eastern stone wall. The dimensions of the whole house are 9 m from east to west and 8.5 m from south to north. The door is 185 degrees. The plan of the large room is square (4 × 4 m), with rounded corners and convex walls, made of hard red daub, 100 cm high and 60 cm thick. In regard to the exterior stone walls, a door was placed in the middle of the southern wall. The inner width is 125 cm and the exterior 80 cm, which is connected directly to the small room. The dwelling floor was first paved with dark-brown mud mixed with straw 2 cm thick and then coated with lime 0.6 cm thick. The lime on the inner wall is 30 cm high and at either side of the doorway it is about 55 cm high. A round burned place with a diameter of 50 cm was in the center of the room. From this house some delicate objects such as a painted black pottery *yu*, a polished stone knife, a stone adze and so on were unearthed. The small rectangular room is 2.2 m long from east to west, and 1.6 m wide from south to north, and the mud-brick wall is 80 cm high

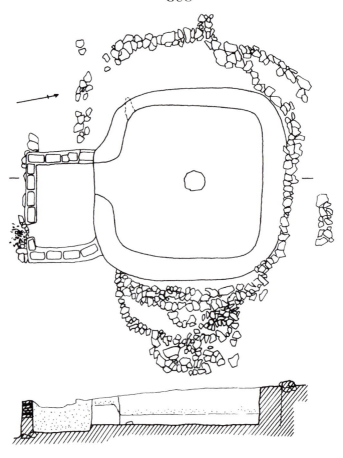

Figure 5.12 House F12 at Fengxia

and 30 cm thick. The door is on the east of the southern wall, not directly across from the main-room door. The doorway is 35 cm wide with a yellow mud threshold 15 cm high. The dwelling floor of the small room is 20 cm lower than the large room, whose floor is made of the mud mixed with straw and then burned.

House 2 (Figure 5.13) is a small round house located 8 m south of House 12. The diameter of the interior room is 1.86–2.15 cm, the earth wall is 67 cm high and 20–50 cm thick. Underneath the earth wall there is a mud-brick structure. The building method is two lines overlapping each other. The exterior line is built with the bricks on end. The bricks are slightly wedge-shaped. The earth wall is coated on the inside with two layers of black sticky mud, and the exterior is surrounded with stone walls. There are

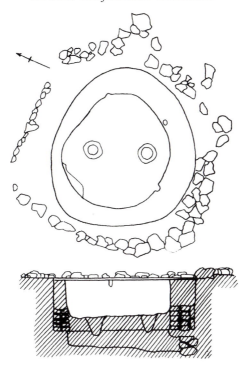

Figure 5.13 House F2 at Fengxia

three layers of dwelling floors inside the room, 90, 165 and 190 cm deeper than the surface floor respectively. The second dwelling floor is well preserved, made of yellow mud mixed with straw, 2 cm thick. There are two post-hole foundations inside the room with a surface diameter of 38 cm and a depth of 31 cm. The foundation pit is filled with yellow soil and broken potsherds, rammed into 15 layers. Near the west wall of the room an earth platform 30 cm long has a surface which has turned dark red through several episodes of baking or burning. Underneath this house floor lies another house of similar size (House 6).

Near the house there are often earth-pits where sometimes complete vessels were unearthed. Frequently the pit wall was coated smooth.

Surface houses were at the current ground level and underwent three to four thousand years' weathering without later human disturbance, remaining almost unchanged. For example, Dongbaijia in Chifeng is located on a small mound which is high in the northwest but low in the southeast. There are 57 houses which could be identified on the ground surface. They are

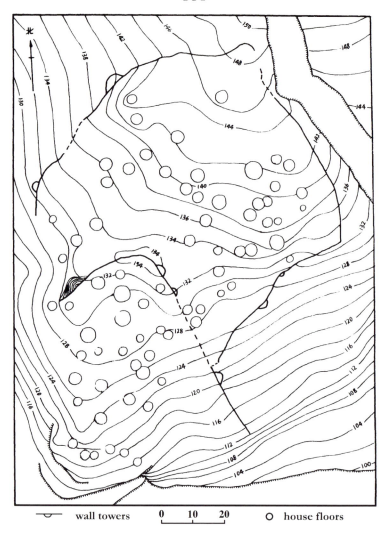

Figure 5.14 Plan of Lower Xiajiadian stone wall and houses at Xishangen, Chifeng

round, surrounded with stones. House 57, which is located in the center of this site, has a diameter of 40 m. The others include one house with a diameter of 10 m, eight with 5 m, seven with 4 m, and five with 3 m.[22] Similar houses have also been found on the bank of the Jinying river in Aohan Banner, in Chifeng, in Kezuo and in Jianping. Judging from the red-brown potsherds collected at these sites, they belong to the third period, whose date is late.

Village walls and ditches

Another characteristic of the settlement sites of Lower Xiajiadian culture is that walls, generally earth and stone structures, surround the sites. Some of the large sites have pounded earth walls with ditches excavated outside the walls. An example is the rammed-earth walls of Dadianzi. About 2 m of the wall is preserved above the ground, 2 m wide at the top, and the section below the ground is about 7 m wide at the bottom. The exterior ditch is 8 m wide. Another example is Xishangen in Chifeng, which is also surrounded by stone walls (Figure 5.14). In these walled settlements, civic architecture has not been discovered, so that it is not appropriate to call them city walls.[23]

Site types and clusters of city walls

Because the sites of Lower Xiajiadian culture are distributed densely and are well preserved, locational types can be identified. According to the location and the geographic features of these sites in western Liaoning region, they can be classified into five types: the Low-Platform Type, the High-Platform Type, the High-Mound Type, the Hill-Slope Type, and the High-Hill Type.[24]

The Low-Platform Type is usually located near a river. The sites are large in scale with rich accumulations. Typical sites include Shuiquan in Jianping and Dadianzi in Aohan. The earliest artifacts of this culture are mostly found at the lowest level of these sites.

The High-Platform Type is built on the ridge of the second terrace, and its location is a little higher than the Low-Platform, although sometimes it is very difficult to distinguish them. The scale is smaller, with thin accumulations. These sites are usually located along a small river or near a river confluence. The walls surrounding the village are usually constructed of stones. Beipiao Fengxia is a typical site.

The High-Mound Type is on a hill above the second terrace or on a hill ridge, far away from the river. They are generally in a place where the previous hilltop was leveled, on top of which the stone walls were built, which makes this kind of site a special shape, representing a typical feature of this culture. These sites are often called by the local people "flat-top hill," or "city-hill," and they are found in great numbers. They have thin accumulations, and due to their high locations, they are usually not disturbed by the people of later times, so that dwelling sites are often well preserved.

The Hill-Slope Type has locations similar to the High-Mound Type. The location was selected to make use of the side facing the sun as well as taking advantage of the back of the windy side. There are often deep ditches on both sides of the site. Thus, although there is a slope from the north to the south, yet it helps to keep in heat and protect from the wind. As these sites have a natural defensive position, their village walls are built only at weak places.

The High-Hill Type is usually located on top of a high hill far away from any river. They have very thin deposits, only a scatter of potsherds over the ground or some wall foundations. For example, on top of Daiwang mountain in the vicinity of Dadianzi there are stone wall foundations and red-brown potsherds belonging to the Lower Xiajiadian culture. It is not a dwelling place, but might be some sort of sentry post.

Clusters of city walls

In distribution the sites mentioned above are not isolated, rather they relate to each other within a small range, so that they are an organic whole, forming "clusters of sites" or "clusters of walled cities" (Figure 5.15). Based upon the information we have, the following compounds could be classified. 1) Sites facing each other: two similar sites are located face to face across the river. Some typical sites are Shangshijianggou in Aohan and Jiufetang in Kezuo. They are both sites on high platforms or hill-slopes. 2) A pair of sites with one lower and the other higher, the one on a low platform and the other nearby on a high mound or hill slope: a typical site is found in Laoyemiaoxiang in Kezuo. 3) Sites located in groups at the creek mouths near the rivers: this is very common among the distribution center of Lower Xiajiadian culture in the Laoha and Daling river basins. Because the extended line corresponds with that of the Yan/Qin Great Wall in the Warring States period, and its structure is mainly stone construction, it is called "the primitive Great Wall." 4) Sites located at a center and its surroundings: these are formed in different sizes based upon the ranges or the special geographic environment. For instance, at Luobogou in Jianping county, a site is located on each of five connected high hills, which is conventionally called "Wu Lian Cheng" (Five-Connected City-Walls). Dadianzi is located on flat land surrounded by mountains, with Dadianzi at the center, and several small sites around it. In addition there is

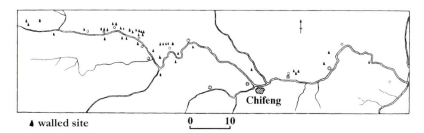

Figure 5.15 Distribution of Lower Xiajiadian walled sites

168

a sentry post in the nearby mountains. In sum, the distribution of Lower Xiajiadian culture has many unique features which are different from contemporary sites in the Central Plain.

Burials

Although over a thousand sites belonging to Lower Xiajiadian culture have been found, very few burials were discovered. In recent years in the distribution of this culture, at the juncture of southeastern Inner Mongolia and Fuxin in Liaoxi, some cemeteries have been found and excavated. In this region the loess is thick and dense, and the water level is low, making it easy to dig deep graves, which was the custom of Lower Xiajiadian culture. The Dadianzi cemetery is an important example.[25]

Dadianzi is located on the upper reaches of the Mangniu river, a tributary of the Daling river, being part of Aohan Banner of Inner Mongolia. The settlement is near the cemetery, which is very well preserved. The burial ground is northeast of the site, beyond a ditch which surrounds the city wall. The cemetery is almost the same size as the site, 200 m from south to north, and about 90 m east to west. The whole cemetery is nearly 2,000m^2, within which about 800 burials have been found. The distance between the burials is only 1 m. Although the burials are very crowded, none intruded into another. It is thus hypothesized that there must have been a strict order to the burial plots, each in succession, and some grave markers might have been above the ground. The burial ground is very flat. Its altitude is about the same as that of the modern village, but it is 3 m or so lower than the terrace on which the site is located.

The burial system

The graves are vertical earth-pits. Most of the bodies are extended burials lying on the side, but there are a few exceptions which are supine and still fewer prone. Most of the burials are single interments, but a few of them have an adult female buried with a male child. The female is somewhat taller than the male. Although some of the children's graves are as large as the adults', most of them are narrow and small. The mean age of people who were buried here is about 20–30 years old, with less than 10 percent estimated at 50–60. The burial direction is northwest to southeast, with the head pointing northwest. Males face the site, while the females face away from the site.

It was customary to bury deep. The bottom of burials for adults is 2–3 m below the current ground surface (the burial opening is exposed 20–40 cm beneath the ground surface). The largest burial is more than 5 m deep, and the deepest one is 8.9 m. There are remains of a wooden outer coffin, which is a wooden frame in the shape of tic-tac-toe [the character for

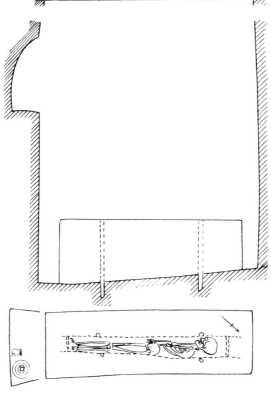

Figure 5.16 Tomb M5 at Dadianzi

"well" in Chinese] with mortise and tenons, and planks laid on the top and the side. The wooden frame is about 1 m high or so, with the highest 2 m. Small burials, without wooden coffins, are made of single platform grave pits, with the raw earth as the second platform, or mud-bricks were used to line the burial pit. Some individual burials have a pit dug at one side in which the body was placed. In other graveyards, the coffins were constructed of stone slabs. At the foot end, there are niches with flat bottoms, arched tops, and a semicircular plan. The niches vary in size according to the scale of the grave. The main burial objects, such as plain pottery vessels, painted pottery, lacquerware, pig bones, etc., were placed inside the niche. The grave goods were buried in sets, generally with one *li* placed upside-down on top of a pot or a *lei* (wine jar). Most burials have only one set, but the large burials have two to three sets, and pig and dog bones, often with whole animal skeletons, in the fill. The burial objects on the bodies are often ornaments, such as jadeware (bracelets, hoops, etc.) and bronze finger rings. Ceremonial stone battle-axes accompanied some large male burials.

Within the whole graveyard there are no obvious boundaries, but several divisions can be differentiated by burial objects, especially the style of the painted designs and the types and the composition of the pottery. The main divisions are the two at the center. There are no time differences between these central groups, but the dates for the outside groups are later.

Examples of burials

No. 5 is a large burial in the south area (Figure 5.16). The grave opening is 0.2 m below the present ground surface, and the grave itself is 2.3 m long, 0.78 m wide, and 4.4 m deep. Two pig bones and a whole dog skeleton were found in the fill. The wooden coffin had decayed. The body is that of an adult man, which appeared to have been wrapped tightly in cloth when buried. The niche at the foot is 0.85 m wide, and the bottom of the niche is 1.9 m higher than the bottom of the grave. Within the niche three pieces of pottery were found: one double painted pot, one *ding* with four legs, and one *li*. There were also two pig foot bones. Grave No. 726, another large example, is 4 m long, 1.4 m wide, and 8.9 m deep. It contains a large double-cross-shaped wooden coffin. A pig and a dog were in the fill. In addition to the foot niche, there was a niche on each side, within which a group of pottery vessels and lacquerware were placed.

Dadianzi is one of the most interesting Lower Xiajiadian sites so far discovered. Other cemeteries, such as Fanzhangzi, Shangshijiangguo and Shangxinqu in Fuxin, and Sanguan in Zhangjiakou, Hebei province, are smaller, but the features are similar.

PRELIMINARY ANALYSIS OF SOCIAL STRUCTURE

Lower Xiajiadian culture coincided with the height of the Xia dynasty in the Central Plains, when Xia and its neighbor state Shang to its northeast coexisted, had contact, and then Shang replaced Xia. This was the period when the tribes along the Yellow river and the adjacent regions established and developed neighboring city states. The historical record, *Qiu Zhuan Yun Gong Qi Nian*, refers to this as the time period of Xia having tens of thousands of states. Lower Xiajiadian was a strong tribal group which played an active role in northern China, but what kind of social structure did Lower Xiajiadian culture represent? I will consider social and economic developmental levels, the social division of labor and social relations.

Lower Xiajiadian culture had intensive agriculture. The application of hoes, axes, and knives with specific functions according to their shapes indicates that the process for agricultural production was already standardized. Small and thin stone hoes were used intensively for the purpose of loosening the soil, indicating that agriculture had already reached a certain degree of high-quality farming. Many pig bones were found in the sites and pig bones, including whole pig skeletons, were included commonly among the grave goods, which were based upon well-developed animal husbandry, and the keeping of animals was closely linked with long-term sedentary agricultural life.

Bronze-casting and pottery-making, especially the painted pottery, constitute two important departments of handicrafts in the cultural and economic activities of Lower Xiajiadian culture, and they are also a major landmark for the developed levels of the society and economy of this culture. In terms of the technology of bronze-casting, there are very few finds so far, but from the discoveries of the inner mold, the composite mold, the rivet, and the casting joins, it seems that almost all the basic procedures of bronze metallurgy were known, so that it is not the most primitive period of metallurgy. The painted pottery, from shaping to painting, has a clear division of several steps. In addition, groups of painted vessels which were made at the same time but bear different styles suggest that they must be from different workshops. Their widespread occurrence suggests that specialization and technical division of labor within the pottery-making industry had reached a certain level, and in addition, it suggests that the handicraft workshop was not just single-product producing and not independent. Moreover, the making of lacquer-ware and jadeware required specialized technologies, indicating that several kinds of handicraft industries came to exist at that time. Specialized production units must have been independent from agriculture.

The specialized division of labor in the social economy would lead to differences of economic and social status among the producers, and cause the differentiation by status of the members of society. In Lower Xiajiadian culture, this kind of difference among the members of society is obviously represented in social strata. In the Dadianzi burials, the stratification was already very marked, as shown, for instance, in the depth of the burial, the use of the wooden coffin, the size of the niche, the quality of the ceremonial objects, and the painted pottery as well as the application of decorative designs, which are divided into different grades. These traits are associated. For example, graves which are only 1 m deep are considered small burials, where such items as whole pigs and dogs, painted pottery and delicate ornaments were rare, and wooden outer coffins never occur; whereas those which are over 3 m deep, designated as large burials, usually have whole pigs and dogs, a large niche, and ceremonial objects including painted pottery, *gui* and *jue*, bronzes, jades, lacquer, sea-shells, stone battle-axes, etc. Most of these objects are found in the large burials, but each burial can be graded according to the individual case. For example, in the number of pigs and dogs, the largest burial has two pigs and four dogs, the next, two pigs and two dogs, then one pig and two dogs, and last one pig and one dog, which is the most common. In some small or medium-sized burials only a pair of pig foot bones were found in the niche. In terms of the painted vessels, those unearthed from the biggest burials are much larger, and they still have bright colors with animal faces painted on them. In terms of the pottery composition, there might be two or three sets in the biggest burials, but most often there is only one set; the scale of the niche varied consequently. The large niche has the burial wall extended outward, and the biggest ones have both walls extended; some even have three niches, whereas small burials have a small narrow niche. In terms of the wooden outer coffin, the largest one is 2 m high, while small burials have no wooden outer coffin but mud-bricks instead. *Gui* and *jue*, vessels for the highest rank, are limited to the large graves. The battle-axe is found only in large male burials, representing a special warrior class. In addition, women's burials with painted vessels and unfinished jadeware including rich ornaments suggest that the important handicraft techniques are in the hands of individuals of the class who have high social status.

The same kind of strict class differentiation is reflected in the dwellings. The houses at Fengxia and Dongbaijia show great differences in size. Those which have lime on the floor are the large houses, but small houses, and houses attached to large houses, have only burned floors. These variations underline the differences found in the graves.

Another important aspect which reflects the cultural and social stratification of Lower Xiajiadian culture is that the settlements often have defensive structures. For example, houses with thick mud walls also have well-built strong stone walls and around the settlements stone walls and ditches were constructed. The largest sites have sentry posts in the mountains nearby. In certain areas, the stone walls along the rivers made a section of a line, the so-called "prototype of the Great Wall." It is quite common in Lower Xiajiadian culture that defense is important, and walled settlements are often found. This is a special phenomenon of this historical period, reflecting the instability and unrest of the society at that time. It can be contrasted with the relations of the interior, for the successive but non-overlapping graves and the multiple layers of dwellings show the stability of the interior as a result of the defended exterior.

All these data indicate that the social formation of Lower Xiajiadian culture was on the same level as that of the Xia dynasty in the same time period, that is, it had entered into the historical stage of the formation of the state. Lower Xiajiadian culture was a strong branch of ancient civilization in northern China at that time. In order to understand the historical background of such an ancient state, it is necessary to explore the origins of Lower Xiajiadian culture and its relations with its adjacent cultures.

ORIGINS AND DEVELOPMENTAL DIRECTIONS

Lower Xiajiadian culture has such a magnitude of sites and rich accumulations that no previous culture, including Hongshan, is a match for it. The features of the vessels do not derive from the earlier cultures. It seems to have suddenly arisen in western Liaoning. Although it has some common features with the Longshan and Erlitou cultures in the Central Plain, it has its own characteristics. What is its origin? If the Hongshan culture in the same region is its antecedent, then what was the line of development? Through several years of research, some conclusions have been reached. Lower Xiajiadian culture is seen as mainly a local cultural development, based on post-Hongshan culture.

The date of the Post-Hongshan culture is between 3000 and 2500 BCE [See Chapter 1]. Very few remains of this period have been found in western Liaoning so far; only about ten dwelling sites and cemeteries have been discovered. It cannot be compared with Hongshan culture, or with Lower Xiajiadian culture. Only in the 1970s, through excavation of sites and burials at Xiaoheyan, Aohan Banner and Danangou, Wengniute Banner, was some understanding obtained. According to this research, early and late development of this culture has the following tendencies: a decrease in red pottery and painted pottery; the designs on the painted pottery tend to become simplified; an increase in grey-black pottery and polished black pottery; the appearance of vermilion paint and simple painted pottery; the scale pattern which was characteristic of Hongshan culture is replaced by the thunder pattern; in terms of the change in pottery shape, there is a trend from bowls and basins to *yu*-shaped vessels, and the latter is the typical vessel of Lower Xiajiadian culture. These changes in the cultural factors mentioned above link Hongshan with Lower Xiajiadian, thus suggesting that this is a transitional type between the two major cultures, and also showing that Lower Xiajiadian is the indirect successor to the Hongshan culture.[26]

However, it must be considered that the formation of Lower Xiajiadian culture, whose contents are rich and varied as well as prosperous, might have more than one root. In the period of Hongshan culture, among those ancient cultures which coexisted with it, some show a connection with Lower Xiajiadian culture, with the Zhaobaogou type as the most prominent. An early type of polished black pottery, as well as the incised cloud-thunder designs on the polished black pottery, are stylistically almost exactly the same as the painted pottery from Lower Xiajiadian. Thus, it is inferred that Lower Xiajiadian culture, in the process of formation, was greatly influenced by Zhaobaogou, an important branch culture.

Nevertheless, the problem of the development of Lower Xiajiadian from the local Hongshan culture has not been solved, because there are several new factors which contribute to Lower Xiajiadian culture. In addition, very few sites in the period between these two cultures have been found. Several features, such as the tripod vessel, have no obvious origins. This might be considered from another aspect, that is, between Hongshan and Lower Xiajiadian there might exist a period of low cultural development, a transitional period in which, although it was not as prosperous as the preceding and following periods, new factors appeared continuously. This is a feature of historical transitions. Thus, it can be demonstrated through current archaeological data and research that Lower Xiajiadian culture mainly developed on the basis of local cultures, with Hongshan as the major source.

After Lower Xiajiadian culture in western Liaoning, Upper Xiajiadian appeared, with groups of undecorated or plain red pottery. It seems not to be linked to Lower Xiajiadian, so that some scholars consider these are two unrelated economic types and cultural traditions, with the later abruptly replacing the earlier. Thus, it has become a difficult problem to know what happened to Lower Xiajiadian culture. However, if the relationship between Lower and Upper Xiajiadian is carefully analyzed, there are related aspects.

First, the features of the two cultures underwent a great change, but there are still linked aspects; for example, they both have the tripod *li* as the major vessel shape. The *yu*-shaped *li*, which is the most typical vessel of Lower Xiajiadian, finds its commonality with the cylindrical *li* of Upper Xiajiadian, for they both are polished and have straight and deep upper walls. Also notable is the fact that in the late period of Lower Xiajiadian there is a great increase in red-brown pottery but a decrease in cord-marking, trending toward the ceramics of Upper Xiajiadian culture.

Second, the most striking differences in these two cultures occurred not in the northern part of Liaoxi, that is, the central district of Lower Xiajiadian culture, but in the southern part of its distribution. There the successor to Lower Xiajiadian culture is the Weiyingzi type, whose major feature is red-brown pottery with cord marks, showing that Lower Xiajiadian culture is continuous in its late period.

Third, the character of cultural development in this region should be taken into consideration, that is, the replacement of one culture by another like one wave higher than the next, instead of directly showing an inheritance relationship. The difference between Lower and Upper Xiajiadian cultures is the main trend, but the phenomenon of inheritance also exists, which is a typical indication of this regional character.

When tracing Lower Xiajiadian culture, in addition to the cultural change in the center, differences in the south and the north within the distribution of this culture have also been analyzed in recent years, that is, north of the Yanshan from the early period of this culture to the late period it changed not only from the rise to its peak but also from peak to decline, and besides, the clues of related cultural types show that it succeeded Hongshan culture and passed some traits down to the Shang/Zhou period. This culture began south of the Yanshan and came later to the north. It had a close relationship with Longshan, and later with the Erligang culture of Shang. The contents are not as unique and typical as north of the Yanshan, and thus the center of Lower Xiajiadian culture is north of the Yanshan rather than south of the mountains.

RELATIONSHIP WITH ADJACENT CULTURES

When exploring the origins and directions of Lower Xiajiadian culture in the discussions above, the relationship of this culture to the adjacent cultures was already touched upon, that is, this culture not only developed upon the foundation of local cultures, but also developed its own characteristics along with constant exchange with neighboring cultures. Most of these influences came from the east and west.

Although the tripod vessel constitutes the major part of Lower Xiajiadian pottery, it was not found either in the local Hongshan culture or in Post-Hongshan culture, so that it seems to come into being suddenly in great numbers in Lower Xiajiadian. According to other studies, tripods existed earlier along the southeastern coasts, in the Qingliangang and Dawenkou cultures where a *ding*-type tripod is found. Even much earlier in Beixin and Cishan-Peiligang cultures in the Central Plain, the *dou*, an antecedent of all solid-leg tripods, existed. However, among tripod vessels, *gui* was the earliest, found in the Middle Dawenkou culture at about the same time. In the delta region, the boundary of Liaoxi, another type of the early tripod vessel named *jia* (round with unconnected hollow legs) appeared. According to recent studies, this kind of *jia*-shaped vessel is based on the combination of the small-mouthed and pointed-based jar and a local egg-shaped urn, when three short baggy legs were placed on the bottom of the original jar-urn shaped vessel. This is different from the later type of *li* which uses baggy legs to replace the vessel walls.[27] Therefore, another feature of *yu*-shaped *li* of Lower Xiajiadian culture is the addition of three short baggy legs onto the base, showing a commonality with the earliest *jia*. Thus, it is likely that the baggy tripod vessels of Lower Xiajiadian culture were mainly influenced by the neighboring western regions. Meanwhile, because there are many similarities between Lower Xiajiadian, Longshan and Yueshi cultures in the Shandong peninsula, the issue should be considered whether Lower Xiajiadian, in which the tripods, including *ding*, are present, is related to the ancient culture in Shandong where there are developed tripods.

The relationship of Lower Xiajiadian to its eastern neighbors began to be discussed in recent years with the discovery of the Gaotaishan type.[28] The distribution of these sites is to the east ridge of the Yiwulu mountains and along both banks of the Liao river, which abuts and overlaps the distribution of Lower Xiajiadian culture. C14 dates for the Gaotaishan are 1500–1300 BCE, corresponding roughly with the late period of Lower Xiajiadian. The Gaotaishan sites have plain red pottery jars and ring-footed bowls as the major feature and the baggy-legged *li* and *ling* are well developed. In addition, the shapes are like Lower Xiajiadian, suggesting that they resulted from the influence of that culture. In the sites of Lower Xiajiadian culture, especially near the eastern boundary of the distribution, features of the Gaotaishan site were also found, such as Dadianzi cemetery in Aohan where a group of polished red pottery jars was unearthed, whose shape and paste are unusual components of Lower Xiajiadian pottery, instead they bear obvious features of Gaotaishan sites. The most typical is Dadianzi Burial No. 459. In this large grave, along with the painted *yu*-shaped *li* and *lei* which are typical of Lower Xiajiadian pottery, a set of polished red vessels was unearthed, consisting of one jar and one bowl. The bowl has a short ring-foot, four decorated handles, and a short rim slanting inward. The bowl was placed upside-down on top of the jar, which has a gourd-shaped mouth and a ring-foot. Such composition of a bowl and a necked jar is quite typical of Gaotaishan-type burials.[29] Thus, Lower Xiajiadian culture, especially its late period, shows increasing influence from the east. This is what we note when considering the relationship of the change in Late Lower Xiajiadian to Upper Xiajiadian, that is, the cause for such a great change between Lower Xiajiadian and Upper Xiajiadian. The increasing impact of the Gaotaishan type from east of the Yiwulu mountains and the lower Liao river is a very important factor.[30]

CONCLUSIONS

Lower Xiajiadian culture, which represents a strong group inhabiting the area south and north of the present Great Wall, must have played a very important role in the process of the formation, development, and replacement of Xia/Shang culture, but it is not recorded in historical documents. Along with the constantly deepening understanding of this culture, an unavoidable question is what historical events occurred, and what tribe or nationality did the sites belong to? So far, although there is no specialized paper on this issue in scholarly circles, some have touched upon this topic and quite a few interesting viewpoints have been raised.

One view, represented by Zou Heng, is that Lower Xiajiadian north of Yanshan is related to the Sushen, whereas that south of Yanshan is not.[31]

Another view, represented by Zhang Zhong-pei, is that Lower Xiajiadian south of Yanshan, in terms of its distribution areas, in date as well as the relationship with its neighboring cultures, is related to the pre-Shang dukes and kings mentioned in *Shanhaijing*, whereas Lower Xiajiadian south of Yanshan is the archaeological culture of the Yi tribe.[32]

A third opinion is that Lower Xiajiadian is a culture which includes several nationalities in the northern part of the Shang period, such as Guzhu, Shanrong, Tufang and others.[33]

The fourth view argues that Lower Xiajiadian is a branch of pre-Shang culture. Jin Jing-fang, professor at Jilin University, raised again the issue that

Shang culture originated in the Dongbei, which finds support from Gan Zhi-geng, who proposed that Shang culture came from Yan. They all consider Lower Xiajiadian culture as important archaeological evidence, that is, Lower Xiajiadian was related to the origin of Shang culture.[34]

The last viewpoint argues that Lower Xiajiadian is pre-Yan culture. This argument was first raised in the brief report on the excavation of the Dachang Datuotou site in Tianjin, and did not attract much attention.[35] I tend to agree with this argument, and because it has not been given in much detail, I would like to provide more evidence here.

First, it was pointed out long before in academic circles that in the earlier period of Zhou, Shao Gong granted Yan as Yan. It did not just appear in early western Zhou when grants to nobles were recorded, but was already present before this period. In inscriptions on oracle bones, the character for Yan already existed. Recently in Beijing at Liulihe, levels earlier than the Shang dynasty in what became the capital of the Yan State in Early Western Zhou were found. Beneath the level of the Early Western Zhou at Liulihe, burials of Lower Xiajiadian were found. However, the Yan culture of Early Zhou has its own features, in addition to the characteristics of the Central Plain, so this is related to cultural features in northern China. All these suggest that in the Shang dynasty, before Yan was granted in Early Zhou, Yan already existed, that is, pre-Yan, whose cultural traditions after the grant of Early Zhou were still kept in the Yan State culture of Western Zhou.

Second, there is a transitional relationship between the Yan culture and the Lower Xiajiadian culture. For instance, the animal mask designs on the painted pottery of Lower Xiajiadian, which appeared earlier and were well developed, are one of the antecedents of *taotie* designs in the Shang dynasty, and *taotie* designs continued in Yan until the end of the Warring States period, about 300 BCE. By this time the eaves tiles in the Eastern Zhou dynasty and states such as Qi and Qin used a cloud pattern which is the simplified form of the *taotie* design, and even in the Warring States, the eaves tiles in the secondary capital still kept the standard *taotie*. At the Yan State burials in Liulihe, the lacquerware is very elaborate, suggesting it might be related to the advanced lacquerware and painted pottery of Lower Xiajiadian, especially the Yan-type *li* which has a pot belly with three baggy legs. This must be related to the *yu*-shaped *li* in Lower Xiajiadian culture.

Third, Yan and Shang have the same origins. The Shang nationality which set up its dynasty in the Central Plain seems to have no origin there, but Shang kept close ties with northern China. In terms of archaeological findings, the *li*, which is a main feature of Shang, is similar to the *li* in Lower Xiajiadian and Yan cultures; they all have pot-like bodies with three baggy legs, instead of using the body walls. Among the bronzeware from Shang, the northern style was also found, such as bell-head decorations, animal-head knives, and bow-shaped objects. Recently, Pan Qi-feng proposed, using human osteological evidence to identify tribes, that the character of the human bones from the medium and small burials of the Yin dynasty ruins representing the Shang royal tribe shows a combination of traits from East Asia and North Asia. This is not the character of the inhabitants of the middle-lower reaches of the Yellow River basin, but instead might be related to the northern people. Yan Xi-zhang made similar arguments.[36]

On the basis of these arguments we come to the conclusion that the Lower Xiajiadian culture, in the process of its development, was divided into several branches, one of which moved south and originated the Shang culture, while another remained in the same place for a long time, and became the antecedent of Yan. Thus, it might be close to the original historical events if we consider Lower Xiajiadian culture as Pre-Yan culture.

(*Translated by Mingming Shan*)

NOTES

1 Inner Mongolia Excavation Team of the Archaeological Institute of the Chinese Academy of Social Sciences. Test Excavation Report of the Xiajiadian Site at Yaowang Temple in Chifeng, Inner Mongolia. *Kaogu* 1962(2): 77–81.

2 Hamada Kosaku and Harada Yoshito. *Pi-tzu-wo*, Archaeologia Orientalis, Far-Eastern Archaeology Society of Japan, 1928.

3 Yawata Ichiro. *Prehistoric Sites and Relics in Southern Jehol*, Tokyo, 1936, and *Prehistoric Sites and Relics in Northern Jehol*, Tokyo, 1940. First Academic Survey and Research Reports of Manchuria and Mongolia, ser. 6, No. 3.

4 Hamada Kosaku and Mizuno Seiichi. *Chifeng Hongshanhou*, Archaeologia Orientalis, ser. A, No. 6, Far-Eastern Archaeology Society of Japan, 1938.

5 Dong Zhu-chen. Survey Report of the Stone City at Dongbaijia, Chifeng. *Kaogu Tongxue* 1957(6): 15–22.

6 Jehol Provincial Museum Preparatory Group. Ancient Bronzes Found at Haidaoyingzi in Lingyuan of Jehol. *Wenwu Cangkan Ziliao* 1955(8): 16–27.

7 Archaeological Excavation Team of the Tianjin City Cultural Bureau. Test Excavation Report of the Datuotou Site in the Hui Nationality Autonomous County at Dacheng in Hebei. *Kaogu* 1966(1): 8–13.

8 Zheng Shao-zong. Neolithic Sites near Chengde in Hebei. *Kaogu* 1959(7): 369–370.

9 Archaeological Training Team of Liaoning Province. Excavation Report of the Fengxia Site in the Spring of 1972 at Beipiao, Liaoning. *Kaogu* 1976(3): 197–210.

10 Liaoning Provincial Museum and Zhaoyang City Museum. Excavation Report of the Shuiquan Site, Jianping. *Liaohai Wenwu* 1986(2): 11–29.

11 Liaoning Team of the Archaeological Institute of the Chinese Academy of Social Sciences. Test Excavation Report of the Dadianzi Site of Aohan Banner in 1974. *Kaogu* 1975(2): 99–101.

12 Zhangjiakou Archaeological Team. Archaeological Report from Weixian County. *Kaogu yu Wenwu* 1982(4): 10–14.

13 Archaeological Survey Training Team of Liaoning Province. Main Results of

the Survey and Excavation in the Chaoyang Area in 1979. *Liaoning Wenwu* 1980(1): 20–24.

14 See notes 1, 9, and 12.

15 Archaeological Laboratory of the Chinese Academy of Social Sciences. C14 Determination Reports: III, *Kaogu* 1974(5): 336; IV, *Kaogu* 1977(4): 2000; V, *Kaogu* 1978(4): 285; VI, *Kaogu* 1979(1): 89.

16 Guo Da-shun. Recognition of the Pottery Phase Differentiation of the Fengxia Site. In *Wenwu yu Kaogu Collected Papers*, Beijing: Wenwu Press, 1986.

17 Chinese Encyclopedia of Archaeology, illustration, p. 33, Chinese Encyclopedia Press.

18 See note 7. Bronze Dagger-axe of the Shang Dynasty with Continuous-Bead Pattern and a Long Handle Unearthed at Jinzhou. *Guangming Daily*, September 23, 1986.

19 Liaoning Provincial Museum. Test Excavation Report of the Dongshanzui Site at Sifendi in Chifeng, Inner Mongolia. *Kaogu* 1983(5): 420–429.

20 Archaeological Institute of the Chinese Academy of Social Sciences. *Archaeological Discovery and Research in New China*, p. 341, Figures 85, 12, 13, and 8, Beijing: 1984.

21 See note 19.

22 See note 5.

23 See note 20, p. 343, Figure 86.

24 See note 13.

25 See note 11.

26 Guo Da-shun. A Post-Hongshan Culture Phase at Danangou. In *Collected Archaeological Cultural Papers*, II, Beijing: Wenwu Press, 1989.

27 Su Bing-qi. On the Archaeology of the Jin Culture. In *Wenwu yu Kaogu Collected Papers*, Beijing: Wenwu Press, 1986.

28 Archaeological Management Office of Shenyang City. The Gaotaishan Site at Xingming in Shenyang. *Kaogu* 1982(2): 121–129.

29 Liu Jing-xiang. Pottery Analysis of Group B of the Dadianzi Cemetery. *Zhonguo Kaogu Yanjiu, Wenwu*, 1986: 101–104.

30 Guo Da-shun. New Developments in Bronze Culture Research in the Liaoxi River Valley. In *Collected Papers of the Fourth Annual Meeting of the Chinese Archaeology Society*, Beijing: Wenwu Press, 1983, pp. 185–195.

31 Zou Heng. *Collected Archaeological Papers of Xia, Shang and Zhou*, Beijing: Wenwu Press, 1980, pp. 262–271.

32 Zhang Zhong-pei, Kong Zhe-sheng, Zhang Wen-jun, and Chen Yong. Lower Xiajiadian Culture Research. In *Collected Archaeological Papers,* I, Beijing: Wenwu Press, 1987, pp. 58–78.

33 Wang Cai-mei. Yan State Historical Origin and Lower and Upper Xiajiadian Cultures. In *Hua-xia Civilization*, Vol.I, Beijing: Beijing University Press, 1987.

34 Fu Si-nian. Discussion on Yin and Xia. In *Collected Papers on the Celebration of Cai Yuan-pei's Sixty-fifth Birthday*, Vol. II, Beijing: 1935, pp. 1093–1134.
Jing Jing-fang. Shang Culture Originated from Northern China. In *Collected Papers on Chinese Literature and History*, Vol.7, Shanghai: Ancient Books Press, 1978, pp. 65–70.
Gan Zhi-geng and Chen Lian-kai. Shang Tribe Originated from You and Yan Area. *Historical Research* 1985(5): 21–34.

35 See note 7.

36 Pan Qi-feng. The Distribution of Ethnic Types and Developmental Trends of the Chinese Bronze Age Residents. In *Collected Papers on the Celebration of Su*

Bing-qi's Fifty-five Years of Archaeological Work, Beijing: Wenwu Press, 1989, pp. 294–301.
Yan Xi-zhang. Yin People Showed Respect to North and East Directions. In ibid., pp. 302–305.

6

"NORTHERN-TYPE" BRONZE ARTIFACTS UNEARTHED IN THE LIAONING REGION, AND RELATED ISSUES

Guo Da-shun

EDITOR'S INTRODUCTION

"Northern-Type" is the name given to bronzes north of the Zhongyuan which are contemporaneous with the Shang dynasty and perhaps earlier. They are stylistically distinct from Shang bronzes. In this chapter, Guo describes "northern-type" bronzes from 11 sites in Liaoning and the circumstances of their discovery. The bronzes are known to be early because some of them are associated with earrings or bracelets with fan-shaped ends which are characteristic of the Lower Xiajiadian culture.

Few of the Liaoning "Northern Bronzes" have been excavated by archaeologists. They tend to have been deposited in caches which were found by villagers and later described by archaeologists. Thus, while it may be known which items were found together, the exact arrangement of the artifacts was not recorded. Not all caches have bronzes from the same time period; thus we know that bronzes were kept, perhaps as heirlooms, for considerable lengths of time.

The main artifacts in the caches are axes, daggers, battle-axes, and knives. Bronze vessels are rare, ornaments are few, and only one mirror from this time period has been brought to light in Liaoning. Ring-headed and bell-headed and animal-headed knives with curved blades and sometimes an upward-curving tip are like those from Mongolia. Socketed weapons are also characteristic in both places, and inlaid turquoise also occurs. Decorative patterns are similar, including rows of short slanting lines, zigzags, and large dots.

The northern-type bronzes are considered to be Late Shang to Early Zhou in date, since sometimes identifiable Shang or Zhou bronzes are found in the same cache. The Gaotaishan pottery style from Liaodong, mentioned also in the preceding chapter as partly contemporaneous with Lower Xiajiadian, is used to date some sites to about 1300 BCE.

The distribution of northern bronzes extends from north and south of

Yanshan to the Shang culture in the south and northwestern Siberia. Pottery is usually not found with northern bronzes in Mongolia, nor is it found associated in Liaoning. This could be attributed to raiding or trading alien groups, or to the adoption of bronze by local cultures. Local bronze-casting cultures include Upper Xinle and Gaotaishan in eastern Liaoning province, where bronze objects are few and usually identifiable as northern bronzes. Nevertheless, they might have been made locally, since the technology was available.

Western Liaoning cultures include Lower Xiajiadian, Weiyingzi and Upper Xiajiadian, of which Weiyingzi falls at the main time of northern bronzes. The Weiyingzi culture is found along the Daling and Xiaoling rivers in southern Liaoxi. Several cemeteries of the Weiyingzi culture have bronze objects, but they are not typical northern bronzes although they might have been influenced by them. For instance, earrings and gold bracelets with fan-shaped ends were found in graves, a characteristic which is frequently associated with northern bronzes, and a bronze mirror and a bow-shaped object were also found. In northern Liaoxi the earliest Upper Xiajiadian sites are contemporaneous with Weiyingzi. Many bronzes were found, which are generally classified by Guo as northern bronzes. Suspended bells are typical, and standing animals on handles are often depicted.

In Lower Xiajiadian there are some small bronze objects. Since they are earlier than the Erligang phase of Shang, Guo argues that they may be related to the origin of northern bronzes, although he stops short of insisting that the northern bronzes arose there. Advanced casting technology was already known, and some bronzes have features of northern bronzes, such as inlaid turquoise and a large bronze dagger. The earring with fan-shaped end and the use of gold, both associated with northern bronzes, were already present in Lower Xiajiadian.

A kind of tripod pottery vessel called "snake-design *li*" is found widely in the regions west and northwest of Liaoning, and also turns up in Lower Xiajiadian as an import, a fact which Guo uses to connect Lower Xiajiadian with the grasslands as early as 1500 BCE.

S. M. N.

The discovery of great numbers of "northern-type" bronze objects in northern China, mainly knives, axes, and daggers which are typical artifacts of the Shang and Zhou periods, is important to scholars at home and abroad for understanding the Chinese Bronze Age. The unique features of these bronze objects, and the close relationships with the Shang culture, as well as extensive connections with the Bronze Age in the Eurasian steppes, are particularly interesting. In Liaoning, particularly in Liaoxi [western Liaoning], this type of bronze object is being excavated continuously,

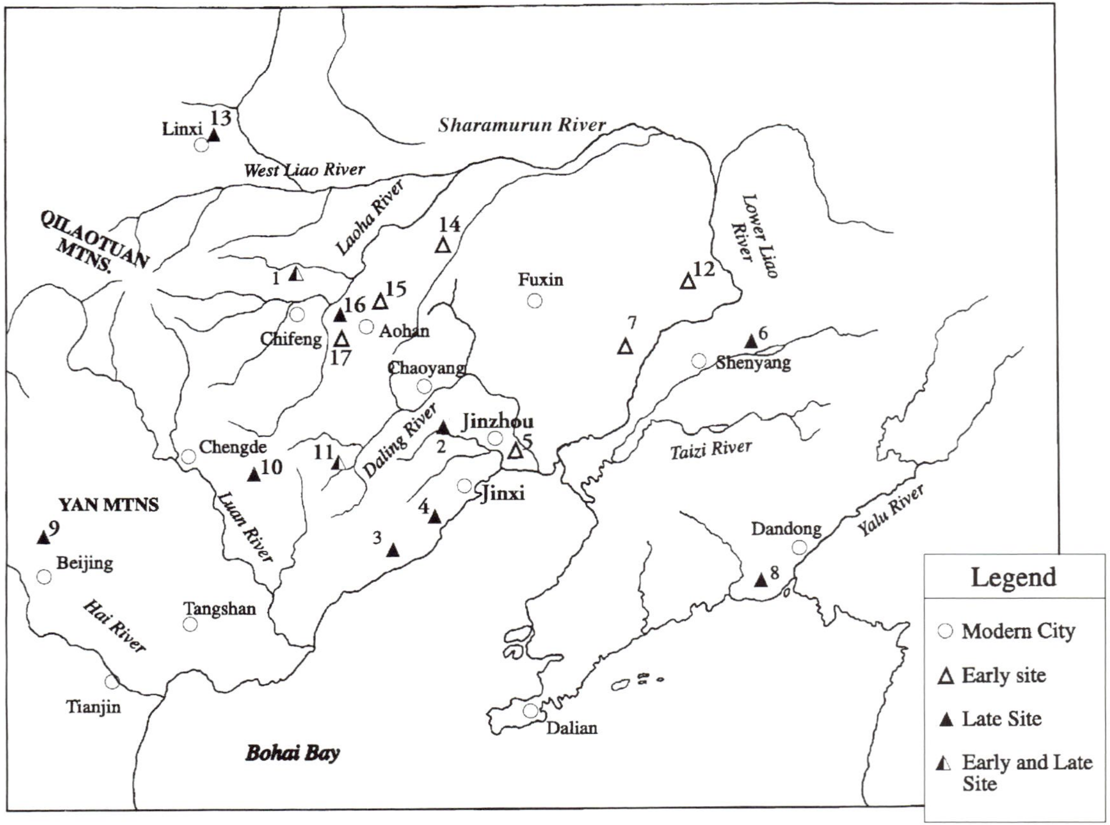

Figure 6.1
Locations of northern
bronzes discussed in
Chapter 6
Key:
1) Chifeng
2) Chaoyang
3) Majiacun
4) Xingcheng
5) Shuishouyingzi
6) Wanghua
7) Gaotaishan
8) Donggou
9) Zhangjiakou
10) Chaodaogou
11) Xiabotaigou
12) Wanliu
13) Dajing
14) Dadianzi
15) Bajiananchang
16) Nanshangen
17) Shaoguoyingzi

making it a very important region for the distribution of northern bronzes. In recent years, the discovery of and research on bronze culture in the Liaoxi region have made great progress, and the chronology has basically been established, including the Shang and Zhou periods.[1] There has been little discussion of northern bronzes in the Liaodong [eastern Liaoning] region, because excavated artifacts are fewer and the excavations were rarely ideal. However, this chapter will discuss the northern bronzes on the basis of the materials available, and analyze the discoveries. Northern bronzes have been excavated at 11 sites in the Liaoning region (Figure 6.1).

SITES AND HOARDS

Bajiananchang Dongjiagou site in Jianping

Two bronze objects were found by local inhabitants. The site is located in the northern part of Jianping county, near the eastern bank of the Laoha river. A formal survey of this area has not yet been conducted, but according to Li Dian-fu, Director of Jianping Cultural Archaeological Administration Institute, several Lower and Upper Xiajiadian sites are found nearby.

Human-head-shaped-dagger (Figure 6.2j): The dagger-handle resembles a head with two faces. Along the slope of the handle one head looks up and the other down. The two faces are exactly the same, the eyes drooping, wide-open mouth, high nose-bridge, high cheekbones, two nostrils, wide ears, and flat skull. Within the skull a bell hangs upside-down, and the eyes, nostrils, and mouth are indented. On the front of the handle, saw-tooth patterns were applied as decoration. Both sides of the body protrude like bronze buttons. The dagger is 29 cm long and 3.15 cm wide, large enough to use as a spoon.

Deer-headed pick (Figure 6.2n): The body is S-shaped, narrowing from head to tail, and becoming pointed at the end. It is 19.8 cm long. It is hollow, although the tail is solid. Each part of the deer head has clear features. It has large nostrils, snout, open mouth, protruding eyes, and no ears but long antlers resting along the neck. Between the antlers there are two hollow posts.

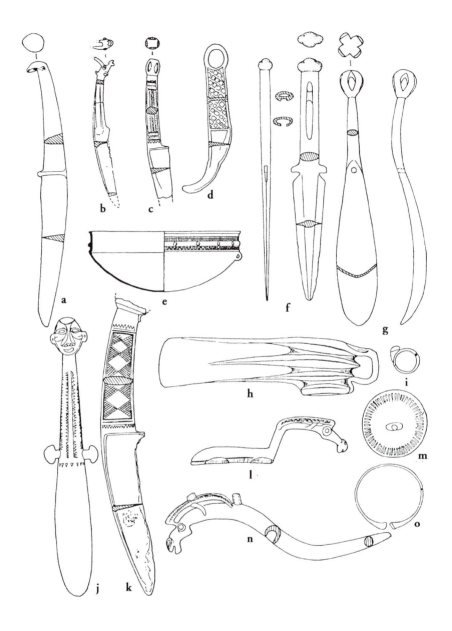

Figure 6.2 Northern bronzes from the Liaoxi mountain regions: a), c), d) and h)
Chifeng, Inner Mongolia; b), k) and l) Chaoyang; e) and g) Xiaobotaigou; f)
Shaoguoyingzi; i) and m) Daohugou; j) and n) Dongjiagou, Jianping; o) Heshangou

Shaoguoyingzi Dahuang tomb 1 in Jianping

This site is also located in the northern part of Jianping, near the Chifeng region in eastern Inner Mongolia. The tomb was destroyed, therefore the relationships among the objects were not clear. Several bronze objects were collected, of which the most important is a bronze dagger which is 23.3 cm long, with a long, thick, hollow handle with an oval cross-section (Figure 6.2f). The front of the handle has a rectangular groove. The handle end has projections, and the handle and blade were cast together. The dagger is short, with both sides slanting. A raised ridge runs along the middle of the blade. The handle of this dagger is different from others such as the chisel-type dagger and T-shaped handle which are commonly seen in Jianping county, nor is it like the dagger with the handle and the body molded together which is seen in the Upper Xiajiadian culture at Nanshangen near Ningcheng county, but it is similar to the animal-head and bell-head daggers of the northern bronzes, and also much like bronze daggers excavated from the tombs of Early Western Zhou at Baifu village near Cangping county in Beijing.[2] Thus, this tomb could be regarded as an Early Western Zhou tomb. A bronze awl in the shape of a nail was also excavated. The point is rectangular without special features. Bronze awls are very commonly seen among northern-type bronze objects, but they are rarely unearthed in western Liaoning; thus this one is notable.[3]

The Xiaobotaigou cache pit, Kezou county

The Xiaobotaigou cache contained 14 bronze objects. One vessel lid is very unusual, but it was found with typical Shang/Zhou *ding* [a pot with three or four solid legs], *gui* [a round-mouthed food vessel with two or four loop handles], and *lei* [a short-necked wine vessel]. The unusual bronze lid is 9.8 cm in diameter and 6 cm high, shaped like a low bowl (Figure 6.2e). The wall is thin, only 1.5 mm. The material has not been tested, but it is light green and not very shiny, obviously different from the Shang/Zhou artifacts in the same pit. At one side of the lid a small single ring was attached. Especially unusual is a band design around the neck. The band consists of a saw-tooth design with small dots added. This is a typical decoration of northern-type bronze objects. Associated with this were other objects with northern-type features or similarities. For example, there are a bell-head dagger and a square-support *gui*. The bell-head dagger is 29 cm long, longer than the usual northern-type bronze dagger, and the bell-head is smaller, with no ball inside the bell (Figure 6.2g). This bronze dagger is finely made, thick and heavy, and the material is like that of the rest of the artifacts in the pit. The square-support *gui* is the usual shape of Shang/Zhou vessels, except that there is a single bell at the bottom of the interior. The bell is a characteristic of northern-type bronze objects. In the

Xiaobotaigou cache the latest bronze objects belong to the Early Western Zhou, and Late Shang objects, stylistically Erligang and Late Yin-Xu, also were found. Thus, the northern-type artifacts from this site could be categorized as Late Shang/Early Zhou.

Similar to bronze objects of this cache pit, another pit was found at Yixian, Huaerlou. A rectangular plate with twin suspended bells in the bottom was excavated along with some other typical Shang/Zhou artifacts. From the designs the dish could be categorized as Late Shang. This type of bronze object has not been discovered in the Central Plains, so it is an artifact with features similar to northern-type bronze objects.

Some collections in the Chaoyang region

In 1969 a bell-head knife (Figure 6.2k) was collected, said to have been excavated from Lingyuan county. It is broken into two pieces and the remaining length is 25.7 cm and 3 cm wide. It has a convex back, with a round thick handle and a wide body. Below the bell-head there is a single ring, which is broken. The remaining part has 13 prongs. The handle was decorated with triangles and saw-tooth designs. The knife point turns up. This handled knife is large and of good quality and the bell-head and decorative patterns are unusual. It is considered to belong to the Late Shang period.

Deer-like belt ornament (Figure 6.2l): The whole body is like a recumbent deer. The mouth and the eyes are pointed, the mouth is open, the two nostrils are shown, and the eyes are inlaid with turquoise. Long antlers extend behind the neck, with a band connecting them. The antlers are decorated with wave patterns. The deer has a long neck and is lying down. It has a round, hollow body. Inside are two rings. The front one is horizontal and the back one is vertical. This artifact is much like one published by the Metropolitan Museum of Art in New York.[4] It probably belongs to the Late Shang period.

Deer-head knife (Figure 6.2b): this is said to have been excavated from Jianping county, Ershijiazi Chaoyang. The deer is open-mouthed, with two nostrils, and big eyes.

Xingcheng Yianghe cached bronze objects[5]

The site is in hilly land, just 25 km from the Bohai coast. Nearby a river runs to the Bohai Sea. Six bronze objects were excavated: 3 ring-headed knives, 1 beaked, socketed halberd, 1 battle-axe, and 1 hooked object (Figure 6.3a–f). One of the ring-head knives is unusually large. It is 23.2 cm long and 2.9 cm wide, and the body is decorated with parallel slanting lines. The head is oval, with three teeth protruding at the outer edge. The other two knives have small narrow handles. The axe was decorated with

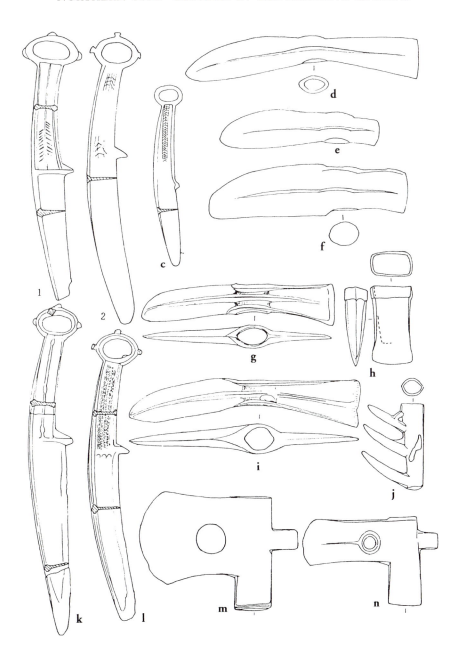

Figure 6.3 Northern bronzes from the Liaoxi corridor: a)–f) Yianghe, Xingcheng;
g)–n) Qianwei, Suizhong

circular patterns on the face. In addition to the halberd in this group, two others, similar in shape, were collected in this county by the County Cultural Archaeological Bureau. This group of objects is rough in terms of the quality. They are thin and the designs are not deep, so that they seem to be different from the typical northern-type bronze objects. Perhaps this indicates a later period.

Qianwei Majiacun bronze caches in Suizhong county

The excavation location is 50 km east of the Yiang River site mentioned above. It is even closer to the Bohai coast, only 10 km. The land is flat. The 48 bronze objects were discovered by local inhabitants, so the manner of their excavation is not clear. This is the largest number of northern-type bronze objects to be unearthed at one site. Included are 13 axes, 18 knives, 13 halberds, 1 battle-axe, and 1 three-toothed object (Figure 6.3g–n). These artifacts are still being sorted out. I will present them briefly based upon the photographs published by Suizhong county.

Axes: two types. Type I, long, narrow blade. Type II, also long, but with a wide blade.

Knives: three types. Type I, convex ridge, circular-head with three teeth protruding, and the handle was decorated with slanting lines. Type II, almost straight ridge, the point is turned sharply upwards, the handle tip is circular, with a single ring below, and the handle was decorated with slanting lines. Type III is the usual ring-head knife.

Halberds: three types. Type I, small, the front part is quite long and the rear part quite short. Type II, long and narrow with the front and the rear equal in terms of the length. Type III, wide, the front part long and wide and the rear quite short.

Axe: rectangular, decorated with concentric circles.

Toothed object: the three teeth slant downwards, with equal distance between them.

The objects in this group are quite similar to those from the Xiang river in Xingcheng in terms of their quality. The site might be a cache.

Xinmin Dahong Banner

Although this site was published, the author did not describe the finds in detail,[6] so I will add a little more here (Figure 6.4b–d).

Socketed battle-axe I: the total length is 14 cm, the socket is 7.4 cm long and the blade is 4.5 cm wide. The blade is relatively wide. There are multi-angle flower designs in the center and the lower part of the socket is long and decorated with geometric slanting lines and parallel lines.

Socketed battle-axe II: 14.4 cm long, the socket is 3.9 cm long and the blade is 2.5 cm wide.

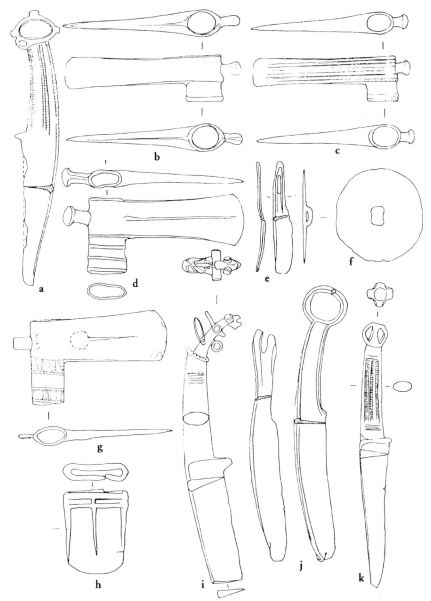

Figure 6.4 Northern bronzes from Liaodong: a) Wanghua, Fushun; b)–d) Dahong
Banner, Xinmin; e)–k) Wanliu, Faku

Socketed battle-axe III: the total length is 15.7 cm. The socket is 4.1 cm
long and the blade is 2.7 cm wide. It is like SBA II. It is also thick and
heavy, with a plain face.

The Sanshu site was also discovered and collected by local people.

According to Wang Zhong-sheng, who investigated the location, the local people found it surrounded by stones on a slope, belonging probably to some sort of cache. Nearby sandy red potsherds belonging to the Bronze Age were also found. These three objects are of high quality, thick and heavy, and are typical northern-type bronze objects. They are late Shang period.

Bronze knife in the Wanghua site[7]

This knife is 24.4 cm long (Figure 6.4a). The back is raised and the pointed part of the knife is slim and narrow, pointing upward. The ring is oval. The handle is thick, decorated with bands of short slanting lines, a characteristic of northern-type bronze objects. The date is probably in the Late Shang period. Wanghua is a bronze culture site along the Hunhe River valley in eastern Liaoning. Most of the pots from this site are *li* and *ding* made of sandy red pottery with horizontal ring-like handles. The vessels are plain, but the legs often have projections. It belongs to the Upper Xinle culture.

Bronze objects from the Wanliu site, Faku[8]

This site is located on the east bank of a tributary to the lower Liaohe valley. It is on a terrace at the southeastern edge of the Song-Liao Plain. Since 1979 when the site was discovered, bronze objects have been collected from the site several times, altogether 5 knives, 1 battle-axe, 2 axes, and 1 mirror were reported (Figure 6.4e–k).

Knives: one deer-head knife. The deer head is especially long and narrow, and the mouth, eyes, and ears protrude. At the neck there are large circular bands and below there is a small circular knob. One bell-headed knife has a relatively straight body with a round, thick handle, also decorated with horizontal and vertical bands of saw-tooth patterns and fine scale patterns. The bell-head is made up of four prongs.

One battle-axe with a long and narrow body. In addition, a ring-headed knife and bronze mirror were found.

Two axes: one is short with concave blade, the other long with a wider blade.

When the Wanliu site was excavated, vessels of plain sandy red-brown pottery were unearthed. The shapes include bowls with horizontal handles, jars with punctate patterns and vertical handles, and pottery spindle whorls whose cross-section is trapezoidal. *Li* is a common shape, with high solid conical legs. Analysis of the features of the artifacts from this site shows that they belong to the Gaotaishan type, different from the Upper Xinle culture. The date is approximately in the Middle Shang period. This is an important reference for the chronology of this group of bronze objects.

At Donggou in Dandong, one northern-type bronze object was collected. It is a halberd, whose shape is unique. Nearby bronze sites were found, where the rim of the pottery was decorated with raised patterns.

SYNTHESIS

Although nearly 80 northern-type bronze objects were collected from the 11 sites described above, they were not discovered through formal excavation, and the places where they were collected are imprecise. However, since some are in groups, there are some phenomena which can be sorted out.

Regions

The division of bronze cultures in the Liaoning region follows the natural boundary of the Yiwulu mountains. The division between eastern and western Liaoning in ancient times also followed this south-to-north mountain ridge.[9] Currently, the typology and chronology of these two ancient bronze cultures of the east and the west are being studied. The Liaoxi patterns are quite clear, but the Liaodong region is still under study.

For the convenience of comparison, we divide the northern bronzes of Liaoning into several regions. There are roughly four: Liaodong, concentrated along the Lower Liao river and its tributaries (called hereafter the Central Liao region); the Liaodong peninsula and coastal region (where only one northern bronze object was found, in spite of many surveys and excavations); and Liaoxi, where there are similarities between the lower part of Suizhong county in the Liaoxi corridor and Xianghe Xingcheng county, but there are differences from the Chaoyang region in Liaoxi, and thus Liaoxi can be divided into two sub-regions of mountains and corridor.

It should be noted that the Liaoxi region in prehistoric times was differentiated from that of the Chifeng region in Inner Mongolia. This is a big problem in comparative research. Fortunately, in the mid-1970s we collected a group of artifacts which were clearly northern bronzes from the Chifeng region. Here I would like to introduce them to the reader (Fig.6.2a, c, d, h).

Bronze Objects from Chifeng

One socketed dagger, said to be unearthed from Linxi county, was 19.5 cm long. It is big, thick, and heavy. The whole body was made up of front and back, with a central ridge. The front section is quite long and the blade has a slightly convex curve, similar to an axe.

Eight knives can be divided into four types by the ends of the handles. Type I is ring-headed knives, of which there are four. Two have convex backs and broken blades. One is small, with the blade curving upward, the handle decorated with slanting lines and checks. The last is even smaller, but it has a wide blade. Type II is the double-ring-headed knife, of which there are two. One has a convex back, and a long sharp blade. The other is small, with a handle decorated with dots. Type III includes two ball-headed knives, one with a convex back and round handle; of the other only a flat handle remains. Type IV is a bell-headed knife. The blade portion of this knife is missing. The handle is round and thick, decorated with horizontal dots along with vertical saw-tooth patterns.

In addition, according to the report, a bronze sword with a bell-shaped head and a handle was unearthed from Aohan Banner,[10] and at Naiman Banner a deer-head-shaped knife was also excavated.[11]

Although northern-type bronzes are found in the regions described above, including the two sub-regions in western Liaoning and nearby provinces and cities such as Chifeng, in Inner Mongolia, and Chengde, Zhangjiakou, Beijing, and Tianjin in Hebei province,[12,13,14] it is in Liaoxi that northern bronze objects were concentrated. Liaodong had very few northern bronze objects. In recent years in the lower reaches of the Liaohe valley, more have begun to appear. In the peninsular and coastal areas there were even fewer. This distribution is important.

Analysis of locational relationships

Site excavation

Wanghua in Fushun is one of the excavated sites in the central Liaoning region. According to the report, a ring-headed knife was unearthed from the yellow-earth layer 1.4 m below ground surface. In test pits nearby, a large number of potsherds were excavated. No sign of burials was noted, nor other bronze objects. The site, which belongs roughly to the Upper Xinle Bronze Age culture along the Hunhe valley, is relatively simple, without any disturbance by late cultures. The date of the site is around Shang/Zhou, which is identical to the date of the bronze knife. Thus, the presence of a knife is not surprising. Similarly, Wanliu in Faku was excavated twice, again there were no burials found, and the date of the bronze object is identical to the date of the site. Thus, the bronze objects could be deduced to be from the same site.

Excavated burials

One site has become clear: Tomb 1 of Shaoguoyingzi Dahuangdi, in Jianping county. It is reported that this was a rectangular earth-pit tomb. There were nearly 20 excavated bronze artifacts, including buttons and other bronze ornaments, along with three agate beads. All are commonly seen in burials in this period.

Caches or storage pits

There are four locations, which can be divided into two types. First, there are pits with only northern bronzes. This includes the three sites of Xingcheng Xianghe, Suizhong Qianwei, and Xinmin Dahong Banner. Based upon site investigations, these three sites with bronze objects are not within dwelling areas, nor is there any sign of burials. Some of them were found between rocks and on slopes where dwellings could not have been constructed. Thus, they were called cache pits. The Chaodaogou bronze-object groups in Qinglong county near the Chengde region are reported as "intentional storage" in similar situations, so that they are also a cache type.

The second kind is the storage of northern bronzes along with typical Shang/Zhou bronze objects. Only the Xiaobotaigou cache in Kezuo county belongs to this category. Here, there are mainly Shang/Zhou bronze objects, but some northern bronzes, which are secondary, are also found.

The three situations mentioned above indicate that northern bronzes in Liaoning are present in both dwellings and burials, but storage caches are the main feature. These three kinds of excavations should be taken into consideration when discussing these bronze objects.

Assemblages

Among the northern bronzes excavated in Liaoning, there are five examples of groups of bronzes: Xingcheng Yianghe; Suizhong Qianwei; Xinmin Dahong Banner; Wanliu, Faku; and Dongjiagou, Jianping. The Wanliu group was collected at different times, and the Dongjiagou group has special object types which are not clear in terms of its excavation. Thus only Xingcheng Yianghe, Suizhong Qianwei, and Xinmin Dahong Banner clusters have definite assemblages. In addition, Chaodaogou nearby could be regarded as having some important reference information.

From the composition of the two groups excavated at both Xianghe and Qianwei, knives and large socketed daggers are quite common. In terms of the group at Qianwei, the knives, socketed daggers, and axes are either almost equal in the number excavated (both have 13 axes and 13 daggers) or close to equal, further providing evidence to show that these three objects are basic components. Both of the sites have bronze battle-axes, but the Xinmin Dahong Banner cluster also has three battle-axes. This indicates that battle-axes are another important component. The Liuwan site has a set including knife, axe, and battle-axe, which is the same, and the group at Chaodaogou also has knives, battle-axes, and daggers. Therefore, it can be inferred from the present information that the fundamental components of northern bronzes in Liaoning region are axes, knives, daggers, and battle-axes.

195

Chaodaogou, there is another. They are found far more often here than farther west. The shape traits, such as long and narrow body, and straight unflaring blade like an axe, are different from those in the western region.

4) There are some unusual shapes of objects, such as vessel lids, head-shaped dagger-handles, and chariot ornaments, some of which are very elaborately made. They are unknown or rare in other regions, which indicates a high peak of development of the northern-type bronzes in Liaoning.

Chronology

In terms of the chronology of northern-type bronze objects, since many of them were unearthed with bronze objects of the Late Shang Period, they are generally considered to be contemporaneous with the Late Shang dynasty. Tomb 112 of Gaocheng Taixicun is considered to belong to Dasikong Phase I, but the bronze dagger is already very advanced. Thus, some consider the bronze knives unearthed from Erligang and Erlitou sites as northern bronze objects,[17] and accordingly infer that northern bronzes began to appear from Middle and Late Shang to Early Zhou; for example, the excavations at the Baifu cemetery in Beijing. Based upon this line of reasoning, it is considered that the age of northern bronzes in the Liaoning region might be as follows.

First, most northern bronzes unearthed from the Liaoning region lack context to place them temporally, yet because of the objects mentioned above which were found nearby, the chronology is relatively clear. For example, the three knobbed ring-headed knives from Wanghua in Fushun, the deer-head knife and the bell-head knife from Chaoyang, as well as the deer-head carriage artifacts, can all be considered Late Shang.

Second, co-existing with typical Shang/Zhou bronze objects is a cache of bronzes from Xiaobotaigou, Kezuo. However, the bronze objects from this pit have different ages. The earliest, a tripod *ding*, could be Shang Erligang phase,[18] and the latest is Early Zhou (the square *gui*). Among the objects is a bell-head dagger, which is commonly seen during the Late Shang period. However, the bell-head is not very typical, thus it is considered Late Shang to Early Zhou.

Third, the Wanliu site belongs to the Gaotaishan type. The time of Gaotaishan type used to be considered around the time of Shang and Zhou, but calibrated C14 dates have shown it to be 1300 BCE.[19] Recently several sites of Lower Xiajiadian culture having Gaotaishan-type pottery were discovered at Aohan Dadianzi in Inner Mongolia and Pingdingshan in Fuxin. Based upon C14 determinations, Wanliushan is in almost the same time frame as Gaotaishan, around 1300 BCE. Thus, some of the northern bronzes from this site can be considered to be earlier than the Late Shang period. For instance, the two pierced knives have no clear separation of the tip from the body; their shape is primitive. Some scholars think that this is the earliest type of northern-type bronze object.

Fourth, Qianwei in Suizhong and Yianghe in Xingcheng are two sites where the typical excavated northern bronzes are very different from the Liaoxi region. They show differences in shape, type, and features and besides, the quality is not as good and the body is usually thin and flat. The designs are shallow, suggesting a later time placement, perhaps Early Zhou.

In sum, northern bronzes in the Liaoning region seem to be contemporaneous with other regions where they are found, around Late Shang and Early Zhou, but no later. What needs to be emphasized, however, is that in this region there are traces which are earlier than Late Shang. Although no evidence has been found which is earlier than Erlitou, yet these bronze objects are very well made, and this factor should be taken into consideration.

DISCUSSION

As northern bronzes are distributed not only both south and north of Yanshan, including the Liaoning region, in the loess plateau along the Yellow river and the bend of the river, but also in the center of the Shang culture as well as in Siberia, there is a close relationship with the bronze culture in the grasslands of Eurasia. Thus, it becomes very important to study the origin, cultural nature, and cultural range of the northern bronzes. Lin Yun once hypothesized, based upon the archaeological evidence that northern bronzes are not often found with pottery, that in addition to the settled agriculturalists who used some kind of pottery and production tools similar to Shang culture, there were also pastoral nomads who used northern-type bronze objects in northern China. Either these nomads did not use pottery or their pottery was not well-developed. They travelled between the settled agriculturalists and raided them, but also had trade as well as conquest relations, and some assimilation caused the northern bronzes to become more common in this vast area.[20]

The northern bronzes excavated from the Liaoning region were not accompanied by pottery either. Perhaps these collections were limited. However, is the lack of pottery due to the nomadic nature of the bronze users? In other words, are the northern bronzes local or alien? Thus, another important topic is the relationship of the northern bronzes to other bronze cultures locally as well as to the neighboring bronze cultures. As the northern bronzes unearthed from Liaoning can be classified into categories different from other regions, the first general question which should be asked is the relationship to the local bronze objects.

Previously the northern bronzes unearthed from eastern Liaoning have been discussed, mainly from Gaotaishan (Wanliu) and Upper Xinle culture

(Wanghua). Very few bronze objects have been unearthed from these two sites. Except for the few northern bronzes noted above, only one small knife and one trumpet-shaped earring were found. Neither bronze tools nor bronze vessels were found. Thus, the northern bronzes and the bronze objects affected by the northern bronzes might possibly be the main component of several bronze cultures in eastern Liaoning. From the bronze objects discovered so far, the technology for making small bronze objects was already available in the bronze culture period in eastern Liaoning, thus the possibility that the northern bronzes were made locally cannot be excluded.

In western Liaoning, the cultures where northern bronzes were unearthed include Lower Xiajiadian, Weiyingzi, and Upper Xiajiadian. Among them the most relevant is Weiyingzi because it belongs to a similar time frame.[21] Excavations with bronze objects in Weiyingzi sites include the Weiyingzi wooden coffin tomb, the Daohugou tomb, and the Heshangou tomb as well as the bronze pit of the Shang/Zhou period in Kezuo related to the Weiyingzi type.

At the Weiyingzi cemetery, bronze objects were excavated from Graves T601 and T602.[22] Although no typical northern bronzes were found, the excavated bronze armor and bell ornament have local characteristics, so that they could be regarded as affected by northern bronzes. A sheep-head ornament excavated from Grave T601 is particularly notable. The head is very lifelike. Northern bronzes have many sheep, so this object might be related to northern bronze.

In Heshangou Tomb 1[23] a pair of gold bracelets was discovered along with some typical Shang/Zhou bronze objects (Figure 6.2o). Both ends of the bracelets are fan-shaped, which is typical of the bronze culture in Liaoxi; for example, the gold bracelets excavated from Liujiahe in Beijing Pinggu and bracelets from Lulongdong Guangezhong (Shang tombs) have this shape.[24] At Dongguangezhong tomb a bow-shaped bronze object was also excavated. The latter is very suggestive of the close relationship between northern bronzes and the Yin-Xu culture. The bronze mirror unearthed from the Daohugou tomb has not been formally put into the category of northern bronzes, but associating it with the northern bronzes of Weiyingzi type is very natural. Also in this tomb, a trumpet-shaped bronze earring was collected. This type of bronze earring was seen in the local Lower Xiajiadian culture. Some scholars consider it a component of northern bronzes.

In terms of the features of northern bronzes among the cached bronze objects, in addition to the vessel lid and bell-head dagger from Xiaobotaigou previously mentioned, a square-stand *gui* and a chopping-board-shaped plate, both with an upside-down bell at the bottom of the vessel, were unearthed from the same pit at Huaerlou in Yi county. A narrow-necked bronze bowl from Pit 2 of this cemetery was also found. The quality of this vessel is very similar to the vessel lid from Xiaobotaigou, but somewhat different from the bronze objects of Shang/Zhou unearthed from the same pit.[25] These examples all indicate that in terms of Shang/Zhou cached bronze objects in Liaoxi, some features of northern bronzes are present.

The Weiyingzi type is mainly distributed along the valley of the Daling and Xiaoling rivers, that is, the southern part of Liaoxi. The time is around the Shang/Zhou period, which is also the time of northern bronzes. Analyzing the bronze objects from the Weiyingzi-type site, although it is not appropriate to say that all the northern bronzes unearthed within the range of Weiyingzi type belong to it, it is clear that: 1) generally speaking, Weiyingzi-type bronze objects bear fundamental features of northern bronzes; 2) among the Weiyingzi type there are typical items of northern bronzes; 3) the Weiyingzi type contributed new traits to northern bronzes, such as the vessel lid, mirror, earring, and gold ornaments.

In the northern part of Liaoxi, mainly along the valley of the Laoha river, cultural relics identified with Shang/Zhou are not clear. Only from the site of Shuiquan Jianping partial remains of Early Upper Xiajiadian culture can be identified, such as the rimmed *li* and impressed-triangle pottery similar to the Weiyingzi type. This might suggest that the cultural remains of the Shang/Zhou period in this region were Upper Xiajiadian, that is, the original Upper Xiajiadian culture,[26] because in this region many typical northern bronzes were unearthed. Northern-style bronzes might be related to Early Upper Xiajiadian culture of the same time.

In terms of the relationship between Upper Xiajiadian culture and northern bronzes, many bronze objects were unearthed from Upper Xiajiadian. Some scholars have categorized the bronze objects of Upper Xiajiadian culture as part of the system of northern bronzes in the broader sense. However, we argue that northern bronzes should be a special concept with a strict boundary, meaning Upper Xiajiadian should not be considered in the category of northern bronzes. However, a close relationship between Upper Xiajiadian culture and northern bronzes is suggested. I will not go into detail about the commonalities and connections. What should be noted is that the commonalities between the bronze objects of Upper Xiajiadian culture and northern bronzes are not always the same. For instance, although they both have suspended bells, the bells of the northern bronzes are mainly used at the head of the object. In Upper Xiajiadian there are bells, as, for example, the bell-headed short dagger from Nanshangen[27], but the suspended bell is attached to other parts. Another example is the animal-head ornament. The themes are very similar, such as horse, sheep, and deer, but the northern bronzes more commonly have animal heads. The animal-head dagger in Siberia might be later. The animal ornaments from Upper Xiajiadian culture are either standing or depict a row of animals. Also, the basic implements are knives, axes, swords, and battle-axes, but the forms are very different. The ring-headed knife is rarely seen in Upper Xiajiadian. The dagger has a straight handle. The divergence between the features of Upper Xiajiadian culture and northern bronzes not only indicates that they belong to different developmental stages which have their own features, but also suggests a developmental relationship between Upper Xiajiadian and northern bronzes. It can be considered that Upper Xiajiadian culture is a very important center of northern bronzes. This difference seems more obvious than in another location where northern bronzes are dispersed – the loess plateau along both banks of the Yellow river.

The last issue to deal with is the relationship between Lower Xiajiadian culture and northern bronzes. This culture represents the early bronze culture in Liaoxi, where several small bronze objects were unearthed. These objects are presumably prior to Shang Erligang, that is, earlier than northern bronzes which became prevalent in Liaoxi. Thus, what should be considered in terms of the relationship between Lower Xiajiadian culture and northern bronzes is naturally directed to the relationship between the origin of this culture and northern bronzes. Accordingly, it becomes an interesting question for scholars who study northern bronzes. In some published articles, objects excavated from Lower Xiajiadian culture, such as earrings and gold ornaments, have been categorized as features of northern bronzes. Our arguments regarding this issue essentially are as follows.

First, although the bronze objects excavated from the Lower Xiajiadian culture are mostly small, people already knew how to use composite molds and inner molds. For instance, a part of a pottery mold was unearthed from Sifendi in Chifeng belonging to Early Lower Xiajiadian culture. This pottery mold has all the basic components of casting funnel, casting body, notched joins, and cross-marking symbols.[28] A bronze attachment to a stone battle-axe from Dadianzi also used an inner mold, and in addition, patterns were applied on the surface, and rivets were used for attachment. Some pottery vessels which mimic bronze, in that they have rivets as ornaments, were also unearthed. It can be inferred that the technology of bronze-casting was quite well developed; it was not the earliest period of this technology. In other words, at that time people had grasped the technology of casting objects which look similar to northern bronzes.

Second, among the bronze objects of Lower Xiajiadian culture, in addition to ornaments there are also weapons and tools which are identical to northern bronzes, especially a bronze-handled dagger unearthed from the Jinzhou region which is 38 cm long, a large bronze object. It is inlaid with turquoise.[29] All these features are related to northern bronzes.

Third, the typical objects of Lower Xiajiadian culture – the trumpet-shaped earring and gold ear ornament – were present until Shang/Zhou when the features of northern bronzes began to appear.

The above analysis indicates that Lower Xiajiadian culture does have something to do with the origin of northern bronzes, but so far no typical northern bronzes have appeared in this culture. Thus, it cannot be concluded that Lower Xiajiadian culture is the direct origin of northern bronzes.

As a result, when referring to the origin of northern bronzes in Liaoning, influence from outside cannot be excluded from consideration. We note that in the western region where northern bronzes are distributed, early Shang bronze objects along with northern-type bronze daggers and swords have been found at the Zhukaigou site (Phases IV and V) in the Ordos region. Some scholars have argued that northern bronzes originated from the Ordos region.[30] It should be noted that in the Ordos region, a "snake-design *li*" [a baggy-legged vessel decorated with fine raised patterns] was unearthed along with early northern bronzes. This typical pottery *li* is found occasionally in Lower Xiajiadian culture in Liaoxi. For instance, at Beipiao Fengxia site and Aohan Dadianzi cemetery in Inner Mongolia, a typical "snake-design *li*" was unearthed. However, this *li* is very different from Lower Xiajiadian in terms of the quality, the shape, and the patterns. It can be deduced that it came from outside this area. It is known that this kind of *li* was very common from the area of the Mongolian grassland to northern Liaoning and southern Siberia as well as from Inner Mongolia to western Liaoning.[31] Thus, this *li* is probably adapted from neighbors in the north and west. This becomes very important evidence indicating the cultural exchange between western Liaoning and its neighbors in the west and north in the Early Bronze Age. Incidentally this kind of "snake-design *li*" appeared in western Liaoning at the same time as northern bronzes are first found. Thus, we deduce further that in the late period of Lower Xiajiadian culture (around 1500 BC), it was affected by the ancient cultures of its western and northern neighbors, and consequently, it helped northern bronzes develop all over Liaoxi and finally to the whole of Liaoning.

In western Liaoning where northern bronzes are concentrated, back in the Neolithic there were already multiple economies, multiple cultures, and exchanges between this region and the outside, especially relationships between horticulturalists and herders. The northern bronzes with the style of northern grassland developed in western Liaoning. In the meantime the development of this ancient culture in western Liaoning had a tendency to rise and fall. When northern bronzes were prevalent around Shang/Zhou, Lower Xiajiadian culture was on the verge of decline. This causes us to consider that in addition to the attention we give to the exchange between horticulturalists and farmers, the influence of northern grassland tribes is another important historical factor that cannot be ignored. This ancient culture of western Liaoning is in a region where there was a close connection with the origin of Shang culture. Among the regional features of northern bronzes is that they are most closely related to Shang. This might indicate that the relationship between Shang culture and Northern Grassland culture used Liaoxi as the place of exchange.

In summary, the development of northern bronzes, especially the development in Liaoxi, is both an important component of the bronze culture in this region and a very special historic phenomenon in the historic period. If we can understand the development of this ancient culture in Liaoxi in wider perspective, it will be helpful in understanding this special phenomenon in historic periods.

(Translated by Mingming Shan)

NOTES

1 Wu Zhen-lu. The Shang and Zhou Bronzes Found in Baodo County. *Wenwu* 1972(4): 62–64.
2 *Kaogu Xuebao* 1976(4): 253, Figure 9.3.
3 Jianping County Cultural Center and Chaoyang Area Museum. Bronze Age Tombs and Related Remains at Jianping, Liaoning. *Kaogu* 1983(8): 679–694.
4 Maxwell K. Hearn. *Ancient Chinese Art – Miscellaneous Metalwork, No. 36*, New York: Metropolitan Museum of Art, 1985.
5 Jinzhou City Museum. Bronzes Found at Xianghe in Xingcheng, of Liaoning. *Kaogu* 1978(6): 387.
6 Liaoning Provincial Museum. Shang and Zhou Bronzes Unearthed at Shanwanzi in Kezuo, Liaoning. *Wenwu*, 1977(12): 23–33.
7 Fushun City Museum. Bronze Ring-end Knife of the Yin Dynasty Found in Fushun, Liaoning. *Kaogu* 1981(2): 190. See Figure 4.
8 Archaeology Group of the History Department at Liaoning University. Wanliu Site Excavation at Faku, Liaoning. *Kaogu* 1989(12): 1076–1086.
9 Guo Da-shun. New Developments in Bronze Culture Research in the Liaoxi River Valley. In *Collected Papers of the Fourth Annual Meeting of the Chinese Archaeology Society*, Beijing: Wenwu Press, 1983, p.79.
10 *Wenwu Bao*, November 13, 1987, pp. 11–13.
11 *Inner Mongolian Archaeology* No. 2.
12 Cultural Archaeological Team of Hebei Province Cultural Archaeological Bureau. Bronzes found at Chaodaogou, Qinglong, Hebei Province. *Kaogu* 1962(12): 644–645.
   Beijing Archaeological Administrative Office. Another Important Archaeological Discovery in the Beijing Area. *Kaogu* 1976(4): 246–258.
13 Archaeological Administrative Office of the Hebei Provincial Museum. *Selection of Relics Unearthed in Hebei.*,Beijing: Wenwu Press, 1980.
   Archaeological Research Institute of Hebei Province. *Shang Sites at Taixi in Songcheng*, Beijing: Wenwu Press, 1985.
14 Beijing Archaeological Administrative Office. Shang and Zhou Bronzes Newly Collected in Beijing. In *Wenwu Ziliao Congkan*, II, Beijing: Wenwu Press, 1978.
15 Lin Yun. Further Research into the Relations Between the Shang Cultural Bronzes and Northern Area Bronzes. In *Collection of Archaeological Papers* I, Beijing: Wenwu Press, 1987.
16 Wu En. Northern Bronzes from Yin to the Beginning of Zhou. *Kaogu Xuebao* 1985(2): 135–156.
17 Erlitou Archaeological Team. Excavation Report of the Erlitou Site at Yanshi in Henan in the Fall of 1980. *Kaogu* 1983(3): 199–205.

18 see note 3, Figure 167.
19 *Wenwu Ziliao Congkan,* VII, p. 88, Beijing: Wenwu Press, 1983.
20 see note 15.
21 Guo Da-shun. On the Weiyingzi Phase. *Collection of Archaeological Papers,* I, Beijing: Wenwu Press, 1987.
22 Archaelolgical Team of the Liaoning Provincial Museum. Western Zhou Tombs and Ancient Sites at Weiyingzi in Chaoyang, Liaoning. *Kaogu* 1977(5): 306–309.
23 Archaeological Research Institute of Liaoning Province. Heshangou Tombs in Kezuo. *Liaohai Wenwu Congkan* 1989(2): 110–115.
24 see note 21.
    Beijing Archaeological Administrative Office. Shang Tombs Found at Pinggu in Beijing. *Wenwu* 1977(11): 1–8.
25 Liaoning Provincial Museum. Yin and Zhou Bronzes Unearthed at Beidongcun in Kezuo, Liaoning. *Kaogu* 1974(6): 364–372.
26. Liaoning Provincial Museum. Excavation Report of the Shuiquan Site in Jianping. *Liaohai Wenwu Congkan* 1986(2): 1–29.
27 *Selection of Relics Unearthed in Inner Mongolia,* Figure 37, Beijing: Wenwu Press, 1963.
28 Liaoning Provincial Museum. Test Excavation Report of the Dongshanzui Site at Sifendi in Chifeng, Inner Mongolia. *Kaogu* 1983(5): 420–429.
29 Bronze Dagger-axe of the Shang Dynasty with Continuous-Bead Pattern and a Long Handle Unearthed at Jinzhou. *Guangming Daily,* September 23, 1986.
30 Archaeology Society of Inner Mongolia Autonomous Region. Chronology and Related Problems of the Primitive Cultures in the Western Area of Inner Mongolia. *Wenwu* 1985(5): 77–78.
31 Yu Wei-chao. Discussions at the Forum on the Western Area Primitive Cultures in Inner Mongolia. *Inner Mongolian Archaeology,* 1986 (4): 6–10.
    Liu Guan-ming. On the Pottery Li of the Lower Xiajiadian Culture. In *Collected Papers on the Celebration of Xia Nai's Fifty Years in Archaeology,* Beijing: Wenwu Press, 1986, pp. 94–100.

7

BRONZE CULTURE IN JILIN PROVINCE

Liu Jing-wen

EDITOR'S INTRODUCTION

Sites which are considered to be Bronze Age in Jilin province do not necessarily contain bronze, but the pottery is different from that of the Neolithic, and the stone tools are more often ground than chipped or flaked. No dwellings have been excavated. Bronze-casting occurs later than in Liaoning.

This chapter divides Jilin into four regions. In the northwest, a region of grasslands, cemeteries provide the most information. Among the graves, double burials of a man and a woman are frequent, and secondary burials are sometimes found. Graves are earth-pits, either shallow or deep. Pottery and bone tools are common, with occasional small bronze artifacts, especially knives. The bronzes are distinctive, and appear to be locally made. *Li* tripods occur, connecting northwestern Jilin with sites in Liaoning province and beyond into the Zhongyuan. Tubular greenstone beads were found, as well as disk-shaped agate beads. Many fish bones suggest the importance of fishing in the subsistence base. The date is said to be Spring and Autumn period.

The south-central plains and hills are between the Songhua and Liao rivers. Houses have rock walls and central hearths, with either a stone paved floor or a burned floor. Stone cist burials are usual here, especially on high hills. Secondary and multiple burials are common. Necked jars, bone and stone beads, spindle whorls, and bronze rings are typical grave goods. Above-ground dolmens are also found. At Xingjiadian the female burials are primary, with secondary male burials placed beside the legs. Pedestal pottery, jars, bowls, bronze buttons, and bone beads and arrowheads were found as grave goods. Spindle whorls and net sinkers were also found, as well as pillow-shaped handle ends for bronze swords.

The Xituanshan culture occurs in central Jilin, near the cities of Jilin and Changchun. Some archaeologists designate the culture by the names of two types of tripods, the *"Ding-Li"* culture. Villages are located on low terraces above rivers. Houses have stone walls or plastered mud. Small

rectangular hearths were found. Most of the burials are of a single individual in a stone cist. Pottery jars, bowls, spindle whorls and net weights,
various stone tools, and white stone beads were the common grave goods.
Small bronze ornaments were buried on the person, and pig bones were
also included as grave offerings. Jar burial under the house floor was used
for infants, and a few earth-pit burials were also discovered under house
floors.

The ceramic inventory is rich and varied. Not only the *ding* and *li* for
which the region is known, but also plates on pedestals, jars with bead-
shaped or arched handles, large basins, and rice steamers were found. One
unusual vessel is a plain tripod. Bronze objects were made in two-part
molds. Several kinds of tools and weapons, as well as buttons and combs,
were included. The author believes that the Xituanshan culture extends
from the Western Zhou to the Warring States period in temporal span.

The eastern region includes the Yanbian Autonomous region, with
valleys between numerous mountain ridges. Several cemeteries have
been excavated as well as dwelling sites. Most of the burials are in stone
cists or stone-lined graves, but some plain earthen pits are found. Secondary burials wrapped in birch bark occur, as do double burials. Wooden
coffin burials and stone cists under earthen mounds are also reported.

Obsidian was still being used for flaked tools in this region. The usual
complement of stone tools was found, as well as jade pendants and tubular
jade beads. Stone projectile points were made in imitation of bronze ones.
Pierced disks with various features are common. The pottery includes
many complex shapes, and some polished red vessels. Carved bone
plaques include various motifs including human faces. Bronze objects
are few, but bronze slag shows that the artifacts were being locally
made. Cattle, sheep and goat bones, along with wild species such as
deer and fox, were found on the house floors.

S. M. N.

Jilin province covers an area of 180,000km^2. To the east is Siberia and to
the southeast across the Tumen and Yalu rivers lies Korea. In this beautiful
and richly endowed region, early in the late Paleolithic, the ancestors of the
Chinese already resided and began to till the land. They have left many
artifacts and relics (Figure 7.1).

Over the last forty years, archaeologists have made many field surveys
and excavations, and obtained abundant data. This chapter divides the
discoveries into four regions: the northwest, the south-central plains and
hills, the central plains and hills, and the eastern region.

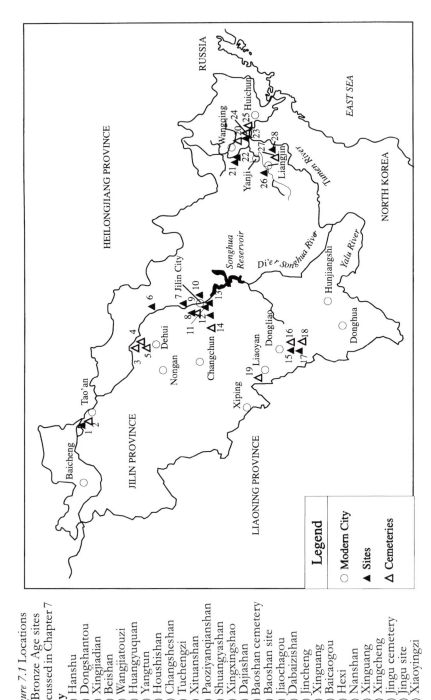

Figure 7.1 Locations
of Bronze Age sites
discussed in Chapter 7

Key
1) Hanshu
2) Dongshantou
3) Xingjiadian
4) Beishan
5) Wangjiatouzi
6) Huangyuquan
7) Yangtun
8) Houshishan
9) Changsheshan
10) Tuchengzi
11) Xituanshan
12) Paoziyanqianshan
13) Shuangyashan
14) Xingxingshao
15) Dajiashan
16) Baoshan cemetery
17) Baoshan site
18) Jiaochagou
19) Dabaizishan
20) Jincheng
21) Xinguang
22) Baicaogou
23) Hexi
24) Nanshan
25) Xinguang
26) Xingcheng
27) Jingu cemetery
28) Jingu site
29) Xiaoyingzi

THE NORTHWEST REGION

The northwest region of Jilin province is intersected by the Tao'er river valley, and bordered by the Songhua and Nen rivers. This area is mainly grassland with saline-alkaline sands. Few bronze culture sites in this area have been excavated. Exceptions are Dongshantou of Da'an county where some burials were excavated,[1] and at Da'an Hanshu.[2] However, survey data supply further information, and there are sufficient data to show that the bronze culture of the northwest region has striking regional features (Figure 7.2).

There are two kinds of burials – shallow and deep earth-pit burials. An example of a shallow grave is Dongshantou 60M2. The plan of the burial is rectangular, 2.2 m long, 1.15 m wide and 0.33 m deep. It contained a male and a female, both extended and supine, oriented northwest. Hanshu M102 is an example of a deeper vertical pit grave. It has only a few bones in the upper layer, but in the lower layer one man and two women were reburied. The burial objects in the two kinds of burials are identical. Pottery and bone objects are more common than bronze objects.

So far dwellings from the Bronze Age have not been excavated in Jilin province. But at Baijinbao in Zhaoyan, Heilongjiang province,[3] which is just across the river and belongs to the same culture, several houses have been excavated [see Chapter 8].

The pottery of this culture was fired at high temperature. It is all hand-made red pottery, some tempered with sand. There are varieties of patterns including composite comb patterns, fine cord marks, raised patterns, and rocker-stamped patterns. The shapes of the vessels include pots, necked jars, cups, drinking-cups, and bottles. There are also legs of *li* tripods with cord marks. The open-mouthed cylindrical pot is decorated with geometric designs consisting of comb pattern and incised patterns. Another type of pot is short, with globular walls, and geometrical patterns consisting of comb-dots. Necked jars are either buff or red. The buff pottery has criss-cross fine cord marks on the outside. Most of them have open mouths and globular walls.

Two kinds of bowl can be distinguished. One is greyish-yellow, with high everted sides and a flat base. It may be painted in red. The other kind is dark red, with wide mouth, tall sides and flat base. The cups are all plain, with straight slanting sides.

In this culture, the abundant bone tools are mainly awls, needles, and bone tubes. There are also ornaments made of tooth or shell, and shell daggers. Most awls were manufactured from animal long-bones, and polished. There are round and triangular shapes. One arrowhead was polished into an almost flat triangle. Needles are slender and round, with a tiny hole at one end.

Bronze artifacts are mostly small tools and ornaments, such as knives.

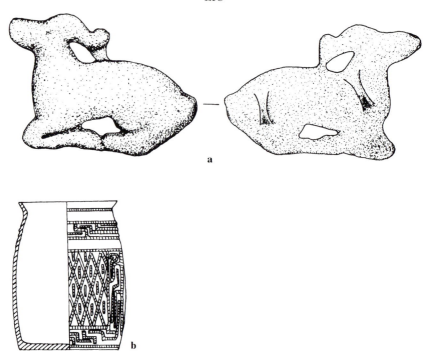

Figure 7.2 Bronze Age findings from the northwestern area: a) animal-shaped bronze plaque; b) pottery vessel with incised geometric pattern

Tubular beads of sea-green glauconite were found. Agate beads were made in two shapes, cylindrical and disk-like, and both were symmetrically pierced in the middle.

Pottery *li* decorated with cord marks began to appear as the result of influence from the Central Plains. However, the differences between the two regions are quite obvious. In Jilin, the unique pottery was mostly decorated with comb patterns and various geometric designs made of incised bands, diamonds, squares, triangles, etc. These ceramics are very delicate, indicating the advanced techniques of the artisans. There are few bronze objects, and most of them are small items such as knives or buttons, but their particular characteristics suggest that they are local products. This culture had certainly entered the Bronze Age. Given the presence of its advanced bone and shell tools, as well as fish bones and scales, and the scarcity of stone tools, it seems that, although there was farming, fishing played the most important role in the economy.

Regarding the burials, most of them are male/female burials or a male with two females buried in one grave. Thus monogamy and polygamy have begun to appear.[4] The main cultural features of cylindrical pots and long-necked jars decorated with geometrical comb patterns, and *li* covered with cord marks, are identical to the Baijinbao culture. The C14 date for Baijinbao is 2790 ± 65 [ZK–0324], and for Hanshu II, it is 2380 ± 100 [BK 78001]. Thus, this culture is earlier than Hanshu II and close to Baijinbao. The time is around Spring and Autumn to the Warring States period.

THE SOUTH-CENTRAL PLAINS AND HILLS

In recent years, some surveys and excavations in the central plains and southern hilly regions of Jilin province have been made. Hand-coiled open-mouthed pots, long-necked jars, and ring-footed *dou* with a trumpet opening made of sandy brown and yellowish-brown pottery represent a new type of bronze culture (Figure 7.3). Excavated sites include the Baoshan site[5] and the Dajiashan site[6] both in Dongfeng county; Xingjiadian cemetery in Nongan county;[7] Wangjiatuozi burials in Dehui county,[8] and others.

This region is located in the Song-Liao Plain, which has low hills in the south. Several rivers pass through this area. The soil is rich, with sufficient water, which is ideal for farming and herding.

House floors were excavated at Baoshan and Dajiashan in the Dongfeng hilly region. One type of house floor is a rectangular shallow pit, covering an average area of $25m^2$. The walls were built with uneven rocks and the floor was burned. In most houses a round or rectangular hearth about 20 cm in diameter was built in the center. No entrance was found for most houses, nor was there any sign of post holes. A retaining wall was built, about 20–50 cm high. Another type has a stone-paved floor, but the rest of the features are the same.

Stone cist burials are more common than earth-pit burials. Cist burials are mostly found at the top of relatively high hills. A stone slab was placed at the bottom and the burial was covered by another, giant one. One type was built with thick and heavy slabs in rectangular shape at the sides; for example, Dongliao Gaogu M2, in which four persons were given a secondary burial.[9] The burial objects include necked jars, bronze rings, and bone beads. One subrectangular type was built with stone slabs which were chipped into neat shapes. At Dongliao county, Dadingzishan M3,[10] there were multiple secondary burials. The burial objects were located in the middle and at both ends of the grave. They include stone weights, stone beads, pottery jars, and spindle whorls. The third type of stone burial is the dolmen. Most dolmens have three upright slabs supporting one slab cover. No excavations of this kind of burial have occurred.

Earth-pit burials are rectangular, vertical graves. There are no burial objects and they are covered with dirt. This type of burial is mostly found in the plains. Some of them are individual primary burials such as Dehui

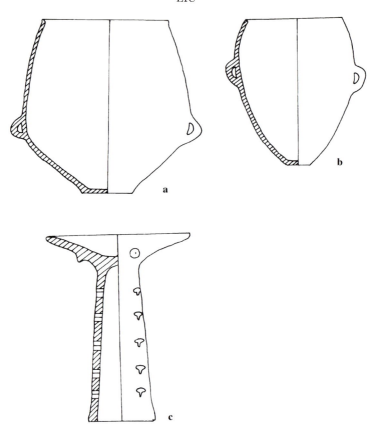

Figure 7.3 Bronze Age pottery from the central-south plains and hills, Jilin province: a) pot with open mouth (M5: 2 at cemetery in Xingjiadian; b) tall pot (M6: 1 at cemetery in Xingjiadian); c) stemmed cup (M1: 2 at cemetery in Dehui)

cemetery M2;[11] others have primary and secondary burials together, such as Nongan Xingjiadian M13. Female burials are primary supine burials with extended limbs; male burials are secondary and the bones are placed to the side of females' legs. Some multiple burials occurred, in which from two to five primary burials were lying on the back with extended limbs. In some cases, below the feet of the primary skeleton, one body or several bodies were buried; for example, at Nongan Xingjiadian M26. Among these burials, a few bodies were cremated, e.g. Xingjiadian M24. The main burial objects include jars, pedestals, bowls, bronze buttons, bone beads, and bone arrowheads. Most pottery vessels were placed above the head, but a few were placed below the feet or along the legs. Ornaments were mainly on the chest.

Many pottery vessels were excavated. Most of the pottery vessels are high-fired and hand-made. They are sandy brown, yellow-brown and grey-

212

brown, plain but well polished.[12] A few are decorated with punctates. The shapes include pots, jars, bowls, pedestals, cups, and spindle whorls. Tall vessels with extended mouths were found in various sizes. The pottery of this culture has a very attractive appearance. Vessels such as big-mouthed tall pots, high pedestal vessels, wide-mouthed and slanting-walled cups and trumpet-shaped pedestals are distinctly regional features. In particular, engravings on the handles of high ring-footed cups are rarely seen elsewhere, except at Dawenkou in Shandong province, which was much earlier.

There are various shapes of spindle whorls and pottery net weights with two holes. Very few stone tools have been unearthed so far. Mainly there are pillow-shaped handle ends for bronze swords, stone beads, turquoise beads, and jade pendants. Bone objects are only arrowheads, awls, and tusk ornaments. Only two kinds of bronze objects were found, buttons and rings.

During our research we have discovered that the pottery and vessels in the southern part of this hilly region include bowls and jars with rocker-stamped patterns under the rim. However, the jars located in the northern regions are tall and varied. The tall slender jars with small bases are only found in the north. The arched vertical handles are more advanced. However, the long-necked jars and the rocker-stamped oval patterns which are found in the south hilly regions are rarely seen in the north. Is this a difference of style within the same culture? A difference of time period? Due to the limited work which has been done, it is not clear. The problem needs to be explored further.

In terms of chronology, a C14 date for Nongan Xingjiadian cemetery burials is 2165 ± 75 [WB 87–18], so we argue it lasted from the Early Spring and Autumn to the Middle Warring States periods.

THE CENTRAL HILLS AND PLAINS

Over the vast hilly regions of central Jilin, as well as some of the adjacent flat regions, there is a culture called *"Ding-Li"* [two kinds of tripod cooking vessels] (Figure 7.4). Chinese archaeologists also call this the Xituanshan culture. The work of many years shows that the distribution of this culture begins in the east and south at the Zhangguangcai and Wei mountains. It terminates in the west at the valley of the Huifa river, and ends in the north at the upper reach of the Lalin river, with especially dense distribution over the middle to upper reaches of the Di'er Songhua river.

In this region, in addition to several large-scale surveys, a number of huge excavations took place. The main ones include the excavations of Xituanshan tomb clusters in the suburbs of Jilin city,[13] the Tuchengzi site and cemetery north of the river in Jilin city,[14] Changsheshan in Jilin city,[15] Saodagou cemetery in the suburbs of Jilin city,[16] Xingxingshao cemetery

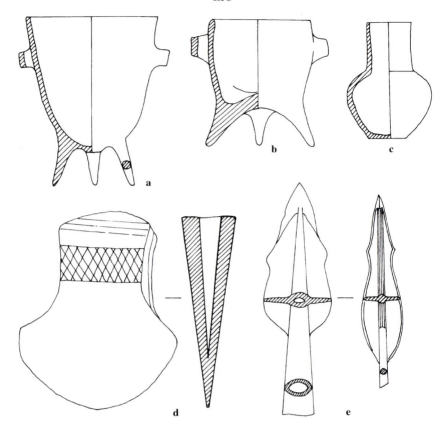

Figure 7.4 Bronze Age artifacts from the central hills and plains area: a) *ding* tripod (excavated from T1 at Yangtun); b) *li* (79 II T2 3: 5 at Houshishan); c) jar (79 M17: 5 at Houshishan; d) bronze axe (57 F4: 25 at Changsheshan); e) bronze spearhead (57 F2: 21 at Changsheshan); f) bronze sword (AM19 at Xingxingshao)

in Yongji county,[17] Houshishan site and cemetery in the suburbs of Jilin city,[18] and Yangtun in Yongji county.[19] Other sites have also been excavated.[20,21,22,23,24] Many artifacts were found.

The houses of early Xituanshan culture are mostly located on the sunny slopes of low hills near a water source. Terraces of 7–40 m long by 5–10 m wide were made along the slope, upon which semi-subterranean houses were constructed. The houses are mainly in two shapes: sub-rectangular, which is common, and oval, which is rare. They are 4–8 m long, 3–7 m wide and 0.5–1.2 m deep. Three types of buildings were erected. The first used weathered rocks or hard native soil as the walls. Some of the walls were plastered with a layer of mud and then fired, for example, Houshishan 80 II F1. The second type is built with a combination of stones and weathered rocks, such as Changsheshan 62 F3. The third type is built solely with stones, such as Changsheshan 62 F1. On the floors of these houses small rectangular hearths of 20–90 cm long and 15–60 cm wide were placed. The floors are mostly baked, and the entrance was dug into the slope. At a later time, when people were moving to live on the terraces nearer the water source, the houses were sub-rectangular and semi-subterranean, with a few irregular in shape. The floor was baked and the hearth was sub-rectangular. There are round post holes which are distributed without pattern. The walls are dirt. The house usually covers an area of 25–40 m^2.

About five hundred burials of the Xituanshan culture have been excavated. Most of them are single burials, and the majority of the graves are stone cists. In most burials the head is directed toward the top of the hill, although a few were buried horizontally across the slope. There are several kinds of stone cist burials. The first is built with slabs placed diagonally into rectangular or trapezoidal shapes, and then covered with a slab on the top. The second type is built with irregular stones into either a rectangular or a trapezoidal grave and covered with a slab. In both these types a rectangular frame was plastered with clay, and some have small pits attached to the foot. Most burials are single and supine with extended limbs. The burial goods include pottery, many stone tools, and some bone and bronze objects. The pottery objects include necked jars, pots, bowls, spindle whorls, and net weights. Stone objects include mostly production tools such as axes, adzes, knives, and arrowheads, but there are also white-stone beads. The position of the burial objects falls into a pattern. In general pottery vessels are found at the foot or in the attached pit; stone production tools range from below the arms down to the foot. Bronze objects were placed above the arms, with various ornaments at the wearing positions. The burial objects vary with the sex. Basically farming/hunting tools were found in male graves, while spindle whorls, stone knives and ornaments occurred with females. There are pig bones and teeth on most grave lids and in some pottery vessels.

Simplified stone cist burials have only a few stone slabs or stones erected at the head, foot, or side. Some have cover stones, but others do not, and the rest of the grave is simply dirt walls. The burial itself is almost the same as the two types described above. A few grave goods are out of place. Stone production tools are placed at the head, and others at the feet, while no pig bones were found.

Very few earth-pit burials were found. Most of them were under a house floor or nearby. All were single and supine with extended limbs. The burial objects were only net weights, bronze spearheads, and ornaments.

Jar burials also occur rarely. They were found under floors of houses. The burials use footless *ding*, bottomless urns or jars, and mostly they were used for children. No burial objects were found in them.

The pottery includes *ding* [vessels with three or four solid legs], *li* [baggy tripods], necked jars, pots, bowls, basins, cups, and *dou* [pedestal vessels] made by coiling. Most are plain sandy-brown or dark-brown pottery, a few are red-brown. Spindle whorls, net weights, disks, animal figurines, and axe-shaped objects were also made of clay. The objects are neatly made and well polished.

Many *ding* were unearthed, of which the largest is 40 cm and the smallest 10 cm high. Most have symmetrical arched or bead-shaped handles. Most of the legs are conical, but a few are square, hexagonal, or paw-shaped.

Necked jars can be divided into three types. Type I has an open mouth and symmetrical vertical handles. Type II vessels have long necks and globular walls. Type III includes large vessels with long, straight necks, and arched handles placed low on the sides. Other jars include tall and short vessels. Bowls have everted mouths, slanting straight walls and/or vertical straight walls. Most of them have bead-shaped or arched handles below the rims. Another type of bowl has a contracted mouth with horizontal bead-shaped or arched handles. Cups are open-mouthed with straight slanting walls, with one arched handle, or they are cylindrical with a pointed rim, everted mouth, and straight walls. Yet another type has a pointed rim, wide mouth, slightly bulging walls, and symmetrical handles below the rim.

Dou include plates of various shapes on trumpet-shaped stands. Basins have wide mouths and slanting straight walls, like large bowls. Rice steamers have a single hole, with straight slanting walls, like a bowl. Spindle whorls are found in various forms, some are disk- or bead-shaped, others are hemispheres or truncated cones.

A number of stone objects were unearthed, most of which are polished all over. The main types include axes, adzes, knives, sickles, hoes, hammers, spearheads, arrowheads, awls, grinding slabs, grinding stones, pestles, net weights, jade weights, tubular jade beads, agate beads, and white tubular beads.

The axes can be divided into two main types. Slab-shaped axes are rectangular, while club-shaped axes are long, chipped with only the blade area polished. The cross-section is oval. Adzes are mostly small and polished all over. Small stone knives were made either in semi-lunar shape, with the wide side polished to be the handle, or with the blade ridge slightly curved and the handle narrow and thick. Arrowheads are common. There are three main types: conical, stemless, and imitation bronze arrowheads.

Bronze objects are rare, but they are among the most attractive objects in the Xituanshan culture. They were made in two-part molds. The shapes include axes, knives, swords, spears, arrowheads, fish hooks, buttons, and gilded bronze combs. The axes are fan-shaped with decorations such as slanting net patterns on the upper part, or they have long bodies, also decorated with a net pattern. A few are short and wide, with straight sides.

Bronze knives are many and varied. There are no handles, but one, two, or three round holes were cast at the end for hafting.

Bone objects are few, only including awls, knife-handles, and daggers. Boar tusk ornaments also occur.

Since the Xituanshan culture has well-developed *ding* and *li*, and bronze knives, axes, swords, and spears, as well as stone imitations of bronze spears, swords, and arrowheads, there is no doubt it was deeply influenced by the advanced *Ding/Li* culture in the Central Plain, particularly the Shang and Zhou advanced bronze cultures. It was also influenced by its surrounding advanced bronze cultures. However, the unique feature of this culture – the plain tripod vessel – is not like any surrounding bronze culture. Also, the various necked jars are rare in other northern bronze cultures. There are many farming tools, such as stone axes, adzes, knives, and sickles, which are not found in surrounding cultures. Although bronze objects are not as developed as those of Shang and Zhou, many bronze production tools such as axes, knives, swords, spears, and arrowheads are found. Finally, the bone objects in this culture are far less developed than those of the previously discussed cultures of Jilin province.

The Xituanshan culture has regional features and has undergone a long process of development. In terms of the objects themselves, the stone arrowheads in the early phase are round or rectangular; chipped stone objects were also found. In the middle phase, very few conical arrowheads are seen, being replaced by ones that imitate bronze. In terms of pottery objects, the necked jars in the early phase are relatively short, and most of them have vertical handles, with a big flat base. In the middle phase, the neck became longer and straighter, the base became smaller, and horizontal handles were attached. Bronze objects were few in the early phase, and increased in the middle phase. A C14 date from Xingxingshao (78 CM21) is 3055 ± 100 [ZK–0679]. The date from the middle phase of Yangtun is 2590 ± 70 [WB 81–08], but the one from a later period at Yangtun is 2165 ± 75 [ZK–0093]. We argue that the beginning date of Xituanshan culture is Western Zhou, and the ending is Late Warring States.

In the early Xituanshan culture, males are buried with stone axes, stone arrowheads and other production tools, and females with spindle whorls but without stone arrowheads. It seems that at that time farming and fishing had become the dominant economic activities for men, while women produced textiles and pottery. The abundant stone tools and pottery spindle whorls indicate that pottery-making, stone-tool-making, and textiles had become independent handicraft industries. This division of labor greatly facilitated the development of production. Consequently, surplus products began to appear, and gradually there came to be a division between rich and poor. This trend was obvious in the burials. For example, at Houshishan, some stone slab graves are large and neat with dozens or even hundreds of burial objects; others are barely large enough to bury the body, and have few burial objects, or even nothing at all. The size of buildings is another indicator. At this time, the concept of rich and poor might not be sufficient to describe the existing conditions, but some form of class conflict had begun to exist.

Considering the abundant farming tools such as stone axes, adzes, stone knives and some hoes, sickles, bronze axes, and bronze knives, the large-scale cemeteries and solid houses as well as crops such as millet and soy beans, the people of this culture were living a sedentary farming life. Considering the number of arrowheads, spears, and net weights, fishing and hunting were also an important supplement to the economy of the Xituanshan people.

THE EASTERN REGION

The eastern region refers to the vast area east of the Zhangguangcai mountains and the Tumen river in the eastern part of Jilin province. It also includes mountainous regions such as Longgang, Laoling, etc. In this region, mountains and ridges follow one another closely, except where the Tumen river forms a vast, rich basin. Around the Tumen basin many archaeological sites are located, especially from the Bronze Age.

Since 1938 when Fujita Ryosaku excavated the Xiaoyingzi graves in Yanji,[25] several more investigations and excavations have taken place. The main excavations include that of Baicaogou in Wangqing county;[26] Nanshan dwelling site and graves at Jingu reservoir in Yanji;[27] Wangqing Jincheng tombs;[28] Bronze Age houses at the Xingcheng site in Helong county;[29] the Nanshan site and Xinxingdong burials at Liangshui Yinghua village in Huichun city;[30] Xibeishan cemetery at Liangshuihe in Huichun city,[31] and others. Over 30 houses and 200 burials of the Bronze Age have been excavated. These sites are mostly located on the sunny slopes of low hills.

Houses are densely distributed. They are subterranean and subrectangular, with three kinds of construction. The first is small and shallow; for example, several houses found at Nanshan are only 10–16m^2, and the remaining height is 0.2–0.5 m. The second type is larger with walls built into the slope. The area covers around 25–35m^2, and the remaining wall is 0.20–1.10 m high. The third kind is deepest and largest, up to 60m^2. The houses are all densely distributed, with patterned post holes in the floor, and round or oval fireplaces at the center. The dwelling floor is plastered smooth and the walls are dug into the raw dirt. No entrance is discernible and around the dwelling site no ash-pits were found.

The graves are also dense. Some overlap or break into another burial, and some grave clusters can be subdivided into small groups, such as at Xiaoyingzi cemetery. Many stone cist burials were found, using unworked stone. Three types can be distinguished, as follows.

218

First, stone slab graves: Slabs were placed on the rectangular pit bottom, and then, using different sizes of slabs diagonally, a rectangular stone cist was built and covered with a large slab. Some graves contained several burials, with slabs erected in the middle to separate them. Some make use of the native rock for one side, while the other three sides were built with slabs. The stone cists are 150–170 cm long, 40–60 cm wide, and 25–30 cm tall. Most are single burials, but some are double burials, and a few contain multiple secondary burials. The primary burials are supine with extended limbs. Burial goods are abundant, especially pottery and stone artifacts, but also some bone objects and bronze ornaments. Pottery vessels were often placed above the head or below the feet, the production tools below the feet, hands or armpits, and the ornaments on the body.

Second, stone-built graves: The bottom of the grave was paved with stones, the four sides were built with stones in a rectangle, and the whole was covered with a large slab on the top. Some tombs share one cover. The stone grave is usually 180–210 cm long and 50–170 cm wide. Most of them do not have any bones left, but two burials could be distinguished at Chuankou site[32] as single and supine with extended limbs. In one grave, burned birch bark and burned bones were found, indicating the practice of cremation. The types of burial objects and their positions are almost identical to those above.

Third, simplified stone cists: Only one side of the grave is lined with a few slabs or stones and the other walls are earth. These are found at Jingu cemetery.

Earthen pits covered with stones are the most common type of earth-pit burials. The rectangular grave is sealed at the top with stones or pebbles. The pit is 170–250 cm long, 60–90 cm wide, and 20–30 cm deep. There are various kinds of burials; single or double primary burials lying on the back with extended limbs, and secondary burials with several bodies with birch-bark wrappings which were cremated. The placement of burial objects does not fall into a pattern, some are found at the head, the foot or the waist, others within the earth fill.

Stone pits with earthen mounds are fewer in number, and were only found at the Huichun cemetery. The grave is rectangular, built with weathered rocks and covered with dirt. The sizes of the graves, burial types and burial objects are quite similar to the third type of stone grave.

Earthen graves with wooden coffins were found only at Jingu cemetery. In a rectangular vertical pit, the four sides and the cover were built with wooden planks. The size, the type of tomb and the places of the burial objects are similar to the third kind of stone graves.

Stone tools are very well made, and most of the stone tools are polished except flaked obsidian objects. The main artifacts include axes, adzes, knives, chisels, hoes, sickles, spades, spears, daggers, pointed objects, ring-shaped objects, arrowheads, spindle whorls, net weights, grinding slabs, grinding stones, disk-shaped objects, stone balls, obsidian tools, jade pendants, stone tubes, and tubular jade beads.

There are many axes in various shapes. The adzes are small and polished all over. Few knives were unearthed, but at nearly every site they are found only in the graves. They are polished all over, with one or two holes. Many arrowheads were unearthed. Some are flaked from obsidian, with a few made from shale. Most of them have indented bases and triangular bodies, with a few shaped like a willow-leaf. Another type is polished with a flat stem, and there are also hexagonal examples.

Circular stone objects with holes in the center are found at almost every site and burial. One kind is thick in the middle, but with a sharp polished edge, another has a raised rim on one side while the other side is polished flat.

Pendant ornaments include objects of nephrite and jadeite. Most are round with a round hole. In addition, there are stone and jade beads, mostly polished and tubular.

The pottery is hand-made, sandy brown or red-brown and fired at high temperature. There are a few red-slipped vessels. They are plain but polished. Those with patterns include saw-tooth designs, incised designs, and rocker-stamped dots. The vessels include jars, urns, bowls, basins, pedestals, cups, and spindle whorls. Some of the jars have handles and decorative patterns around the upper wall. Many bowls were unearthed, some with handles and a pseudo ring-foot. Cups are common. One type has an everted mouth, slanting walls and a relatively high pseudo ring-foot, another has a straight mouth and slightly bulging walls. There is also a cylindrical type with straight walls and a flat base.

Bone tools were very finely made, with many shapes including swords, spears, arrowheads, awls, chisels, knives, needles, spindle whorls, daggers, combs, carved plaques, bone containers, beads, tusk ornaments, and shell beads. Some of the polished bone plaques have human faces carved on them. Other bone plaques are carved with parallel lines or net lines. The patterns are beautiful and finely executed. Bone containers are made of bird bones, with one end cut off. Animal long-bones are incised with parallel lines or saw-tooth designs. There is one oracle bone from Xinanlu which must be mentioned. It is made of sheep (or goat) shoulder blade, with no inscriptions on it.

Few bronze objects were found. Bronze buttons have round and bulging fronts, and the back has a horizontal ridge. Some have radiating lines on the front side. There are also a few bronze ornaments, either rectangular or globular.

In spite of the fact that bronze objects are rare in this culture, bronze slag was found. In addition, imitation bronze stone spears, stone arrowheads, and bone swords were found. This indicates that this culture had entered the Bronze Age. This culture also has strong regional features. The pottery includes plain jars, urns, bowls, cups, and pedestals. The cylindrical pots, the big urns and wide-mouthed shallow plate pedestals are rarely seen in other cultures. Obsidian spears and arrowheads were popular in the early period, and the willow-leaf or hexagonal stemmed or stemless stone spears are very characteristic of this culture. Small stone axes and circular stone tools are very rare in other bronze cultures, and the conical stone arrowhead of 10 cm or longer and the long pointed tools are the products of only this culture. The huge bone swords, carved bone plaques, and bone containers reflect the ability of the artisans in this culture. We call this Xingcheng culture (Figure 7.5).

Considering the change in the objects and burial customs, this culture underwent a long developmental process. Obsidian tools were quite common during the early period, and with the development of productivity, they were replaced by even harder polished stone tools. Bone tools also followed the usual pattern from large practical tools to smaller ornaments. In terms of the pottery, those with double rims or saw-tooth designs outside the rim were replaced by cylindrical vessels. The slanting wall bowls of the early period were gradually becoming pseudo ring-footed and ring-footed bowls after the middle period, when short pedestals began to appear. In the later periods, the pedestal stands became even higher.

C14 dates indicate that Jingu is 3270 ± 155 [ZK–0675] and Xingcheng is 3585 ± 115 (calibrated) [ZK–2252]. Thus, we think that Xingcheng culture is 3500 BP at the earliest and 2300 BP at the latest.

To speak of the economy in both early and late periods, there were great numbers of stone arrowheads, stone spears, pointed tools, bone daggers, bone spears, and other hunting tools. On the house floors several kinds of animal bones such as sheep or goat, deer, and fox were found. In the burials there were stone axes, knives, adzes, a few hoes, sickles, and many grinding stones, slabs, and pottery. As indicated by the construction of many houses, agriculture had developed and people were leading a stable and sedentary life. In addition, the appearance of pottery, stone and bone spindle whorls, as well as bone awls and needles, shows that this culture had a textile industry. Moreover, the discovery of bones of ox and sheep indicates the existence of animal husbandry.

Although the Xingcheng culture has definite and unique features, and was affected very little by outside factors, it is probable that in some aspects other advanced cultures impacted upon it, as shown by the existence of ring-footed bowls and pedestals, the appearance of imitation bronze stone spears, and bronze arrowheads. They were all influenced by the advanced Shang and Zhou bronze cultures in the Central Plain. In its distribution, the bronze cultures of Odong,[33] Hogupdong,[34] and Sopohang[35] on the south side of the Tumen river in Korea can be categorized as Xingcheng culture.

(Translated by Mingming Shan)

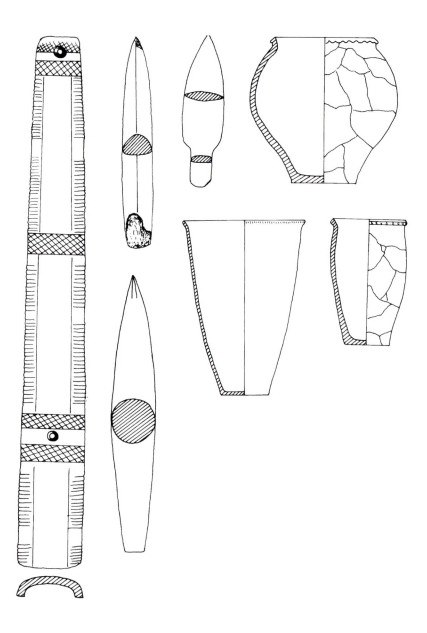

Figure 7.5 Bronze Age discoveries from the eastern mountain area

NOTES

1 Jilin Provincial Museum. Excavation of Ancient Tombs at Dongshantou in Da'an, Jilin. *Kaogu* 1961(8): 407–410.
  Zhang Zhong-pei. Archaeological Survey in the Bai-cheng Area. *Jilin University Social Science Journal* 1963(1): 79–81.
2 Archaeological Section of the History Department of Jilin University and Archaeological Team of the Jilin Provincial Museum. Main Results of the Excavation at the Hanshu Site in Da'an. *Dongbei Kaogu Yu Lishi* 1982(1): 136–140.
3 Archaeological Team of Heilongjiang Province. First Excavation of the Baijinbao Site at Zhaoyan in Heilongjiang. *Kaogu* 1980(4): 311–324.
4 Engels, Friedrich, *The Origin of the Family, Private Property, and the State*, Beijing: People's Press, 1975, p. 63.
5 Archaeological Institute of Jilin Province, Dongfeng County Cultural Center. Excavation Report of the Baoshan Site at Dongfeng, Jilin (unpublished).
6 Archaeological Institute of Jilin Province, Dongfeng County Cultural Center. Excavation Report of the Dajiashan Site at Dongfeng, Jilin (unpublished).
7 Archaeological Institute of Jilin Province. Excavation Report of the Beishan Burials at Xingjiadian in Nongan, Jilin. *Kaogu* 1989(4): 300–309.
8 Liu Hong-yu. Ancient Relics Found at Wangjiatuozi and Beiling in Dehui, Jilin. *Beifang Wenwu* 1985(1): 39–41.
  Archaeological Institute of Jilin Province. Excavation Report of the Beiling Graves at Dehui, Jilin. *Kaogu* 1993(7): 578–601.
9 Archaeological Annals Society of Jilin Province. *Archaeological Annals of Liaoyuan City*, p. 38 (restricted publication).
10 Archaeological Annals Society of Jilin Province. *Dongliao County Archaeological Annals*, pp.160–163 (restricted publication).
11 Jin Yudong. Excavation Report of the Stone Cist Cemetery at Dongfeng, Jilin. *Liaohai Wenwu Xuegan* 1991(2): 12–22.
12 ibid.
13 Northeast Archaeological Excavation Group. Excavation Report of the Stone Coffin Graves at Xituanshan, Jilin. *Kaogu Xuebao* 1964(1): 29–49.
14 Jilin Provincial Museum. Tuchengzi Ancient Cultural Remains and Stone Coffin Tombs at Jiangbei in Jilin. *Kaogu Xuebao* 1957(1): 43–52.
15 Jilin Provincial Archaeological Team. Excavation of the Changsheshan Site in Jilin. *Kaogu* 1980(2): 123–134.
16 Duan Yi-ping, Li Lian, and Xu Guang-hui. Excavation Report of the Stone Coffin Tombs at Saodagou, Jilin City. *Kaogu* 1985(10): 885–900.
17 Jilin City Museum and Yongji County Cultural Center. Third Excavation of the Xingxingshao Stone Coffin Tombs at Yongji, Jilin. *Collected Archaeological Papers*, Vol.3, pp. 109–125, Jilin City, 1990.
18 Short-term Archaeological Training Course of the Jilin Area, 1980. Excavation Report of the Houshishan Site. *Kaogu* 1980(2): 135–141.
  Jilin Provincial Archaeological Research Team. The Second Excavation at the Houshishan Site and Cemetery in Jilin City. *Kaogu Xuebao* 1993(3): 331–349.
19 Liu Zhen-hua. Test Excavation Report of the Yangtun Site in Yongji. *Wenwu* 1973(8): 63–68.
  Jilin Provincial Archaeological Team, Jilin City Museum, and Yongji County Cultural Center. Third Excavation of the Yangtun Site at Yongji. *Kaogu Xiegan* 1993(7): 23–50.

Jilin City Museum. Report on the Yangtun Site at Yongji, Jilin. *Kaogu Xiegan* 1993(5): 120–151.

20 Liu Fa-xiang. Excavation Report of the Neolithic Stone Coffin Graves at Wangqitun in Yongji County, Jilin Province. *Kaogu* 1960(7): 27–30.

21 Jilin Provincial Archaeological Team. Excavation Report of the Zhushan Site at Huangyuquan in Shulan, Jilin Province. *Kaogu* 1985(4): 336–348.

22 Zhang Zhong-pei. Excavation Report of the Liangbanshan Site in Jilin. *Kaogu* 1964(1): 6–12.

23 Jilin City Museum's collected papers.

24 Jilin Provincial Archaeological Team. Xiaoxishan Stone Coffin Graves at Panshi in Jilin. *Kaogu* 1984(1): 51–58.

25 Fujita Ryosaku. Survey Report of the Xiaoyingzi Site at Yanji. Tokyo, 1942.

26 Wang Ya-zhou. Excavation Report of the Baicaogou Site at Wangqing, Jilin. *Kaogu* 1961(8): 411–422.

27 Yanbian Korean Autonomous Region Museum. Excavation Report of the Jingu Ancient Tombs at Dexing in Yanji. *Dongbei Kaogu Yu Lishi* 1982(1): 191–199.
Yanbian Korean Nationality Autonomous State Museum. Test Excavation Report of the Nanshan Site at Jingu Reservoir. *Museum Study* 1985(3): 69–72 (restricted publication).

28 Archaeological Institute of Jilin Province. Excavation Report of Jincheng Ancient Tombs at Wangqing in Jilin. *Kaogu* 1986(2): 125–131.

29 Archaeological Institute of Jilin Province, Yanbian Korean Nationality Autonomous State Museum, and Helong County Archaeological Administrative Center. Excavation Report of the Jilin Helong County Xingcheng Sites (unpublished).

30 Archaeological Institute of Jilin Province. Excavation Report of the Nanshan Site and Cemetery at Yinghua in Huichun, Jilin. *Kaogu* 1993(8): 701–708.
Archaeological Institute of Jilin Province, and Yanbian Korean Autonomous Region Archaeology Administrative Center. Excavation Report of the Xinxingdong Graves at Huichun, Jilin. *Beifang Wenwu* 1992(1): 3–9.

31 Archaeological Institute of Jilin Province, Yanbian Korean Nationality Autonomous State Archaeology Administrative Center, and Huichun City Archaeology Administrative Center. Excavation Report of the Beishan Cemetery at Hexi Village, Huichun City in Jilin (unpublished).

32 Based on data of the Archaeological Institute of Jilin Province.

33 Archaeological Institute of the Social Sciences Academy of the Democratic People's Republic of Korea. *Excavation Report of the Prehistoric Remains at Odong in Hoeryong*, Pyongyang: 1960.

34 Hwang Ki-dok. Excavation Report of the Prehistoric Site at Musan Pomuigusok. *Kogo Minsok* 1975(6): 124–226.

35 Kim Yong-gan and So Guk-tae. Excavation Report of the Prehistoric Site of Sopohang. *Kogo Minsok* 1972(4): 31–45.

8

THE BRONZE AGE OF THE SONG-NEN PLAIN

Tan Ying-jie, Sun Xiu-ren, Zhao Hong-guang, and Gan Zhi-geng

EDITOR'S INTRODUCTION

In this final chapter the Heilongjiang team presents the discoveries of the Bronze Age in Heilongjiang in the southeastern part of the province. They have chosen this area because evidence of bronze in the rest of the province is scarce. However, many of the sites with bronze also have iron, and may be as late as the Warring States period. The sites are found where the Songhua [Sungari] river and the Nenjiang [Nonni river] come together, and along both rivers. This is the best agricultural land in the province. It is in some sense a continuation of the Liao region, as the drainages are separated by only low hills, and the entire area can be perceived as one vast plain.

The Baijinbao culture has the earliest bronze in the region. *Li* are found in this area as well as in Jilin and Liaoning. Three layers were identified in the site. The lowest level was dated at about 1000 BCE.

The second stage of the Hanshu culture, called here Hanshu II, follows Baijinbao in the same locations. It still includes stone tools as well as sandstone molds for pouring bronze axes and fish-hooks. Some iron is even found in Hanshu II, and the time period seems to be Warring States.

Wanghaitun has been identified as another separate culture. Some of the pottery is painted red, and the *li* is present here as well. Based on the pottery, the earlier phase seems to fall between the Baijinbao and Hanshu II, and the later assemblage has many similarities to the Tuanjia culture in eastern Jilin, which is a bit later than Hanshu II.

The Dongbali cemetery had more than 1,100 artifacts, including 400 restorable pottery vessels, in 59 graves. Most of the burials are in earthen pits, both large and small. Multiple burials and secondary burials are common. One large earthen pit contained 27 bodies, each of which had been interred in its own coffin. Bronzes in the graves include small ornaments, arrowheads, and knives with upturned points. It is thought to be Warring States period.

Another cemetery at Erkeqian has earth-pit graves, some marked by stones but without mounds. Both bronze and iron artifacts were found in the burials, as well as stone and bone tools, pottery, and birch bark. Bronze hemispheres, probably attached to clothing, were found here; they were also found at Dongbali. A new ceramic form is the duck-shaped jar. The early graves are assigned to the Baijinbao culture, although there are some local traits as well. Bronze arrowhead shapes are like those of Upper Xiajiadian, and some ceramic types are like those found at the Shiertaiyingzi site in Liaoning, placing them in the Spring and Autumn period. Later assemblages include a great deal of iron, with types found in Inner Mongolia during and after the Warring States period. Daggers with hook-shaped handles were derived from the grasslands cultures.

The Sanjiazi cemetery has earth-pit graves neatly laid out in rows. Horse trappings were prominent among the burial goods, including bronze ornaments such as bells, buckles, plaques, and rings. Small hemispheres are made of iron. Animals feature widely in the art. Most of the pottery is painted red. Tripods and pedestals are rare, but there is quite a variety of vessel shapes. The age range is from middle Western Zhou to Warring States.

Two cemeteries are found near Pingyang, 3.5 m apart. Primary, secondary, and multiple burials were found. The one on the east has mostly small to medium earth-pit burials with very few grave goods. Bones of dogs, horses, and cattle were found in the graves in varying combinations. Sometimes whole skeletons were found, including sheep, pigs, and rabbits as well as the animals noted above. Various kinds of ornaments were discovered, made of bronze, iron, stone, antler, shell, and cowries. Bronze plaques with realistic animals are particularly notable. Some burials have the face and head covered with ornaments such as beads and hemispheres.

The Qinghua site is beneath the walls of an ancient city. The ceramics are red, and include complex shapes such as tripods and pedestals. An unknown adhesive was used for repairing breaks. Iron farming tools were found. The site is rather late, and lasted to the first century BCE.

Differences between these cultures are both temporal and regional. The chapter concludes by drawing some of the distinctions between various sites. These differences are seen as ethnic ones.

S. M. N.

DISCOVERIES AND ANALYSES

The Bronze Age is one of the common stages of the human past. Judging by discoveries of ceramic molds for casting and artifacts, most of the bronzes in Heilongjiang province were small production tools and ornaments. Archaeological work on the Bronze Age in Heilongjiang is mainly concentrated on the Song-Nen Plain in the southeastern part of the

Figure 8.1 Locations of Bronze Age sites in Heilongjiang province

province. As for discoveries of bronze in other areas of the province, there are only fragmentary finds, whose features are still unclear.

The discoveries discussed in this chapter are concentrated on the middle and lower reaches of the Nen river and the upper and middle reaches of the Songhua river (Figure 8.1), therefore the region is called the Song-Nen Plain. The lakes and dense network of waterways, and the porous soil of the plain make an ideal place for primitive agriculture, fishing, and hunting. Therefore, the distribution of archaeological sites is denser here than in other areas. Because of the flat terrain, slight and slow loss of water, and erosion of soil and floods over the years, the ancient cultural sites were covered with layers of alluvium and were well preserved. The low Song-Liao watershed divides the Song-Nen Plain from the Liaohe Plain in the south. In location landforms and communication, the Song-Nen and Liaohe Plains are actually connected to each other. The combination is

227

referred to as the Song-Liao Plain, or the Great Northeastern Plain, according to the natural geographical division. The Song-Nen Plain is in the northern part of the Song-Liao Plain and is the densest area of distribution of the Heilongjiang bronze culture sites.[1]

The studies of the Song-Nen Plain bronze cultures began with the excavation of the Baijinbao site in the 1970s. Although the area of the first excavation of the Baijinbao site was not large, many characteristic and complete implements were found in the rich and complex stratigraphy. This excavation had the effect of rousing the deaf and awakening the unhearing, for it made people for the first time realize the rich contents of the Heilongjiang bronze cultures. The field archaeology of the province developed by leaps and bounds in the 1980s. Many new discoveries were made, not only in the Song-Nen hinterland but also in other areas. There were both large-scale general excavations and planned and successive excavations of some major sites. The sites known to belong to the Bronze Age and early Iron Age by excavation include Gucheng, Wolong, and Houqikeshu, and others. Large-scale excavations were also made in cemeteries belonging to this age, of which some important ones are Sanjiazi, Erkeqian, Xiaodengke, Dongbali, and Pingyang. The last two contain large graves. The excavations of these typical sites and graves amassed various rich assemblages, complex layers and complicated stratigraphy, the analysis of which has gradually made clear the order of the bronze culture and the archaeological chronicle of the Song-Nen Plain. These achievements not only supplied comparative data to set up the bronze cultural order of the other areas in the province but also laid the foundation for understanding the bronze periodization of the Song-Nen. The Bronze Age archaeological work on the Song-Nen Plain has entered a new stage in both depth and breadth. Since the ancient cultural data of the Song-Nen Plain are very rich and the relevant problems are complex, the necessity for making intensive studies is obvious.

Up to now, since most of the data have not been published or were published only in preliminary reports, the understanding and discussion of some problems will necessarily be incomplete. The studies of some specific problems will have to be discussed after the formal publication of all the data in the future. What is presented here is a general discussion of the Song-Nen Plain bronze cultures based on both published data and restricted reference materials.

SPECIFIC BRONZE CULTURES

The Baijinbao culture

The site of Baijinbao has the earliest characteristic bronze assemblage on the Song-Nen Plain. It was first excavated in 1974 and re-excavated in

1980^2 and $1986.^3$ The designation "Baijinbao culture" was suggested in the first excavation report. Baijinbao village is 15 km west of the confluence of the Nenjiang river and the Di'er Songhua river and is east of the Dongshantun site, which is on the opposite bank. The main stream of the Nenjiang is 0.5 km to the south of the village while 0.3 km to the southwest of the village is Damiao pond, whose southeastern end connects to the Nenjiang river. The site is located on the second terrace, 20 m above the river. The terrace, which contains the central part of the site, is flat in the southwest, wide in the south and north, and narrow east to west. It is 450 m long and 400 m wide. The site was eroded by rain over the years, and several large gullies exposed the cultural layers.

Early in 1964, the Heilongjiang Provincial Museum discovered the Baijinbao site. Ten years later, the archaeological team of the Heilongjiang Provincial Museum excavated the site for the first time. The excavated area is 150m^2, in which the remains of houses, ash-pits, and cellars were found. A group of locally characteristic ceramics were discovered, along with bone, antler, shell, and stone implements and bronze ornaments. There were about 140 complete or restorable vessels. In 1980, an area of 350m^2 was excavated. Discoveries include one house, 37 ash-pits, and about 300 ceramic vessels and bone implements. In 1986, another excavation of 1200m^2 was undertaken, with great quantities of discoveries – 54 semi-subterranean houses, 350 ash-pits, and more than 400 restorable ceramic vessels. Because of the richer data, we can grasp the overall characteristics of the site easily and also take a step forward to the understanding of the context, features, periods, and relative and absolute ages of the culture.

The Baijinbao pottery is mostly brown, but there are also some red and red-painted vessels. Most of the ceramics are plain and polished. All the pottery vessels of the Baijinbao culture were hand-made by coiling. Some ceramic jars still have finger impressions in the inner walls. After they had been completed separately, the lip, handles, base and legs of the ceramic were attached to the body. As for the ceramic *li*, some cord-marked decorations were first made along the rim, then clay pieces were added to make a thickened lip. Three mammiform legs were also joined to the body after being constructed separately. Some small ceramics, such as cups, necked jars, and sculptures, were molded with the fingers. Small holes had been bored in some broken vessels in order to repair them. The ceramics are solid, pure, and highly baked, to about 1,000 degrees centigrade judging by experiments.

The decorative patterns of the Baijinbao ceramics include cord marking, animal figures, and geometric figures as the most common, followed by various other incised or impressed designs. Cord marking is largely limited to the *li*, with either thin or thick cord impressions. Other patterns appear on bowls, basins, pots, and necked jars. The dotted-line pattern is one of the most characteristic. It was made by pressing comb-like implements continuously on the smoothly polished vessel walls to make close and fine indentations, from which various imaginative geometric figures were made. Some of the geometric animal figures, mostly sheep, frog, deer, and camel, are simple and vivid. A few ceramics were decorated with squares and cicada patterns.

The ceramic shapes of the Baijinbao culture are rather standardized. The majority are flat-bottomed, tripod, or pedestal vessels. Most vessels have handles. The major shapes are the bowl, pot, and necked jar with dotted-line patterns; the urn with small mouth, erect collar, and nipple or round patterns; the plain cup with handles and plain surface; the cylindrical jar with straight mouth, hollow feet, and cord markings; and some vessels with pedestals. Imitation birch-bark vessels and jars are local traits. Red-painted ceramics should also be mentioned.

The production implements of the Baijinbao culture are mostly made of bone and shell. There are more than 40 shell knives and a few shell sickles. There were also many implements for fishing and hunting, such as finely polished sharp bone harpoons, bone spears and projectile points of bone as well as others of shell and stone, which show that fishing and hunting were dominant in the economy. Ash-pit No. 1, excavated in 1974, contained a 0.1 m-thick layer of fish bones and shells and a great many animal bones, which firmly verify the above inference. Stone implements are very limited and only include some scrapers and polished stone axes and adzes.

On the body of the ceramics, designs depict grass, grasslands and fences made up of dotted-line patterns which are very simple but quite vivid and reflect developed animal husbandry at that time. Based on these designs, the original excavators suggested that sheep were the main animals raised by the ancient people.

The houses of the Baijinbao culture are all semi-subterranean. In House No. 1, excavated in 1974, the rooms were square or rectangular. The house is 8 m long, 4 m wide in the northwest section and 4.9 m wide in the southeast section with an area of $35m^2$. The floor and walls are simply the original yellow soil. The entrance ramp is in the southeast, low inside and high outside, 1.3 m long and 1 m wide with the end in arc shape. The surface of the entrance connects to the floor of the house, which was solidly stamped. It was made by first flattening the surface, then ramming the soil, and finally baking it. The hearth is in the center of the house. It is a pit, 0.6–1 m in diameter and 0.3 m in depth. Being burned for years, the soil around the hearth became red-fired soil, 10 cm thick. Six post holes were found in the house floor. A soil platform on which to store pots was 1 m wide, 4 m long, and 0.25 m high, close to and as long as the northwest wall. House No. 2 is also semi-subterranean, with an area of 4 × 4 m. There is a sub-rectangular hearth-pit in the middle of the floor, 1.1 m long, 0.8 m wide, and 0.25 m deep. The north and east walls were both destroyed, but the door probably faced east.

A ceramic kiln is incomplete. It is 1.67 m deep with a bag-like vertical section. The kiln mouth is elliptical, 1 m × 0.8 m. About 0.3 m below the kiln mouth, there is a platform which is smaller than the kiln bottom. A fire chamber 10.4 m high and 0.55 m long is near the bottom.

When the Baijinbao site was excavated for the third time in 1986, a simple report was published which identified three cultural layers. The lower layer ceramics mainly include tall jars, pots with constricted mouths, necked jars, and one-handled cups. The middle layer is represented by the cylindrical and high-crotched *li*, cylindrical jars, ridged wall pots and necked jars, one-handled cups, platform-like pedestals, and some small bronze molds. The upper layer has the following pottery shapes: big-mouthed and low-crotched *li*, one-handled cup, high-collared *hu* [vessel for liquids], constricted-waisted pedestals, and red-painted ceramics.

The distribution of the Baijinbao culture is mainly on the Song-Nen Plain, concentrating on the middle and lower reaches of the Nenjiang river and the upper and middle reaches of the Songhua river. Following the rivers to the east, the culture reaches Harbin city, Bing county and Bayan county, but does not go beyond the Zhangguangcai mountains; in the south, it crosses the Nenjiang and extends to one of its branches – the middle and lower reaches of the Tao'er river in Jilin province; in the west, it ends in the lower reaches of the Chao'er river, a branch of the Nenjiang; and in the north, it follows the Nenjiang to Angangxi, Fuyu and Nenjiang counties.

The age of ash-pit No. 1 of the Baijinbao culture is 2790 ± 65 (918~810 BCE, calibrated) [ZK–0324]. Therefore the absolute age of the Baijinbao culture is equivalent to the middle stage of the Western Zhou dynasty in the Central Plain.[4] Newly excavated materials give the earliest age of the Baijinbao culture as 3110 ± 115 BCE (1420~1100 BCE, calibrated) [ZK–2156].

The Second Phase of Hanshu culture (Hanshu II)

Hanshu II is a bronze culture later than Baijinbao on the Song-Nen Plain. The Hanshu site is on a hillock on the right bank of Yueliangpao lake, which is 35 km to the northeast of Hanshu village. Following the mainstream of the Nenjiang to the east, it is not far from the Baijinbao site.

The second layer is the main assemblage of the Hanshu site.[5, 6] Eight house floors and more than 20 storage pits were found. Among the semi-subterranean house sites, there is only one round house, while the rest are square.

House No. 104 is 7.2 m long from north to south and 6.6 m wide from west to east, with an area of 47.5m^2. The incomplete walls are 0.2–0.4 m higher than the floor. The entrance in the middle of the east wall is 1.2 m wide. A storage pit in the middle of the house is surrounded by 12 post holes. To the east of the hearth, a row of 5 post holes is aligned north-south;

while to the west, a similiar alignment has only 4 post holes. A storage pit was found south of the house.

The ceramics of Hanshu II are mainly red-brown, painted or unpainted. They were made by coiling. Many vessels have decorations which include straight-line incising, impressing, painting and a few awl-pricked patterns. The painted ceramics are an important development and outstanding feature of the ceramic technology and decorative art of Hanshu II. On vessels such as necked jars, bowls, cups, and pots, there are usually painted decorations. The designs were painted before they were fired in the kiln. The color of the paint is bright red. The designs are mainly on the exterior of the vessels, but there are also a few on the inside. The painted designs include stripes, triangular hooks, nets, thunder pattern, cloud pattern, and some geometric figures made up of triangles.

The ceramics of Hanshu II mainly include *li*, necked jars, pots, bowls, cups, pedestals, and boat-shaped vessels among which the last are the most characteristic.

The stone implements in Hanshu II include polished stone axes and adzes, as well as stone molds for bronze fishing hooks and axes. There are many bone and antler implements, such as awls, arrowheads, spears, spoons, hammers, spindle whorls, bone slivers with holes, and bone hair-pins. The bone slivers with holes are one of the characteristics of this culture.

The metal implements of Hanshu II include both bronze and iron. More than 50 clay molds (simple or complex) for casting bronze implements were unearthed, which firmly establishes the presence of bronze-casting. The clay molds are mostly for casting small implements such as projectile points, buckles, spears, and horse-shaped plaques. The bronze artifacts include knives, awls, buckles, and pillow-shaped pieces which are part of the handles of bronze daggers. Some iron implements were found, including socketed axes and knives. The shape of the socketed axe is similar to those of the Central Plain in the periods of the Warring States, Qin and Han.

The distribution of the Hanshu II culture is similar to that of the Baijinbao culture. The sites containing assemblages similar to Hanshu II include Hatugangzi in Zhaodong county,[7] Honqikeshu, Wanghaitun in Zhaoyan county, and the second phase relics of the Wolong site.

The Wanghaitun Site

The Wanghaitun site is in the upper and middle reaches of the Songhua river. It is 4 km southwest of Sanzhan village in Zhaoyuan county. The site is on a hillock on the left bank of the Songhua river, south of the village.

At the beginning of the 1940s, the Russian archaeologist V. V. Ponosov twice surveyed and excavated here and wrote a report. After the foundation of the People's Republic of China, new archaeological surveys and reports were published.[8] Since the 1970s, along with the development of the archaeological work and study in the local area, it has become possible to distinguish the Bronze Age from the Neolithic and formally put it forward as a cultural type.[9]

The ceramics of the Wanghaitun type are mostly red-brown and coiled. A few are painted red. Most ceramics have a plain surface, but some have various impressed or incised patterns. The shapes include the *li*, pots, necked jars, bowls, cups, and pedestals, among which the necked jars, bowls and pots are usually painted red.

In a recent survey, the *ding* [a cauldron with three or four legs], pedestal, urn, and other shapes were found. Thus, the cultural contents of Wanghaitun can be divided into two types. The traits of the first type are similar to those of the first report on the Wanghaitun site which is represented by the vessel shapes such as the *li*, the pot with a decorative border, pedestal, and long-necked jar, with designs made by impressing, punctates, dotted lines, fingernail marks, and red paint. These are similar to the Hanshu II assemblage, but traits such as larger dotted-line patterns and flat hollow legs on the *li* make it seem closer to the Baijinbao site. This difference suggests that the earliest date of the first period relics of the Wanghaitun type possibly precedes the earliest date of Hanshu II. Therefore, under the circumstances of not completely understanding the contents of the first phase assemblage of the Wanghaitun type, it is not reasonable either simply to equate it with or to separate it from Hanshu II. Most of the ceramics of the Wanghaitun second period relics have plain surfaces, and include all kinds of *ding*, pedestals with solid handles, curved horizontal handles, bead-shape handles, and double rims which are not mentioned in the early reports on Wanghaitun. By contrast, the assemblage is similiar to the excavated artifacts of Tuanjie Tuozi village in Nongan county, Jilin province, whose age is possibly the same as or later than Hanshu II [Figure 8.2]. If future discoveries show this to be correct, the above arguments will be a breakthrough in the studies of the Wanghaitun culture.

The Dongbali Cemetery

The Dongbali hamlet belongs to Sizhan village in Zhaodong county. The site was discovered while digging clay to make bricks, and excavated in 1982, 1983, and 1984.[10] According to incomplete statistics, the excavations unearthed 59 graves, more than 1,100 artifacts, and more than 400 complete or restorable ceramic vessels. Most of the graves are rectangular earthen pits, while there are also a few small oval earthen pits. The former can be divided into two sizes – large and small. There are many multiple burials and secondary burials. Most of the burials are supine, flexed burials, but skulls without bodies were also found. The quantity of burial goods is different from grave to grave; sometimes the differences are great. For

Figure 8.2 Two ceramic jars from Tuanjie cemetery, Jilin, which resemble those of Wanghaitun, Heilongjiang

example, of the graves excavated in 1983, M20 is a small earth-pit grave which is 1.2 m long, 0.65 m wide, and 1.24 m deep. A few limb bones were placed in the middle with a skull on each end. There are 6 ceramic vessels, several bronze ornaments, and 5 bone tubes beside one skull. In contrast, M32 is a large earth-pit grave which is 2.9 m long, 1.45 m wide, and 1.98 m deep. It contained 27 extended supine bodies buried in wooden coffins stacked up in different layers. There are 110 burial articles which include some ceramics, bronzes, and bone implements.

Most of the burial goods in the Dongbali graves had been used during the lifetime of the interred. The ceramics in the graves are all hand-made vessels of daily life which can be divided into yellow-brown clayey and yellow-brown sand-tempered groups, including the *li*, necked jars, pots, bowls, cups, ladles, and pedestals. The typical vessel is the *li* with cylindrical walls and low crotch, the boat-shaped ladle with pouring lip, red-painted necked jar with high collar and bulging walls, and jars with slanting collars, angular walls and plain surfaces. There are many red-painted ceramics, and some bronze, iron, stone, bone, tooth, and shell implements, and glassware. Among the metal implements, bronze is common, but there are no large production implements. In addition to bronze arrowheads and knives, there are small ornaments such as buckles, earrings, hemispherical ornaments, tubes, etc. Among the bronzes, the most characteristic are the bronze arrowhead with a stem and two wings, and the small bronze knife with the upturned point. A few iron implements were also excavated. The age of the graves is estimated by the excavators to be in the Warring States period.

The Erkeqian Cemetery

The Erkeqian cemetery, found at the beginning of the 1960s, is another important bronze site in the upper reaches of the Nenjiang in the Song-Nen Plain. During the 1985 excavation, seven rectangular test pits were dug and 26 graves were excavated.[11] The particulars of three typical graves – No. 6, No. 8, and No. 24 – were reported. The cemetery is on the second terrace on the left bank of the upper reaches of the Nenjiang, a little north of Erkeqian village in Nahe county. The north end of the cemetery is the highest point of the hillock, and the west is an eroded bluff. Some of the graves were destroyed by quarrying. Judging from the exposed incomplete

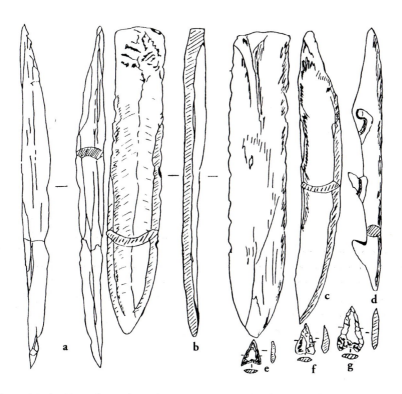

Figure 8.3 Artifacts from the Erkeqian cemetery, Tomb M6: a) bone awl; b) bone dagger-shaped implement; c) bone dagger; d) bone harpoon; e)–g) stone arrowheads

base of the bluff and the excavation, the whole long narrow area (160 m long north-south and 70 m wide) on the south slope of the Fengkuang mountain contains graves.

All the graves in Erkeqian are earth-pit types. Soil fill was above some of the graves, or stones were piled above or put in rows around them, but there are no vestiges of mounds. Most of the graves have no burial goods, but some were divided into two layers by stones or were covered with birch bark.

The burial goods of the Erkeqian cemetery include ceramic, bronze, iron, stone, bone, and birch-bark artifacts (Figure 8.3). Grave goods were usually placed beside the skulls or in the south end of the graves. Each grave has one or two ceramic vessels. According to the observation of the excavators, some of the incomplete ceramics seem to have been deliberately broken when buried, which is a phenomenon worth noting. The primary burials contained ornaments such as bronze hemispheres which the deceased had worn in their lifetimes. Dog skulls and the lower jawbones of horses were found in some of the graves.

The ceramics of the Erkeqian graves are mostly yellow-brown, while a few are grey or black-spotted and low-fired with loose texture. They are all hand-made by coiling. The vessels are slightly polished on the surface. Traces of the slow wheel can be seen on some of the ceramics. Among the decorations, cord marks or dot patterns are the most characteristic. The former usually are arranged in parallel or twisted lines while the latter form triangular figures (Figure 8.4). These two kinds of patterns are sometimes on one vessel, creating new patterns, including some animal figures. The undecorated ceramics are mostly painted red. The ceramic shapes include the necked jar, pot, bowl, cup, *li*, and duck-shaped jar.

The metal implements unearthed in the Erkeqian cemetery include both bronze and iron, of which the former are mainly small ornaments, such as bronze hemispheres, earrings, bronze arrowheads, small bronze knives, two pieces joined together, and some bell-shaped objects decorated with spiral patterns. The iron pieces are extremely rusted, and only daggers and small knives can be identified.

Of the two types of cultural relics in the Erkeqian cemetery, one type is represented by M8 and M12 according to the excavators' studies. These two graves have the same orientation, are of the same burial type, and have the same kind of one-handled necked jar decorated by the dotted triangle and line pattern. They belong to the same culture. The second type is represented by M24 and M26. The two ceramic jars unearthed from M26 have straight necks, flat lips and plain surfaces which are similar to those of M24. Therefore, the styles of the burial goods of these two types of grave are quite different. Since M26 overlaps M12, it can be concluded that the two types represent different stages in the Erkeqian cemetery.

Thus, the early relics of the Erkeqian cemetery represented by M8 and

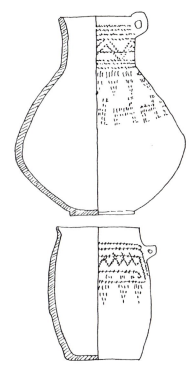

Figure 8.4 Ceramic jars from the Erkeqian cemetery, Tomb M8

M12 are a new type, belonging to the system of the Baijinbao culture. The ceramics are yellow-brown, sand-tempered and low-fired with a loose texture and plain surface. The decorations are mainly straight-line and twisted-line patterns making up triangular lines. The typical ceramic shapes include the one-handled necked jar, the cylindrical jar with bulging walls, the cylindrical jar with bent rim and walls, the bowl-shaped pot, the necked jar with two handles and angular shoulder, the *li* with short hollow legs and plain surface, and bowls. There are also some small bronzes made in complex molds, such as small knives, hemispheres, and arrowheads. According to the excavators, these artifacts are both like and unlike the Baijinbao type. Their similar characteristics are that both of them have cylindrical jars, bowls, *li*, one handle on the rim, and impressed decorations, which indicate that they belong to the system of the Baijinbao culture. However, they are also different in some ceramic shapes, the density of impressed decorations, and pattern composition. These factors indicate that the early artifacts of the Erkeqian cemetery were later than those of the Baijinbao type, but developed directly from it. Therefore, it is likely that the differences between the early Erkeqian artifacts and the Baijinbao type reflect local changes. Erkeqian probably represents a local variety of the Baijinbao culture and should be designated the Erkeqian type of the Baijinbao culture.

The problem of sites and distribution of the Erkeqian type must be solved by more work and study. The artifacts in the graves in Ninweibagang village of Lindian county, and Xiaodengke village of Fuyu county are the most important clues to explore the distribution of the Erkeqian type to the south. To the north, it is possible that it continues along the banks of the upper reaches of the Nen river and in the low mountain areas of the Nenjiang tributaries.

The late artifacts of the Erkeqian type are quite different from the early ones. The later artifacts include many iron implements, so that it can no longer be categorized as bronze culture. The iron daggers have hook-shaped handles, which is the style of the grassland people north of China. Similar graves were found in the Xiaodengke village of Fuyu county and Guandi of the Duer Bute Banner in the lower reaches of the Nenjiang. These artifacts should not be included in the Baijinbao culture, but they have some points similar to those of Hanshu II. The content of these of later assemblages and their relations to the Baijinbao culture and Hanshu II await future study.

As to the age of the earlier artifacts in the Erkeqian graves, in addition to similarities to the Baijinbao culture noted above, it should be observed that the typical decorations, such as the straight-line pattern, twisted-line pattern and dotted-triangle pattern, were not found in the Baijinbao site, but the dotted-triangle is found in the Dongshantun graves in Da'an, some of the Xiaodengke graves, and even in the Hanshu II which is later than Baijinbao. Based on that distribution, we conclude that the relative age of the early artifacts in the Erkeqian cemetery is later than the Baijinbao culture, but earlier than Hanshu II.

Among the early artifacts of the Erkeqian cemetery, three willow-leaf-shaped bronze arrowheads were found, whose forms are the same as those of the Upper Xiajiadian culture. The ceramic necked jars decorated with dotted triangles unearthed in Xiaodengke are similar to those excavated in the Erkeqian early period and close to the bronze necked jars of Shiertaiyingzi in Chaoyang. The age range of Upper Xiajiadian culture and Shiertaiyingzi is from Western Zhou to the Spring and Autumn period. As a result, the age of the Erkeqian early period relics is about the same as the Spring and Autumn period in Chinese history, although the earliest date is possibly before Spring and Autumn.

As to the age of the Erkeqian late assemblages, the M26 burial, which belongs to the late period, disturbs the M12 burial of the early period. There are great differences between these two vessel groups. The form of the ceramic jar unearthed in M26 is similar to those of Hanshu II. The forms of iron daggers are similar to those of the metal weapons in Inner

Mongolia after the Warring States period. Therefore, the age of the Erkeqian late period relics must be later than the end of the Spring and Autumn period, from the Warring States period to the Han dynasty.

The burial customs of the Erkeqian cemetery are rather complicated. The excavators consider that there were some rules in the arrangement of the graves – the secondary burials are in east-west lines and in rows in south-to-north direction. The graves are mainly oriented northeast to southwest. The head orientations of the primary burials are quite different. Most of the secondary burials had earth or stones placed around the graves with piled stones above them.

The Sanjiazi Cemetery

Sanjiazi village is in the southern suburbs of Qiqihaer located on the left bank of the Nen river. The graves are on the northern slope of a dune northeast of the village. There are dense graves (some are in rows) on the north and east slopes of the dune, which is probably the center of the cemetery. During the period from 1979 to 1980, the cemetery was leveled to the ground due to digging soil for construction. Judging from a few ceramics and bronzes collected or excavated later, although it was impossible to make clear all its features, its characteristics are quite distinct and it is a rather unusual ancient cemetery.

According to the excavation report,[12] three graves were excavated, numbered M1, M2, and M3. The burial methods include primary, secondary, and double burials. All the graves were earth-pits. There were 195 burial offerings among which 145 pieces were collected, including artifacts of pottery, bronze, iron, stone, bone, and antler. According to the excavators' observation, most of the pots were laid beside the skulls. Most of the other burial goods are ornaments, while a few are horse trappings.

The ceramics of the Sanjiazi cemetery are mostly yellow-brown and sand-tempered (Figure 8.5). Most of the ceramics are painted red; in some the inner rim or neck is painted red, in others the whole body. There are also some ceramics with plain surfaces. All the ceramics are flat-bottomed, and tripods are very rare. The pottery is all hand-made by coiling, with irregular shapes. A few jars and pots have circular handles. There are straight-necked jars, two-handled jars, wide-shouldered jars, duck-shaped jars, constricted-necked pots, short-necked pots, constricted-mouthed pots, cups, and bowls.

The metal implements unearthed in the Sanjiazi cemetery are mostly small bronzes, with many ornaments and some horse trappings, and very few weapons or production tools. The bronzes include bells, buckles, seals, rings, arrowheads, plaques, and cross-shaped harness pieces (Figure 8.6). The iron implements, mostly rusty, include knives, swords, and hemispheric ornaments.

239

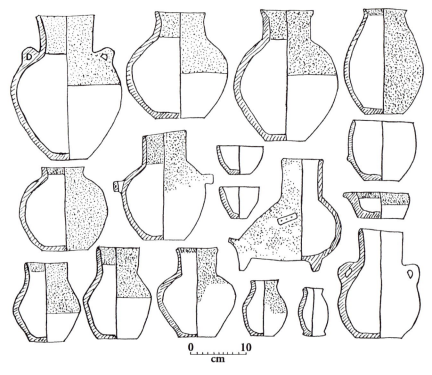

Figure 8.5 Ceramics from the Sanjiazi cemetery

The excavators estimated the age of the Sanjiazi cemetery from the middle of the Western Zhou to the early Warring States period by comparing and studying artifacts such as bronze seals, bronze and iron animal-head-shaped ornaments, bronze buckles with animal face decorations and belts with standing animal figures.

The Pingyang Cemetery

The Pingyang cemetery was excavated in 1984 and 1985. It includes two parts, the Zhuanchang and the Zhandon grave groups which are together referred to as the Pingyang cemetery in the published data,[13] as they both belong to Pingyang town. The distance between these two cemeteries is 3.5 km. This cemetery is the largest public clan cemetery in the northwest region of the Song-Nen Plain. The Zhuanchang cemetery is 2 km east of Pingyang. In 1984, 97 graves were unearthed. The Zhandon cemetery is 1.5 km south of Pingyang.[14] Twenty-one graves were excavated in 1985. Altogether 118 graves were found in two excavations. Both cemeteries

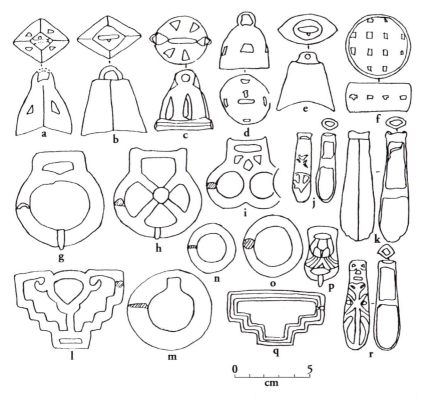

Figure 8.6 Excavated bronze artifacts from Sanjiazi: a)–e) bells; f) bell-shaped ornament; g), h) and p) buckles; i), l) and q) ring ornaments; j), k) and r) belt ornaments; m), n) and o) rings.

are located on hillocks on the left bank of the Nenjiang. More than 2,400 relics were unearthed there.

All the Zhuanchang graves were earth-pits. The graves are rectangular for individuals but square for multiple burials. Medium and small graves are in the majority. Small graves are usually 1.06–1.9 m long and 0.4–0.95 m wide while the medium ones are 2–2.5 m long and 0.5–1.3 m wide. The burial methods include primary, secondary, and multiple burials. There are a few primary and secondary burials together in the same grave. The primary graves usually have the body supine and extended with the head to the northwest. Some of the secondary burials have the skeletons arrayed with the skulls above the limb bones. The ceramics were usually placed beside the skulls, while the other grave goods, such as ornaments and production tools, were laid along the torso. The custom of burying animal sacrifices was quite common, and dogs and horses, horses and cattle, or dogs, horses and cattle were found together. Often only skulls, jaws with some teeth,

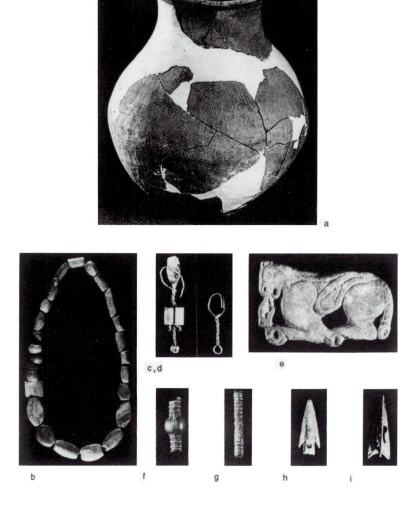

Figure 8.7 Grave goods excavated at Pingyang: a) pottery jar; b) stone beads; c) and d) gold earrings; e) bronze plaque; f) and g) bronze tubes; h) and i) bronze arrowheads

242

horns or hoofs, were placed in the graves. However, complete animal skeletons of dogs, horses, cattle, sheep, pigs, and rabbits were also found.

More than a thousand burial articles were unearthed in the Zhuanchang graves among which the most common are ornaments, especially small bronzes (Figure 8.7). The ornaments include plaques, hemispheres, earrings, and beads, most of which are made of bronze, iron, gold, stone, antler, shell, and cowries. There are many types and shapes of ornaments. The bronze plaques reflect the grasslands bronze style. The hollow bronze plaques with animal sculptures, such as those with gilded standing animals, tigers biting other animals, or running deer, are quite vivid. They are made in realistic style, and are typical of this culture. Other ornaments, such as earrings made of gold beads on a string, are rare. The rather limited production tools and weapons include adzes, awls, knives, and arrowheads. There are many bone implements, such as arrowheads and bow ends. The bone arrowhead, the major hunting implement, has various forms. One burial of a male about 40 years old contained 83 artifacts including 35 bone arrowheads and 1 bronze arrowhead. In another grave there is a necklace made of more than 40 beads of gold, bronze, and stone.

In the Zhuanchang cemetery, there are some graves which exhibit the custom of covering the face. The face and head were covered with ornaments, such as bronze hemispheres, bronze beads, and turquoise beads. In M170, the face and eyes were covered with stone beads.

The ceramics of the Zhuanchang burials are mostly yellow-brown sand-tempered vessels, and are all hand-made. Some are painted. The ceramics include necked jars, bowls, pots, and pedestals, among which the variously shaped ceramic necked jars are most common. The duck-shaped jar reflects a cultural characteristic of the graveyard (Figure 8.8).

The Zhandon burials all take the shape of rectangular earth-pits. There are only four big graves with passages which are 4 m long, and in which there are no burial implements. Most of the graves are primary and extended. There is only one secondary burial. These are single or multiple graves for adults and children.

Altogether more than 280 burial articles were discovered in the Zhandon cemetery. The ceramics include necked jars, bowls, and pots. Necked jars are painted red. The bronzes are all small artifacts, such as bells, arrowheads, awls, spoons, buckles, earrings, and tubular beads. In addition, there are some bone arrowheads, bow ends, shell knives, and stone beads and unworked stone for beads. The custom of animal sacrifices, demonstrated by dog heads placed in graves, is found here as well.

Dates from M40 and M41 are each 2385 ± 70 (410~364 BCE) [ZK–1349]. The earliest date of the Pingyang cemetery is late Spring and Autumn period, while its latest date is in the middle and late period of the Warring States.

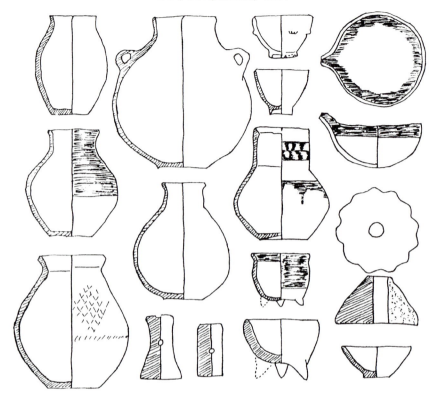

Figure 8.8 Ceramics from Pingyang cemeteries

The Qinghua site

The Qinghua site is located in the southwest of the Song-Nen Plain, in the western foothills of Zhangguangcai mountains. The site is 7 km to the southeast of Binxian town, and is on the southern slope of the north hillock of Qinghua hamlet in the Xinghi village. There is a wide road north of the site, and a small river runs north-south and empties into the Songhua river to the east of the site. The site is about 15 m higher than the river surface. An oval ancient city, 0.5 km in circumference, surrounds and covers the site. As a result of the excavation, the Qinghua site is designated as a new type of archaeological culture.

The Qinghua site was excavated in 1981.[15] Two house floors, one ash-pit and one kiln were found. Both of the house remains are incomplete. In F1, only parts of the floor and hearth remain, therefore its original shape and structure cannot be reconstructed. The F2 house was crushed under the eastern wall of the ancient city and the upper part was destroyed, so its structure is also unknown. The houses are of semi-subterranean style with square plans. The incomplete walls are altogether 3.4 m wide and 14 m long. The floor is solid and red-brown – hardened by fire. The hearth is a basin-shaped pit in the southeast corner of the house, 0.2 m deep and 1 m in diameter.

There were altogether more than 300 artifacts unearthed from the Qinghua site, including ceramics as well as bronze, iron, and bone implements. The ceramics are mainly sand-tempered, with some painted red. All the ceramics are coiled. Most of the sand-tempered ceramics are dark-brown and yellow-brown and have plain surfaces while a few are decorated with patterns along the rim (Figure 8.9). The ceramics include urns, pots, pedestals, basins, bowls, ladles, steamers and *li*. The orange-red ceramics are completely polished and lightly baked, have thin walls and mainly include necked jars and pots. The designs on painted ceramics include triangles, diamonds, geometric figures, and horizontal bands (Figure 8.10). Many large decorated vessels were found. They are highly baked and a few have arched handles. The painted ceramics include urns, jars, basins, bowls,

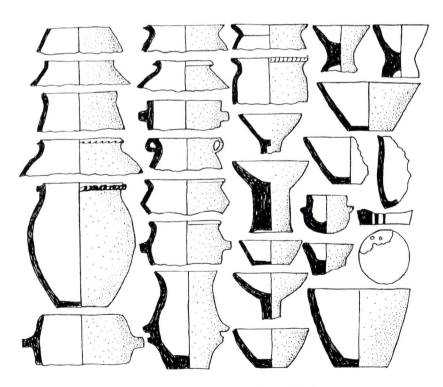

Figure 8.9 Plain ceramics from Qinghua

Figure 8.10 Painted ceramics from Qinghua

and *li*. There are a few brown painted ceramics which were first painted then baked.

The bone implements of the Qinghua site are rather advanced. They include awls, arrowheads, spindle whorls, and combs. As to stone implements, only one flaked stone arrrowhead was found. Some animal-shaped ceramic sculptures, such as of horse and pig, were also found.

The technology for repairing ceramics in the Qinghua site is different from that seen before – an adhesive was used instead of boring holes for mending. The ancient people of the Qinghua site used a kind of black material to repair the broken edges of the pottery. The repair was quite solid. It is hoped that a chemical element analysis of this black material may be made.

The iron implements unearthed in the Qinghua site were all made in combination molds whose traces can be seen on the backs of some small iron knives. The iron implements include farming forks and arrowheads, while only one bronze implement was found.

Painted ceramics similar to those of the Qinghua site include the painted ceramic jars unearthed in the lower layer of the Beishan cemetery in Jilin province. The excavators estimate that the earliest date of the Qinghua site is about the early Warring States period, and its latest date is at the end of the Western Han dynasty, well beyond the Bronze Age.

SUMMARY

The Song-Nen Plain has an important place in Heilongjiang local archaeological studies, not only because of its distinct and colorful cultural features, but also because the material for study is abundant. Today, studies of the bronze culture in the Song-Nen Plain are increasing, and the stage of setting up a complete bronze culture order of the Song-Nen Plain has just begun.

Although the general developmental sequence of the bronze cultures in the Song-Nen Plain has been sketched out, many problems remain unsolved. The fact that the published materials are too few and some of the materials have not been published at all has brought many difficulties to the studies. For example, the divisions of the archaeological cultures of the Bronze Age in the Song-Nen Plain, and their origins and developmental directions, the groups they belong to and the social structures, are questions to which the archaeologists have paid the most attention and which still have not been solved. According to the published data and analyses, the bronze cultures in the Song-Nen Plain have now been divided into several groups which not only have the rich variety of the grasslands bronze cultures but are also unique.

The excavations of the sites and graves of the Baijinbao and Hanshu II have supplied us with a reliable basis for recognizing the vessel groups of two of the cultures. They have many similarities in ceramics; both have *li* tripods, jars, bowls, cups, and pedestals. However, Baijinbao has none of the boat-shaped vessels which are characteristic of the Hanshu II. Both cultures have spiral patterns, red-painted ceramics, and cord-marked decorations. One difference is that Baijinbao has fewer red-painted ceramics than Hanshu II. They both have large numbers of characteristic ceramic *li* as cooking vessels. Because of their large numbers, they are quite outstanding in a group of vessels.

The shape of cooking vessels and their overall characteristics usually indicate the basic features of the ceramics in the assemblage, and they are often regarded as an important basis for recognizing cultural similarities and differences. The straight-mouthed, cylindrical-walled *li* of the Baijinbao culture has big long hollow legs and a high crotch, while the big-mouthed, high-walled *li* of Hanshu II has short legs and a low crotch. In addition to the differences in the shapes of the ceramic *li*, the pedestals of the two cultures also have different features. The ceramic pedestals of the Baijinbao culture are low, and some have hollow pits in the tops for supporting the *li* with the deep legs and high crotch. The three legs form a space which is large enough for convenient burning and making full use of the heat energy when the *li* is used with the low pedestal.[16] The pedestals of Hanshu II have high bodies, constricted waists, and edges on the tops. The appearance of that form suited the needs of the ceramic *li* at that time, which had changed, becoming short-legged and low-crotched, so if low ceramic pedestals like those of the Baijinbao culture were still used, not only could the purpose of convenient burning by raising the ceramic *li* not be accomplished, but the fire in the space formed by the three hollow legs could not burn fully since the crotch of the *li* was lower, and finally the function of the ceramic pedestals was lost. As a result, the ceramic pedestals became correspondingly higher and the upper part of the body became thinner while the bottom was enlarged to become more solid. At the same time, in order to protect the legs of the *li*, which were less stable because the upper body was thinner and the top smaller, brims were added to the top to enlarge the supporting surface. Through the above studies of the evolution of form and use of the ceramic *li* and pedestal, it can be inferred that the functions of the cooking vessels of the two different cultures were identical and the development was sequential. According to that study and the analysis of other factors, Baijinbao and Hanshu II are two cultures of different stages between which there are genetic relations.

In the Laoheshen middle layer, Xinglongshan in Tongyu, Sanjiazi in Qiqihaer, and Pingyang cemetery, there were a great many vessels and ornaments unearthed, such as the red-painted jar, duck-shaped jar, bronze bells, bronze *li*, *wuzhu* coins, whistling arrows, beads, bronze buckles, bronze hemispheres, and bronze plaques decorated with animals such as deer and tiger. The forms of the ceramic wine vessels and duck-shaped vessels are the same as those unearthed in the Wangong graves of the Hulun Beier grassland, and the bronze and bead ornaments are also similar. It has been pointed out above that there are obvious cultural similarities between the rich relics of the grasslands bronze culture and Baijinbao and Hanshu II cultures. They are another variety of bronze culture in the northwest of the Song-Nen Plain and the obvious differences between them are possibly related to different groups, local areas and developmental levels. The new discoveries and studies have once again demonstrated the above thesis.

As to the Wanghaitun site, the new survey data divide it into two phases. The features of the first phase are similiar to previous reports about the Wanghaitun site. The shapes of the pedestals, the decorated rims and red-painted ceramics indicate that the Wanghaitun site has some features similar to Hanshu II. But there are also some differences from Hanshu II; for example, the ceramics have more dotted-line patterns and the *li* has fatter hollow legs. Other features are closer to those of the Baijinbao site, which are rare in Hanshu II. This indicates that the earliest date of Wanghaitun I is probably earlier than the earliest date of Hanshu II. So it is argued that it is not suitable to simply equate Wanghaitun I with or separate it from Hanshu II, since the contents of the former is still unclear.

The second kind of artifact from the Wanghaitun site is more similar to the Tuanjie Tuozi relics in Nongan county in Jilin province, while the age of the former is probably the same as or later than Hanshu II. The accumulation and study of more excavated data are needed to solve the problem of the relations between these two types of relics.

There are relics found in the Qinghua site which are similar to artifacts from other sites which are the result of mutual contacts of different archaeological cultures. An analysis of the cultural factors shows that the painted ceramics are its unique feature and are most important. The Qinghua site should be considered a new culture in the southwest of the Song-Nen Plain, which is different from other known archaeological cultures in age and type.

The Song-Nen Plain was an area inhabited by several nationalities in ancient times, and the colorful and complicated phenomena appearing in the archaeological cultures reflect that character. One of the scientific bases for understanding the historical process and mutual relations of all kinds of nationalities in local history comes from studying all kinds of local archaeological cultures, distinguishing seriously among the different cultural types and defining the contents and distributions of different cultures, and scientifically setting up the cultural order and annals of archaeology.

(*Translated by Peng Ke and Du Jie*)

NOTES

1 Tan Ying-jie. On the Bronze Culture of the Song-Nen Plain. In *Collected Papers of the Fourth Annual Meeting of the Chinese Archaeological Society*, p. 196, Beijing: Wenwu Press, 1983.
2 Cultural Archaeological Team of Heilongjiang Province. First Excavation of the Baijinbao Site at Zhaoyan in Heilongjiang. *Kaogu* 1980(4): 311.
3 Cultural and Archaeological Institute of Heilongjiang Province, and Archaeological Department of Jilin University. Bronze and Early Iron Age Site at Baijinbao in Zhaoyan. *Chinese Archaeological Almanac*, Beijing: 1987, p. 131.
4 Laboratory of the Archaeological Institute of the Chinese Academy of Social Sciences. C14 Age Testing Report. *Kaogu* 1988(7): 658.
5 Archaeological Section of the History Department of Jilin University and Archaeological Team of the Jilin Provincial Museum. Main Results of the Excavation at the Hanshu Site in Da'an. *Dongbei Kaogu Yu Lishi* 1982(1): 136–140.
6 Cultural Archaeological Annals Committee of Jilin Province. *Cultural Archaeological Annals of Da-an County*. Changchun: 1982.
7 Cultural Archaeological Institute of Heilongjiang Province and Northern Archaeological Research Group of Jilin University. Test Excavation Report of the Hatugangzi Site at Zhaodong in Heilongjiang. *Beifang Wenwu* 1988(3): 2.
8 Dan Hua-sha. Neolithic Sites at Wanghaitun in Zhaoyan, Heilongjiang. *Kaogu* 1961(10): 544.
9 Si Jin. Brief Report on the Wanghaitun Site. *Beifang Wenwu* 1987(1): 17.
10 Cultural Archaeological Team of Heilongjiang Province. Bronze Age Tombs at Zhaodong. In *Chinese Archaeological Almanac*, p. 100, Beijing: 1984.

11 An Lu and Jia Wei-ming. Discussion on the Erkeqian Cemetery and Related Problems at Nahe in Heilongjiang. *Beifang Wenwu* 1986(2): 2.
12 Heilongjiang Provincial Museum and Cultural Archaeological Management Center of Qiqihaer City. Clearance of the Sanjiazi Graves at Dadao in Qiqihaer City. *Kaogu* 1988(12): 1090.
13 Cultural and Archaeological Institute of Heilongjiang Province. Excavation Report of the Pingyang Brickyard Cemetery at Tailai, Heilongjiang. *Kaogu* 1989(12): 1097.
14 Cultural and Archaeological Institute of Heilongjiang Province. Excavation Report of the Zhandon Cemetery at Tailai, Heilongjiang. *Kaogu* 1989(12): 1089.
15 Cultural and Archaeological Institute of Heilongjiang Province. Excavation Report of the Qinghua Site at Bingxian, Heilongjiang. *Kaogu* 1988(7): 592.
16 Si Jin. Ancient Pottery Stands on the Song-Nen Plain. *Beifang Wenwu* 1986(1): 16.

CONCLUSION

Sarah M. Nelson

I would like to conclude with a recapitulation of some of the general-
izations that have been made regarding the Dongbei which are now known
to be wrong, based on archaeological discoveries. A great deal has been
learned about the archaeology of this region in the last decade or two, but it
continues to be considered to be a backwater of little interest.

One of the most important misconceptions about the prehistoric peoples
in northeastern China is that they were nomadic. As was seen in the
preceding chapters, settled villages are found in the very beginning of
the Neolithic, as soon as pottery is found, which is almost the beginning
of the Holocene. Few sites appear to be campsites, with the exception of
two tent-like structures from different sites in eastern Jilin province. Thus,
plant and animal domestication (and to some extent fishing) probably
provided the main subsistence base in the Neolithic, and the population
was remarkably sedentary.

Associated with the idea of mobility is the notion that all the land beyond
the Great Wall was vast grasslands. As has been noted both in the
introduction and in several of the chapters, the Manchurian plain is well
watered with large rivers which arise in the mountains surrounding the
plain on all sides except the south, where the plain opens to the Yellow Sea.
Forests still cover the mountains, and probably forests needed to be felled
to create space for fields in the plain, after treeless areas along riverbanks
had been completely planted. The climate was probably warmer than the
present (Chang 1986:71–81), so climatic stresses on farming may have been
few.

This region, therefore, was not marginal for agriculture. Local grains such
as millets, buckwheat, and echinocloa were probably domesticated, and pigs
foraged on the fruits and nuts on the local forest floor. Soy beans may have
been locally domesticated, as well (Ho 1975). Thriving villages of the
Neolithic past attest to the agricultural potential of this region, which
even today is an important "bread basket" of China.

All of the above data show that there is no cause for surprise at the very
early agricultural societies which have been archaeologically attested in the

251

Dongbei. Although much more attention has been turned to the process of the domestication of rice, the sites in northern China, apparently just as early as those of early rice cultivation on the Yangtse river (Yan 1992), are as important and as worthy of study.

The Dongbei was not an area suddenly inhabited by people swooping in from Inner Asia in either the Neolithic or the Bronze Age. Paleolithic sites demonstrate that this region was populated over a long span of time, at least since 200,000 BP. Although it is impossible to say to what extent the descendants of Paleolithic sites contributed to the Neolithic gene pool, it is not *necessary* to derive the Neolithic population from outside the region. A continuously developing population also gradually added bronze to its repertoire. This is not to deny that ideas and influences from beyond the Dongbei had their effects in the Neolithic and Bronze Age. It is doubtful, however, that large-scale migrations of nomadic horse-riders can account for the archaeological sites.

The location of the earliest bronze in China is arguable, and in any case the present knowledge will no doubt be superseded by new candidates for "earliest" as more sites are excavated and more sophisticated means of identifying metals and dating sites are discovered. The important point is that bronze is found in the Dongbei at a relatively early stage, and that there is no reason to believe that bronze, especially in Liaoxi, is derived from the Zhongyuan.

Although there is no evidence suggesting the local invention of bronze production, there is evidence that the regions north of the Great Wall contributed to the bronze styles of the Shang dynasty, as well as being influenced by the Zhongyuan style. The notion that the Dongbei is just a pale and barbarian reflection of central China is erroneous, even at the time of the flowering of Shang. The sites are different from the Central Plain to be sure, but they are not inferior in any way except for the lack of writing. The writing found on oracle bones in the Shang period must have had centuries of development, presumably on perishable material, so we cannot argue from negative evidence in this case.

The possible contributions of the Dongbei cultures to the origins of the Shang state are considerable. A comparison of Hongshan and Shang jades demonstrates their kinship, as well as the Lower Xiajiadian painted jars which foreshadow Shang designs on bronze vessels. The bronze mirrors and weapons in Fu Hao's tomb, the only intact tomb ever excavated in Anyang, have a connection with northern bronzes (Lin 1986). The long walls of the Lower Xiajiadian culture are even known in Liaoning as "small Great Walls," to suggest their similarity to much later protective walls, and the ceremonial precincts of the Hongshan culture are possibly ancestral to the unroofed altars to earth and heaven – square and round – of later emperors. The Dongbei was not a backwater, waiting to be civilized.

PROSPECTS FOR THE FUTURE

The chapters in this book describe the progress which Dongbei archaeology has made in recent years, and some suggest lacunae and future research which the authors would like to see pursued. From a western perspective, the data lead to a number of further questions which could be addressed with additional data collection.

First, study of environmental variables is urgently needed. A joint Chinese-German team has begun studying the geomorphology of Hongshan sites, and has found that significant climate change is indicated just before the beginning of Hongshan (Wagner 1992). This kind of study needs to be widely replicated. The possibilities for learning about sea inundation around the Liaodong peninsula (see Chapter 2), and discovering its causes, are great, and should be continued. These examples could be multiplied around the Dongbei.

Second, we need further study of the subsistence base. Flotation is rarely part of the excavation techniques, and when macroflora are found they are not necessarily studied by paleobotanists. This region is important for the study of early agriculture, yet we know very little about the actual plants cultivated, or the process of their domestication. A whole program of study would be useful here.

Additional radiocarbon dates would be helpful, too, since a series of dates is always more secure than single dates. Dates are particularly valuable when several layers of a site are indicated by the stratigraphy. However, one or more dates are usually obtained from sites when appropriate material is available, so this is a less critical problem.

Skeletal material is rarely studied. Even sexing and aging of skeletons in burials is not always reported, and further studies on nutrition, accidents, warfare, and disease, as they may be reflected in skeletons, are rarely accomplished. Such studies will aid in our understanding of the Dongbei past.

Sources of exotic stone, especially jade and turquoise, need to be located, as well as metals such as copper, tin, zinc, and gold. We simply do not know where these raw materials were procured, let alone by what mechanism. Xiaoyan jade from eastern Liaoning is one type of stone which is located, but it is far from the only source of Neolithic and Bronze Age jades.

These projects might be accomplished by joint teams doing research in the Dongbei. I hope that this volume has displayed the richness of the present archaeology beyond the Great Wall, and that it has opened the doors to future research collaboration.

REFERENCES

Chang, K. C. (1986) *The Archaeology of Ancient China*, 4th ed. New Haven, CT: Yale University Press.

Ho Ping-ti (1975) *The Cradle of the East*. Chicago: University of Chicago Press.

Lin Yun (1986) A Reexamination of the Relationship between Bronzes of the Shang Culture and of the Northern Zone, in *Studies of Shang Archaeology*, ed. K. C. Chang, pp. 237–273. New Haven, CT: Yale University Press.

Wagner, Maike (1992) Impromptu talk with slides at the International Academic Conference on Archaeological Cultures of the Northern Chinese Ancient Nations, Hohhot, Inner Mongolia, August, 1992.

Yan Wenming (1992) China's Earliest Rice Agricultural Remains. *Indo-Pacific Prehistory* 1990, (I): 118–126.

INDEX

255